JUST LET ME PLAY

The Story of Charlie Sifford
The First Black PGA Golfer

by Charlie Sifford with James Gullo

British American Publishing

JUST LET ME PLAY

Copyright 1992 by Charlie Sifford
All rights reserved
including the right of reproduction
in whole or in part in any form.

Published by British American Publishing
19 British American Boulevard
Latham, New York 12110
Typesetting by C.F. Graphics, Inc., Albany, NY
Typestyle: Garamond

British American Publishing is grateful to Associated Press and
United Press International for use of certain photographs.

British American Publishing is also grateful to Rose Sifford
for her generosity with valuable and sentimental photographs.

Manufactured in the United States of America

96 95 94 93 92 5 4 3 2 1

Library of Congress Cataloging-in-Publication Data

See card

Sifford, Charlie 1922–
   Just let me play : the story of Charlie Sifford, the first Black
golfer / by Charlie Sifford with Jim Gullo.
   p.   cm.
   ISBN 0-945167-44-X
   1. Sifford, Charlie, 1922–   . 2. Golfers—United States—
Biography. 3. Discrimination in sports—United States.   I. Gullo,
Jim, 1957–   .   II. Title.
GV964.S53A3   1992
796.352'092—dc20
   [B]
                                                    92-4045
                                                       CIP

To Rose, my loving wife of 45 years,
who is responsible for my success.

Contents

FOREWORD

Charles Sifford has been called "The Jackie Robinson of golf". That description is inadequate. Both of these superior athletes had their own crosses to bear to reach the pinnacle of success. But while the incomparable and fleet-footed Robinson had the powerful presence of Brooklyn Dodgers' president Branch Rickey behind him, Sifford ultimately had only his homegrown survival instincts and family to sustain him.

Just Let Me Play could almost have been a primer on America's racial quandary in the post-World War II era. Many of the travails that Sifford describes—racial slurs, discriminatory housing arrangements, balls kicked out of bounds by ornery spectators, animal excrement found in the cup on a green at a tournament in Phoenix—had their counterparts in the experiences of Robinson's first two years in Major League Baseball.

Stories abound of the difficulties sustained by the first wave of Black Major Leaguers in our nation's pastime, as baseball has been so often referred to. The popular press hung on Robinson's every word and on-field statistic. Sifford more likely than not suffered in silence, and on occasion sought out the advice of behavioral counsellors. Baseball was played at public parks. Professional golf was primarily played at private clubs.

Robinson could take some comfort in knowing that the Negro Leagues, which flourished in the 1920's, 1930's and part of the 1940's, had produced players who were just as good or better than he. Sifford, conversely, had no such organization with as large a public following in the Black community. True, the United Golfers Association (UGA), the Black counterpart of the United States Golf Association, had been around since 1926, but facilities and opportunities had been limited to a relative handful of self-taught players.

Nearly all Black professional golfers began the game as caddies. Very few had paid lessons from competent instructors. The public courses they invariably were forced to play on could best be described as hardscrabble. The balls they used had as many cuts as dimples, and "hustler" may be a more appropriate term than "golf professional" to describe their livelihood. But the most pervasive obstacle they faced was racism.

I have read Charles Sifford described as "surly", "mean", "aloof", and of course, "cigar-chomping". He makes no apologies about the ever-present cigars which he began smoking at age 12. But knowing the distasteful, discourteous, and disgusting treatment he received in the past from the American golf establishment, it's a wonder he hasn't been indicted for felonious assault. He recounts these shameful incidents, and one is left feeling that the sports writers who used these adjectives either didn't do their homework or were just insensitive to Sifford's real life circumstances.

More than anything, *Just Let Me Play* sets the record straight and makes the Shoal Creek Country Club incident at the PGA Championships in Alabama in 1990 appear as though very little progress had been made since Sifford got his PGA card. The truth is that real progress has been made and much of that is due to Sifford's courage, determination, and golf swing. Because of Roscoe and Eliza Sifford's son, Eldrick "Tiger" Woods should never have to suffer these indignities.

Arthur Ashe

CHAPTER 1

That Old Black Golfer

There is no place for a black man in professional golf. It doesn't take a Philadelphia lawyer to figure that one out. I'm 69 years old, and I've been playing this game since I was a little kid in North Carolina. I played for 15 years on the PGA circuit, and I've been a regular on the Senior PGA Tour since its inception in 1980. And I still don't see any room for a black in golf.

If I had known 40 years ago what I know now about golf's unwillingness to open itself to blacks, I doubt that you'd be reading this book because I doubt that I would have had the courage and the strength to break into the game. During my golf career I have faced everything from death threats to harassment to being denied equal rights to make a living. I've had my golf ball kicked by a spectator when I was in the thick of a tournament. I've received phone calls telling me not to bring my "black ass" out to the golf course the next day. I've been barred from golf courses when I had a PGA card and an approved tournament entry, and I've been followed by packs of racists who called me a nigger as loudly and as often as they could.

Along the way I've eaten in more locker rooms than I care to remember because they wouldn't let me eat in the country club restaurant with the rest of the golf professionals. In some places I couldn't even use the locker room but had to change

1

my shoes in the parking lot. I've been barred from playing major
tournaments like the Masters, blackballed from invitations to fat
tournaments with big purses, and excluded from the kind of
financial bonuses that allow some golfers to make hundreds of
thousands of dollars a year in addition to tournament prize
money.

My crime? I was a black man who had the audacity to try
to make a living at the all-white game of golf. Underneath the
facade of gentility of which golf is so proud, I found an ugly streak
of racism that starts in the country clubs and runs all the way
up through the PGA itself. The more I got involved with the game,
the deeper I saw that racist streak. I never dreamed when I started
out that the discrimination in golf could reach as deeply as it
does, nor did I ever think that my struggle would be a lifelong
occupation.

But here I am, 69 years old and still seeing injustices in the
game. Hell, they should have been addressed 30 years ago, but
golf has managed to slip through the cracks of government
scrutiny and media attention. Golf has somehow gotten away
with being a professional sport that routinely witnesses and
sometimes even encourages open discrimination.

And I'm not referring only to things that happened in the
fifties and sixties. Some of the most outrageous things that have
happened to me have occurred in the last 10 years and were either
perpetrated by the PGA itself or done with the PGA's knowledge.
I've had to fight almost as hard in the eighties to play professional
golf as I did in the fifties, and I don't think that's right. I think
equal rights for blacks in golf should have come many years ago,
but the game has stubbornly refused to open itself.

I've been asked hundreds of times what I think about the
controversy that began when the whole country found out that
the Shoal Creek Country Club in Birmingham, Alabama, — the
site of a major tournament — practiced open discrimination in
its membership policies. The club didn't have any black members,
nor would it entertain the notion that a black could ever be a
member. "That's just not done here," the white president of the
country club said.

I can sum up my reaction in one sentence: "So what else is new?" Is it such a big surprise that country clubs all over the nation exclude blacks as members, as well as other minorities, Jews, and women? Could the PGA possibly not have known about this for the last 40 years? I've known about it ever since I started playing golf. There weren't, and frequently still aren't, any black people around many of the tournaments held at private country clubs, for one thing. For another, the country clubs themselves would remind me in as crude a manner as possible that I didn't belong.

I knew about segregated country clubs every time I went to a place like Pensacola, Florida, or San Antonio, Texas, and was told that I either couldn't play at the country club or I couldn't use the club's facilities. Some clubs wouldn't even allow me to use their restrooms, and I was a touring PGA professional. It was clear to me in 1965 and 1975 and 1985 that many clubs holding tournaments on the PGA Tour every year didn't have any black members and that I was usually the only black guy they saw all year. It certainly wasn't a new story. Why, then, did the PGA act so surprised when the media exposed Shoal Creek in 1990? And what took the press so long to figure out that many of the nation's greatest golf tournaments were held at golf courses where blacks weren't allowed past the front gate?

I don't consider myself a troublemaker or a tub-thumper. I wasn't involved in any kind of Black Power movements in the sixties, and I'm not trying to win any votes today. All I've ever wanted to do is play golf for a living and show that a black man can play the game just as well as a white man. I fell in love with the game the first time I set eyes on a golf course, and luckily I had the kind of natural talent and determination that it takes to be a successful golf professional. But I had hazards placed before me that no pro before or since has had to deal with, and my career has had as much to do with breaking down barriers as it has had to do with driving and putting. I think it's time that everybody heard my story and realized that golf isn't as clean as it should be.

I didn't ask for the problems I got. I just wanted to play the game. I believed that in America a man had the right to equal opportunity in his chosen profession, and I did what I had to do to get that equal opportunity for myself and the other blacks who followed me into the game.

I was the guy who broke down the outrageous Caucasian clause in the Constitution of the Professional Golfers Association in 1961, a provision that declared that only whites could be members of the PGA. I was the first black man to play full-time on the PGA Tour and the first to get a full PGA membership. I was the only black to play on the tour until 1964, and what I did paved the way for future black golfers like Lee Elder and Calvin Peete. It didn't happen because golf opened its arms to blacks. It happened because I pushed harder than anybody has ever pushed against the all-white game of golf.

Along the way I've seen the best black golfers of my day wind up bitter and frustrated because the doors to professional golf were never open to them. I've seen men with great games and great potential give up the sport because they didn't have the temperament or the will to fight for equal rights in the game. Men who I think had the talent to take their place right up there with Hogan and Snead were allowed to drift out of the game and disappear. Because they were black, they weren't missed by golf. The game just never made a place for them.

I was the one black man who wouldn't disappear. I've won over a million dollars in official prize money in my career and probably close to two million unofficially. I've received many honors from the game, the latest of which was my induction into the Northern Ohio PGA Hall of Fame. I've been written up in national magazines like *Sports Illustrated* and *Golf Digest*, and my story has been told on television shows like the "Today" show. Still, I don't feel that I've received the recognition that I deserve from the game, and I don't believe I ever will.

Instead, I'm portrayed by the press as the cranky old black golfer. I'm the black man who plays with the cigar in his mouth, a habit, incidentally, that started when I was 12 years old. I'm not invited to any of the special tournaments or paid appearances that other golfers my age regularly attend. I'm never asked by television to comment on a tournament, and the PGA sure as hell doesn't present me as being an important figure in the game. I'm the black guy with the cigar. If a racial question pops up, then they interview me.

Golf has many ways of keeping the black man in his place. We're still not invited to some tournaments, and the endorsements and appearance fees and special bonuses of golf continue to elude us. When we go to tournaments we're still routinely asked if we're caddies by security guards or tournament officials. Can you imagine? I've been playing the game forever, Lee Elder has won over $2 million in a long and distinguished golf career, and Jim Dent is one of the brightest young stars on the senior circuit. Yet we're still mistaken for caddies because as far as most people know, golf is played by whites who are attended to by blacks. That's the way it will always be as far as some people are concerned.

If I want to remind myself how far the black golfer has risen in the eyes of the public and the PGA, I need only think back a couple of years to a tournament I entered in Utah in 1989. You might think what I'm about to tell you would have happened in the forties or the fifties. It did happen then, but it continues to happen in the eighties. It was an incident that reminded me that no matter how much I've accomplished in the game, I'm still just an old nigger golfer to a lot of white people.

It was the first week of August, and I went to Park City, Utah, to play in the annual Showdown Classic tournament at the Jeremy Ranch golf course. It was a tournament that I had entered many times on the senior tour without any trouble, although I've never been treated particularly warmly in Utah. In a place with as few blacks as they have there, I can usually expect either cold treatment or cracks about being somebody's caddy.

Those things I can take, but it really shook me up when, on the first day of the pro-am round, a businessman said something to me that I couldn't believe. As in most pro-ams that take place in the days prior to the tournament, I was paired on that particular morning with four white businessmen. Two of them introduced themselves to me on the first tee and the other two ignored me, which was pretty much par for that particular course.

We played the round of golf and nobody said much. One of the men who was friendly to me revealed that his company was associated with the tournament. I think he was one of the big concessionaires, and it was obvious from the way he talked and carried himself that he was a wealthy man and a prominent member of the local business community. "Charlie," he asked at the 16th tee, "where do you make your home?"

I told him that I was born in Charlotte, North Carolina, lived in Philadelphia for a while, moved to California in 1947, put in a stint in Cleveland, and that now I live in a suburb of Houston, Texas.

His eyes lit up. "You live in Texas, do you? Why I have a nigger maid who is from Texas, too. And so is my nigger cook. She's the best damn nigger cook I've ever had in my life. When I die, I'd like to take her along with me." He broke up laughing over that one.

At first I was stunned. How could a man, particularly a successful man, be so rude and arrogant as to start dropping the word "nigger" around me and then make a big deal about how he had black women working for him? Was I supposed to be grateful? Laugh at his joke? I had to shake my head to believe what I was hearing. I conduct myself as a gentleman on the golf course and expect to be treated like one. But some people can't be civil around a black man.

My shock turned into anger. He may as well have asked me to shine his shoes. I got so mad that I could hardly see straight, and I blew my score up on the last three holes. I just couldn't wait to get the hell off that golf course and away from that racist. I would have much rather told him off or gotten in his face, but I didn't. I'd learned long ago that I couldn't accomplish much by taking a swing at every white redneck. If I were a violent man I wouldn't have lasted three months on the golf tour, because as far back as I could remember there were people who tried to rile me up on the golf course.

I finished the round and stalked off to my car, which was one of the courtesy cars that the tournament supplied to the players. I was so unnerved by what I'd heard that I decided to go to the shopping center and pick up a small bottle of bourbon that I could take back to my hotel room. I'm not much of a drinker, but I occasionally take a sip of bourbon or scotch at the end of the day.

I pulled into the shopping center and saw a lady about to pull out of her parking space, so I waited. As she started her car, I noticed a car behind me that was driven by an older, white man. He was honking his horn and hollering something at me. He had plenty of room to go around me, but he just sat there honking away. The lady pulled out and I swung the car into the parking space. But when I got out of my car, the old white man was still there waiting for me in his car.

"What the hell are you trying to do, nigger, pulling into my parking space? Don't you know that you're not supposed to be parking here, nigger?" the guy screamed.

I looked around, wondering what on earth was going on. "Just leave me alone, mister," I told him. "I saw this parking space first and I took it. I didn't do anything wrong here."

"That's the problem with you niggers," he spat, "you don't even know how to talk to people."

I shook my head and walked away. I somehow was seeing the worst that Utah could offer up in the space of one afternoon. I walked into the store and bought a half pint of Jack Daniels, wondering how I was going to get through the week if this was what it was going to be like. When I went back out to the parking lot, the old guy was still there.

He had pulled three or four other men aside and was telling them that I'd tried to hit him in the parking lot. "There he is!" he shouted when he saw me. "That's the nigger tried to run me over out here."

I saw these four white guys looking at me and I felt a sickening, sinking feeling in my stomach that I hadn't experienced in many years. I thought for a moment that they were going to come after me, but then one of them said to the old man, "Aw, leave him alone. He didn't do anything." As I walked to my car

I heard the man continue his profane shouts, and the words rung in my ears all the way back to the hotel room.

Even then it wasn't over. I got back to the hotel, took a shower, had a swig from the bottle, and got ready to go to a cocktail party at the golf course, where no doubt I would meet with the guy who had felt so compelled to tell me about his black maid. I wasn't too crazy about that, but I had promised that I'd attend the cocktail party. I drove down there and had no sooner gone into the tent when one of the tournament officials rushed over to me. "Charlie, where've you been? I've been looking everywhere for you," he said, his face red and flustered. "We just got a complaint called in on you."

"A complaint? What kind of complaint?"

"A man called us up a few minutes ago and said that one of our courtesy cars was being driven by a drunken nigger who tried to run him over in a parking lot. He said that you tried to kill him out there. What happened, Charlie?"

That was it for me. I was so furious that I could hardly walk back to the car and return to the hotel. The next morning I got a call from one of the local newspaper reporters who had gotten wind of the story, and I told him precisely what had happened. The story about Charlie Sifford's racial problems in Utah ran in the next morning's edition.

To cap it all off, I got a letter about three months later from Deane Beman, the commissioner of the PGA and Senior PGA Tours. He had apparently been forwarded a copy of the newspaper article, and now he was threatening to fine and censure me for my public statements. He said that my conduct and statements could not be condoned by the PGA because they could endanger relationships with sponsors and tournament officials and leave a bad image about the Senior PGA Tour. He decided that he would not levy a fine, but I was put on six-month probation, which meant that if anything else came up, I could be suspended from playing.

I had been under the impression that free speech was allowed, if not under the PGA's constitution, than by the Constitution of the United States of America. Deane Beman apparently disagreed.

So it was okay for a wealthy businessman and a crazy fan to tell me all about their nigger cook and how I was a drunken nigger, but I couldn't give my side of the story? That doesn't seem right to me, but then, a lot of things about the way golf is run don't seem right.

Now I'm giving my side of the story. It's a long story about how a good black golfer has to fight through practically every obstacle, including the organization that is supposed to be protecting his interests as a professional golfer, in order to be accepted. I think it would be great if it changed the way blacks are treated by the game, but I have no illusions that it will. Because as I said, blacks are not welcome by the game of golf. I've been around long enough to know that to be the truth. The only thing I've never been able to understand is why that has to be.

CHAPTER 2

The First Bus out of Charlotte

Golf was around the corner waiting for me when I was growing up in Charlotte, North Carolina. Both of my parents were born and raised in Charlotte, and when I came along on June 2, 1922, I was the third of what would eventually become six children. I had three brothers and two sisters, and we were all raised in a strict Baptist household where my mother was the boss.

Her name was Eliza, and she tended the house, cooked and cleaned for us, and when an important family decision needed to be made, she was the one to make it. She was a wonderful woman, very religious, a regular churchgoer, and she pushed all of us to go to school. She knew how important an education was, and I probably lasted as long as I did in school because of her insistence that I stay in and make something of myself.

The man of the house was Roscoe Sifford, a strong, quiet guy with a sparkling humor about him. Dad worked in the local fertilizer plant as a laborer, lifting things here and pushing them around there. He came home exhausted at the end of the day, and I imagine that the thought of playing a round of golf for fun would have been about as foreign a notion to him as the idea that he could go off waterskiing in the Caribbean.

10

Dad and I were on the same level, though. Everybody who knew him says that I look just like him. He was an easy-going guy who liked to have fun. As long as we didn't do anything too bad he'd let us slide, but if we did anything really bad, he was right on top of us. The thing about Dad was when he whipped you, it only took but two shots with an old army strap and you were whipped good. Twice was plenty. He wasn't a big guy, but he sure was strong.

I knew from an early age that there was no way on heaven or earth that I was going to grow up to follow Dad into the fertilizer plant. In fact, once when I was in my early teens, he got me a job at the factory that lasted all of one day. Carting around those 100-pound bales of manure was not my idea of a good time, and the next day I didn't go back.

I knew that I wouldn't have to do hard labor for a living, because by the age of 10, I had discovered golf. It was right down the street at the Carolina Country Club. Like many of the boys my age, I got a job caddying, and by the time I was 13, I was bringing home almost as much in tips from the rich, white members of the club as Dad was bringing home from his job.

I got 50 cents for carrying a bag, and a dime tip at the end of the round. Sometimes the tip was as much as a quarter when I did a good job for one of my regular customers, so on a good day I could make as much as $1.50 if I worked two rounds. The dollar always went to my mother, but I kept the tips for myself. Most of my money went to the tobacconist, because I was smoking cigars by the time I was 12, and I haven't quit smoking them yet.

The Carolina Country Club was just a few blocks away from our neighborhood, which was a mixed, working-class place where whites and blacks lived side by side. The people who lived there were on the poor side of middle class, but they kept their houses and yards neat and they worked hard to make a living for themselves. I guess I was fortunate that we lived in that particular part of town, because when I was growing up there was no such thing as tension or segregation between blacks and whites. I knew about whites-only restrooms and black water fountains, but they seemed part of a different world than mine. It wasn't until later in my life that I would encounter the ugly racism and segregation that was so ingrained in the South.

Hell, where we lived, our next door neighbors, the Wilsons, were a white family and when their two kids came to my house and did something bad, my mother whipped them just as bad as their mother whipped me when I was over at their house and got into some kind of trouble. No racial tensions there; we were all equal when one of the mothers got her back up over something we did. I grew up playing with those Wilson kids and lots of other white kids in the neighborhood.

Of course, the Carolina Country Club only had white members, but then at that time I didn't know of any black people who could have afforded to join even if they'd been able. Most of the white people in the city couldn't afford to join that club, either. The membership consisted of local businessmen who had done well for themselves, such as cotton merchants and executives.

I remember one man whom I frequently caddied for — Ralph Gerard was his name, as I recall — who was the vice-president of the local Coca-Cola bottling plant. He was a big shot at the club, and when he brought his boss, the president of the bottling plant, I'd caddy for him, too. I never stopped to question why it was only white people I worked for, or where they came from in their big, expensive cars. That was just the way it was at the club. They may have come from Mars for all I cared, as long as they gave me a decent tip at the end of the round of golf.

I didn't care about any of that country club stuff anyway — the lounges, the cocktail parties, the dances. I was in love with the golf course. There was something about it that appealed to me on a very basic level. I loved being there, and I loved being able to make money just by walking on those green fairways and helping older men get through their round. Hell, that wasn't work. Work was what my father did, and what most of the older black men I knew did to get by and put some food on the table. What I was doing was fun.

For me and the other caddies, most of whom were black, the golf course was like our private clubhouse, where we could gather and talk and horse around. It was like we owned the place, regardless of what the members believed. I loved getting there early in the morning and smelling the freshly mown grass on the course and joking around with the gardeners and superintendent. I loved going into the back rooms of the pro shop and locker room, where the members' bags were kept, and where we would clean clubs, polish shoes and get things ready for the early-morning players. Those back rooms were our country club, and the hard benches that we sat on were our lounge chairs.

The pro at the club was also the owner. Sutton Alexander was himself a scratch golfer and frequently entered professional tournaments. He liked me and let me work in the pro shop when things were slow on the course and I wasn't carrying a bag. I'd sell balls and candy behind the counter, keep things straightened up, and help arrange tee times and pairings. It was all fun, and in my own way I felt I belonged there just as much as any white member.

By the time I was 13, I was the best caddy out there, and the players used to seek me out to carry their bag. Men like Mr. Gerard and a guy named Jimmy Helms would swing by my house after school and take me to the golf course, where I'd carry their bag for nine holes, and then they'd bring me home. I was there nearly every day after school, and all day on the weekends.

Why was I such a good caddy? I think it was because I had both a natural talent for the game of golf and a fierce interest in the game that made me want to learn everything about it. The natural ability isn't something you can teach. People get it in baseball, in football, in boxing . . . you can't explain why. But I have always thought that if you don't combine that natural ability with a fierce determination to succeed, you aren't going to get anywhere in your sport. Talent just isn't enough; it must be coupled with dedication. You see all kinds of guys out there on the golf course who have some basic skills for the game, but the vast majority of them don't succeed because they don't study the game or work hard at it. They piss away the few gifts that they have, and that's something I'll never understand. You don't get many chances in this life to be exceptional; why anybody would squander his talents is utterly beyond me. I've been working hard to understand and master this game of golf since I was 12 years old, and I still haven't ever gotten to where I'm satisfied with my game.

I was a good caddy because the game was so important to me. I knew everything about the golf course, like where the trouble was, where the bad lies were, which direction to best approach each green, and how each putt would break. I made it a point to know the strengths and weaknesses of the player I was caddying for, and to suggest ways that would keep him out of trouble that he couldn't handle. I knew how far he could hit each of his clubs, which ones gave him trouble and which ones he had the most confidence in, and I would always pull the right club out of the bag to get him to where he needed to go. I knew all of the distances to the greens from every spot on the golf course, and I could read the speed and the breaks on every green, to every pin placement.

No wonder my players loved me: I saved them lots of strokes every time they used me, and that usually translated into the difference between them winning their bets and losing them. If there's one thing a businessman likes to do, it's win his bets on the golf course, and anything that gives him an edge against the other businessmen will make him very happy. I had a lot of very satisfied clients.

My interest in the game naturally led me to see if I could play it, and by the time I was 13 years old I became the best player among the caddies. Hell, I was one of the best players at the entire country club by that time, because I could routinely shoot in the 70s, and occasionally break into the 60s. Nobody gave me lessons on how to swing or hold a golf club or how the game is played. I picked it all up by watching, and like many of the black players who play professionally, that probably explains why I have such an unorthodox swing.

I started out by hitting range balls in the field next to the clubhouse at the club, and by the time I was 12 I was hitting hundreds of balls a day. Whenever I got a break from caddying, and at night after everyone left, you'd find me out there swatting balls and trying to figure things out. I saw how the best players gripped the club, how they took it back, and the hip and shoulder rotation that got them through the ball, and I'd take these things back to the range and modify them to fit myself.

Some kids can shoot the lights out of a basket or can run circles around people with a football. I found out that I could smack a golf ball and make it go straight and far. And once I learned that, nothing was going to stop me from playing the game and getting better. It was never a matter of me thinking — or even dreaming — that I could make a living out of playing golf. God knows that a black kid in North Carolina in the thirties didn't exactly have many role models in golf. It was just that I found something that I could do well, and I was stubborn enough even then to stick to it until I got it right.

People have been telling me my whole life that I can't play golf for a living — no blacks allowed here, Charlie; you don't qualify for this tournament, Charlie; you're too old for this tour, Charlie — and I've just asked them to move aside. Golf is what I know how to do best, and I will continue to do it until I'm satisfied with the game or I'm physically unable to play anymore.

I played other sports when I was a kid, but I never fell in love with any of them like I fell in love with golf. I was a catcher on the baseball team for a couple of years before I got my two front teeth knocked out. I tried boxing but found it was way too rough for me. Golf was my sport, and I knew I'd stick with it.

There was also some peer pressure involved. Some of those black kids who caddied could also play terrific golf, like Ralph Alexander, Jim McClure and Mack Brown. Those guys shot in the 70s when they were 13 years old too, and from the moment I began swinging a club I wanted to get good enough to beat them on the course. There were some pretty hefty bragging rights to secure out there at the Carolina Country Club, and I wanted my share.

None of us had our own clubs, of course, but on Mondays, when the caddies were officially allowed to play the course, the members would let us use their clubs. I would borrow Mr. Gerard's bag and feel like a million bucks out there. At other times, especially in the late afternoon when we'd sneak onto the course after the members were finished playing, we'd have to borrow a club here and a club there, and all of us would switch off clubs throughout the round. Ralph would have the 7-iron, I'd have a wedge, somebody else would have a 3-wood. We'd play a round that way, trading clubs the whole time.

We could never get ahold of a decent putter, though. I don't know why. More likely than not, we'd end up using a 2-iron to putt. I think that one of the reasons that many black pros don't have an inherent knack for putting is that like myself, they rarely got to use a real putter when they played as kids. Putting takes time and practice, which were two things we never had on the golf course. Except for those Monday rounds when we were allowed to play, we had to sneak onto the golf course to play, and that meant we had to hit the ball and move fast to avoid being thrown off the course. There wasn't any time for standing around on a green hitting 50 putts.

I've heard the same story from many black golfers who learned the game in places where they really weren't allowed to play. One guy said people always question him about his short, flat swing, and he has to explain that when he learned the game he had to hit the ball quickly and move on in order to avoid the marshalls and club pros. That's the way he learned how to swing, as if he were a pickpocket being chased by a policeman.

To this day I have trouble with my putting. It has traditionally been the weakest part of my game. I believe that if I had had more time as a kid to work on my putting stroke on decent greens and with decent equipment, it would come a whole lot easier to me.

When we couldn't play on the golf course, we'd set up a couple of holes in a field and play there. We'd do anything to take a few swings and see who could hit the ball best. At that time I didn't know anything about the subtleties of playing golf. All I knew was whack the hell out of the ball at the tee, loft it onto the green, and try to putt out. Still, I was good enough to shoot a two-under-par 70 and win a caddy tournament in 1936, when I was 14 years old.

Another way I got to play in those days was with some of the members. Mr. Gerard in particular loved to play against me. He'd pick me up after school and I'd carry his bag and play against him. We'd both use his ciubs. We only had time for nine holes after school, so the deal was that if he beat me, he wouldn't have to pay the 30-cent caddy fee. And if I beat him he paid double. You can bet that I didn't go home with nothing very often. I think I beat him nine out of 10 times, and he still came back for more. He was a wonderful man and a good player. He helped me out a lot in those days.

A lot of the members were friendly and helpful. Mr. Alexander, the club pro and owner, would give us golf balls from time to time or lend us clubs. Other guys would give us balls and help us out getting odd jobs to bring in a little extra money. I remember one time a man named Jack Baker got me a job moving bales of cotton around in his factory. I didn't enjoy that one bit, but I did it for the money.

We were fortunate to have one of the great pros of our time playing frequently at our club. His name was Clayton Heafner, a Charlotte native who was right up there in the late thirties and forties winning professional tournaments against the likes of Ben Hogan, Sam Snead, Walter Hagen and Jimmy Demaret, the top golfers of the day. He was a tall, strong, blond man with a famous temper that could go off at any time. I caddied for him a few times, and then he took a liking to me and we frequently played together.

That was in 1938, and there I was, a 16-year-old kid playing head-to-head with a great golfer who would twice come within a stroke of tying for the United States Open championship. It was as if a high school kid of today got the chance to play regularly against Greg Norman.

Someone told me once that Heafner got so mad at his putter during a round that he held it under water and screamed, "Drown, you son of a bitch, drown!" I don't doubt the story, because he had a huge temper. And when he went off, he was scary. The man was over six feet tall and weighed about 230, and when he got angry a storm cloud would build on his red face and you thought he was going to tear you apart with his bare hands. When I caddied for him, he would frequently fire me on the front nine and then hire me again on the back.

Despite the temper, he was a nice man and I loved playing with him. It was quite a prestigious thing for the caddies to be asked to play with Heafner, and we would jockey for position to carry his bag when he came to the club, in hopes of being invited to play along. Although he never gave me any lessons on the golf course, I learned an enormous amount about the game from him. I saw the way he sized up each hole, and I studied his bag of tricks around the green, and the way he could fade or draw the ball depending on the wind conditions and the temperament of the hole. He had a wonderful short game of lobs and soft pitches, and after a round with him I'd run off to the driving range to practice the shots I'd seen him make.

When we got to know each other we began to bet on the rounds we played together, and, surprisingly, I found that I could hold my own with him on the golf course. I'm not saying that I won every round, but I wasn't turning all of my money over to him, either. It was Heafner who also taught me a valuable lesson about having the money to back up your bet. He had me down on a two-dollar bet, and when he beat me on the 14th hole, I didn't have the money to pay up. Heafner promptly picked me up, carried me to the nearest water hazard and deposited me!

It was a great thrill for me over a decade later when I began to enter some of the same professional tournaments as he did. In 1953, in one of the few "white" tournaments that I was allowed to enter, Heafner and I shot the same score, an even 300, at the Tam O'Shanter World Championships in Chicago. He died in 1960 at the age of 46, and I've always regretted that he didn't live to see me enter the PGA Tour, for which he'd given me so much incentive in my early days of golf.

In 1940, I was 17 years old and in the 11th grade, and my life revolved around going to school and playing and working at the golf course every day. That is, I went to school in between getting suspended for smoking cigars. Hey, I was a southern boy

living around all that tobacco! By the time I was 17, I didn't feel
right if I didn't have a stogie in my mouth.

During that time there had been some incidents where
members of the country club complained about seeing me out
on the golf course. I don't know who they were or what their
problem was, but Mr. Alexander came up to me and said that I'd
better watch myself more carefully out there. We'd been getting
thrown off the course for years up to that point, but now things
seemed different. Maybe it was because I wasn't a kid anymore.
By the time I was 17 I had grown into my full size, which is five
feet, seven inches and 185 pounds, and I was solid through the
chest and legs.

I knew that Mr. Alexander was on my side and thought I had
a talent for the game of golf. As far as he was concerned I could
play anytime, but now he was getting pressure from some of the
older members about me and the other black kids playing the
course. Frankly, I resented it, because I was one of the best players
at the club and as far as I was concerned, if anybody had a
problem with me they could come out and try to whip me fair
and square on the golf course. I knew that besides Mr. Alexander
and Clayton Heafner there wasn't anybody out there who could
beat me.

Mr. Alexander didn't come right out and say it, but I was made
to understand that I might be in physical danger out there on
the golf course. He said that he was concerned with my safety
and that people had been saying things. What kind of things?
That the little black kid was getting too good and would have
to be taken down a peg? That my kind wasn't allowed at the
Carolina Country Club? (As far as I know, they're still not allowed.
Like so many other clubs in our country, Carolina still doesn't
have any black members, and I seriously doubt that it's because
no blacks can afford the entry fees anymore.)

It was okay for me to whack balls around the course when
I was a black caddy playing with the other black caddies, or when
I was carrying a member's bag. But now I was becoming serious
about my game and I didn't want to live with playing only when
somebody threw me a handout.

It wasn't like there was a public golf course where I could play. The South wasn't ready for that. For the first time in my life, the white people rose up to try to stop me from playing. It was a situation that I would face my entire career in golf. Had I known that in the beginning, I'm not sure that I would have gone on the way I have.

Maybe I'm foolish or stubborn or so wrapped up in my sport that I'm blind to what is going on around me. Maybe I should have been watching which way the wind blows and known from the get-go that I was going to run into troubles playing golf. I knew that there were racial problems in the world and that black people faced disadvantages in many different professions. But for some reason I never thought it would happen to me.

For the first time in my life I was categorically told that I couldn't play golf anymore. Not at the Carolina Country Club. Here I was, a 17-year-old kid with a whale of a game. You'd think that some of those members would have been proud of the way I played. Here was a black kid who came out of nowhere and with a little help might have been able to start entering the amateur tournaments and maybe make a name for himself and the country club that had given him a start.

But this was 1940 in North Carolina, and that simply wasn't going to happen. The dreadful thing is that I doubt it could happen in 1990 either. Where is a black kid going to get the kind of support and encouragement that he needs to turn his raw skills into a polished golf game? They're going to tell him to run off and play basketball, and get the hell away from our private country club.

Every time that this has ever happened to me, beginning with the Carolina Country Club and on up to the senior PGA tournaments that I wasn't allowed to enter, I've felt a bitter twinge of irony. For God's sake, all I'm trying to do is play a round of golf, and if I do it well and have a good tournament, then maybe I'll make a little money. And here are all these white people getting all worked up about a simple little game of golf. What's that black boy gonna do, tear up our greens? Hit our women over the head with his 3-iron? Take a leak on the 15th green?

As far as I was concerned, I wasn't making any waves or trying to deliberately flaunt rules. All I ever wanted to do was play golf, and every single time I've ever faced a situation where I've been barred from playing golf it has come like a slap in the face to me. When these situations occur, I am shocked. It's as if strangers walked into your office and took your desk away and said you can't work here anymore because we don't like you. It's so unfathomable that I have to stop what I'm doing and look around to see if there's something I missed.

Shit, the fear and downright ignorance that are the basis for these unfair prejudices are simply ridiculous. I'm just one guy who wanted to play golf, and to think that I'd be capable of disrupting anything or ruining anybody's fat-cat golf tournament by my sheer presence is just plain stupid.

Sutton Alexander could have banished me from the club, but he was a better man than that. He came to my parents and suggested that I be allowed to leave Charlotte and move to Philadelphia, where my uncle lived. He told me that there were good golf courses up there that wouldn't have any trouble allowing me to play, and that the only way my game was going to improve was by playing regularly against good competition. Mr. Alexander thought that I had a future in golf, and that it surely wouldn't come true in North Carolina.

To leave Charlotte, I'd have to drop out of school, and that didn't sit well with my mother. She had always fervently believed that education was the only way to get ahead in the world, and at first she opposed the idea of my going off to Philadelphia. "I don't want you to do it if you can't see taking care of yourself," she said. "I don't want you coming back home in a month with no job and no school."

I told her that I'd get a job and support myself up there, and that I could make good money caddying on the golf course. If there were rich people in Charlotte who would pay a good tip on the golf course, there were bound to be tons of them in Philadelphia, I figured.

My dad always went along with what mother said, so it wasn't tough to get his permission once I got hers. He knew that I'd always land on my feet. He called me the Little Hustler, because I was always coming home with change in my pocket that I'd won playing golf or carrying a bag. I think he knew that I wasn't going to end up pushing bales of cotton or fertilizer around for the rest of my life.

I was pretty set on going to Philadelphia, but I wasn't sure of the timing. It was midwinter of 1939, and it didn't make much sense for me to head north where it was cold. But something happened that made up my mind for me. Being black nearly ended my dreams of a career in golf before I ever left Charlotte.

There was a general store down the road from our house that was owned and operated by a big, mean white man named Jim Green. This guy was a wrestler who must have weighed close to 300 pounds. He and his wife were friendly with my folks when he was sober, but Jim Green wasn't sober very often. And when he went on a drinking spree he got very ugly very quickly. Mrs. Green used to spend three or four days at a time at our house to hide from her husband when he was drunk.

One cool morning in early February I walked into the store to pick up something for my mother, and I found Jim Green as drunk and as mean as I'd ever seen him. He looked ornery, and right off the bat, I knew that there would be trouble.

He staggered up to me and blocked my path. He waved a big hand at me and said, "Go down to your house, nigger, and tell my wife to come home."

"Mr. Green, do you know who I am?" I asked politely. "I'm Shug Sifford's son, and he ain't gonna like what you called me just now."

"Just shut up, you little nigger, and do what I said."

A little flash went off inside me. I wasn't going to take that from this big creep. I knew that my father would have hauled off and smacked him by that time, and I was feeling grown up and ready to take on some adult responsibilities myself. "Mr. Green," I said evenly, "if you call me a nigger one more time I'm going to pick up that Coca-Cola bottle over there and hit you with it."

Somewhere inside his drunken haze it registered that I was challenging him. "Oh, is that right? Well you nigger, I'll . . ."

He never finished the sentence, because I picked up one of those big, heavy Coke bottles and I hit him flush between the eyes as hard as I could. That big old wrestler's head snapped back and he was knocked cold to the ground. He later needed 10 stitches to sew up his head.

I didn't stick around. I ran like hell to my house and told my mother and father what had happened. They knew Jim Green was a lot of trouble to a lot of people, but they also knew that he was white and I was black. There weren't too many ways that a black man could get away with decking a white in Charlotte. "You go off to your aunt's house, boy, and don't come out until I tell you to," my father said. I saw how agitated he was and I didn't stop to ask why. I went across town to my aunt's house and waited.

I stayed there two weeks until I couldn't stand it anymore, and then I went back to the golf course. I was caddying my first round when the police caught up to me on the 12th green and arrested me. They threw me in jail, with bail set at $50.

My dad and Sutton Alexander both knew that I wasn't going to win any trial and that if I didn't get out of jail soon, I might be spending lots of years there. They sprang me that night and the next morning my suitcase was packed and I was waiting for the first bus out of Charlotte.

I didn't have much, just a few clothes and a few dollars I'd saved. Passing by the country club on my way to the bus station, I looked out over the green fairways and the clubhouse and wondered if I'd ever play golf again, or if my dream would evaporate before I crossed the state line.

A caddy friend named Walter Ferguson had decided to come along with me. We got on that bus and watched North Carolina slip away. It was the first time I ever traveled, and I remember wondering how long the road would be. Little did I know that I'd be on the road for the rest of my life.

We stopped in Richmond at Walter's urging and hung around for a few days looking for jobs. When that didn't work out, we got on another bus bound for Philadelphia. I was an 11th-grade dropout who couldn't go back home. I knew only one thing, and that was how to play golf. I prayed to God that he would see fit to let me continue playing, and I promised that if he would, I would do everything in my power to stick with the game.

CHAPTER *3*

Cobbs Creek

This may not come as much of a surprise, but when I arrived in Philadelphia in the middle of February, it was damn cold outside. It was so cold that the first thing I did was borrow a coat and hat and gloves from my uncle James Sifford, who put me up at his house in North Philadelphia, near 18th and Norris.

It was not only the first time that I had experienced cold weather, but it was the first time that I was ever in a place where they didn't play golf year round. When I asked Uncle James where the nearest golf course was where I could get me a job caddying, he looked at me like I was crazy.

"Ain't no golf course gonna be open until springtime. Who you think's gonna be playin' golf out here in 30-degree weather?" By the look on his face, I could tell he was wondering just what he had gotten into, offering to put up his nephew for a few months.

Uncle James had two businesses, and I wasn't much help to him in either one. During the day he was a mason, laying bricks in new housing projects across the river in Camden, New Jersey. He got me a job as a laborer right off the bat, but after two weeks of hauling bricks and mortar around in a wheelbarrow in that cold, cold weather, I decided I'd had enough of the construction business. It wasn't any more fun than working in a fertilizer factory

or baling cotton for a living, and I reminded myself that I hadn't
left my family and home to do hard work for a living. I refused
to report to work on the third week and again I got that look
from Uncle James that seemed to say, "What in the world have
I gotten myself into with this boy?"

In the evenings Uncle James went down to the pool hall that
he owned and would proceed to whip everyone in the neighborhood at straight pool. That man could really handle a stick, and
I remember many a night spent watching him clean out all comers.
He tried to teach me the game, but I couldn't pick it up. I had
no talent for shooting pool, and it's probably lucky for me that
I didn't, or I still might be there in North Philadelphia racking
up balls and hustling for a dollar. After losing what little money
I had on a few ill-considered wagers, I put down the pool cue
for good. I could hit a little golf ball 250 yards to a 10-foot target,
but damned if I could make those billiard balls fall into a corner
pocket.

I didn't forget the promise that I had made to my mother
about paying my own way, and within a few days of quitting the
bricklaying, I found a job that I would keep for the next three-
and-a-half years. I became a shipping clerk for the National Biscuit
Company (today it's called Nabisco). I worked in the receiving
department, where I logged and helped unload the deliveries of
all the raw materials that the company used to make its products.
Every day we'd get truckloads of lard, flour, paper, boxes, sugar,
all that stuff they used to make cookies and crackers, and I'd see
that it was properly received and put in the right place in the
warehouse for distribution.

It wasn't a bad job, as regular jobs go, but I knew that I wasn't
going to do it forever. I was just biding my time until the golf
season began.

On Friday nights, which was payday at the National Biscuit
Company, the guys at work had all-night poker parties in somebody's house (somebody who wasn't married, I can pretty much
guarantee), and once in awhile I'd join in. Those were sky's-the-
limit games that would begin in the early evening and not break
up until daylight. You could double and triple your paycheck on
a good night or lose the whole damn thing before midnight.

It was during a warm weekend in April that I staggered out of the poker game one Sunday morning (that particular game had been going so good that it was carried over on Saturday night) with a few dollars in my pockets and started walking back to Uncle James's place. But I never made it to his doorstep, because golf came back to greet me.

That morning I ran into a guy named Waymon Mack, who was rushing to catch the street car with a bag of golf clubs on his shoulder. "Say, where you going with them clubs?" I called out to him. I didn't know Mack, who was about 10 years older than I, but I'd seen him around the neighborhood.

"I'm going to Cobbs Creek," he called back over his shoulder.

"Where's that?"

"It's all the way out to the end of the Market Street trolley."

I rushed to catch up to him. "How 'bout if I come along with you," I volunteered, and Mack agreed. We got on the trolley with his bag of precious clubs and headed to the outskirts of the city. We had to get out at 63rd and Market and then walk the last six blocks to the golf course.

Cobbs Creek, which was named for the creek that ran through several holes of the course, was one of the first public golf courses in Philadelphia when it opened in Fairmount Park in 1915. The course was intended for everyone to use, and I was both surprised and delighted to see both blacks and whites playing side by side there. I'd never seen anything like that in North Carolina. But in Philadelphia, on the public courses at least, things were different. Just as Sutton Alexander had promised me back in North Carolina, here was a place where I could play without having to worry about some groundskeeper coming by to run me off the course.

I didn't play on that first day but was content to follow Mack around and watch him play. I felt the excitement of golf start seeping back into me after the forced winter layoff. The course itself was nothing spectacular. It wasn't particularly long, but there were a lot of tough sand and water hazards to negotiate. Like any municipal course, the greens were cut haphazardly and the fairways and roughs had bald spots. On that April morning I'm sure it was still pretty soggy, too.

But it was a golf course, with a pro shop and a clubhouse and a driving range, and I could play there without anyone demanding to know who had let me in. I don't remember what it cost to play; probably not more than 50 cents in those days. I started going back there with Mack every weekend, and when he couldn't go, I'd borrow his clubs.

After two weekends of hitting balls all day, I felt my old swing coming back and I started to get cocky. After all, I had been one of the best players in North Carolina when I left, good enough to take on the great Clayton Heafner even up, and after just a few hours of beating balls, I was seeing the shots come back. I figured I could walk out on that Cobbs Creek course and take on all comers.

That's when I first met Howard Wheeler, one of the greatest black golfers of all time and the resident champion at Cobbs Creek. It wasn't that he was a working pro at the course, or had any official affiliation there, but as far as he was concerned, he owned the course and everybody knew it. He took on anybody who had the nerve to challenge him to a match, and more likely than not, Wheeler would finish the day with a great deal of his money in his pocket. On his home course he was practically unbeatable, and on the road he was nearly as good. By the time I had met him, he'd already won the first of what would be five Negro National Open championships.

But I was 17 years old and, as far as I was concerned, the man to beat. I'd heard about Wheeler's prowess on the course, but I took one look at his swing, and with the wisdom of the adolescent, said to myself, "Hell, he ain't nuthin!"

Wheeler was a cross-handed player, which means that he gripped a golf club opposite the way nearly everybody else does it. While most players will put their left hand at the top of the club and then intertwine their right hand below the left, Wheeler and other cross-handed players put their right hand at the top. The effect is like they're constantly backhanding the ball when they hit it, and it looks awkward as hell. Take a look at Charles

Owens on the Senior PGA Tour, and you'll see how a great cross-handed player hits.

I was so busy telling myself that Wheeler couldn't possibly hit the ball right that I didn't pay attention to the shots he was making with his short, quick swing. Even with that weird, backhanded swing, Wheeler was a magnificent striker of the ball. I'd later find out that he could and would hit the ball off any surface. Before anyone knew what a trick-shot artist was, Wheeler was hitting 300-yard drives with balls that were teed up on top of Coke bottles. Wouldn't scratch the bottle, but the ball would take off like it was shot from a cannon. He could hit the ball off matchbook covers, off paper cups . . . it was the damndest thing you ever saw. If he'd been alive 40 years later than he was, Wheeler could have made a fortune giving trick-shot exhibitions.

I took one look at him warming up and marched up to him on the driving range. Mind you, this was but three weeks after I'd first run into Waymon Mack on the street and started swinging a club again. "You Howard Wheeler?" I asked.

He sized me up and smiled. He was older than I and much more experienced. I bet he saw dollar signs in his eyes when he took a look at the stocky kid in front of him. "Uh huh."

"I'm Charlie Sifford, and I'm gonna whip your ass on that golf course."

Wheeler promptly turned and headed to the first tee, beckoning for me to join him. I snatched up Mack's golf bag and followed him. Boy, I was sure going to turn some heads at this new golf course. Why, by the time the day was through I'd be the new champ, maybe even set a course record, I figured.

Wheeler asked me how much money I had in my pocket, and I told him $20. Fine, he said, we'll play for 10 dollars a nine, match play. He stepped up to the tee, and backhanded a ball a good 270 yards.

He proceeded to systematically take me apart. My first 10 dollars went into his pocket after the fifth hole, and he cleaned me out on the 10th. Game over. It's not that I played that badly, but Wheeler played great. If I hit a solid approach shot into a green, he'd better it by putting his approach within five feet of the stick. If I messed up a little and put one into the rough, he'd make things doubly tough by screaming a drive into perfect position. When I made birdie, he made eagle.

Afterwards, as he was putting my money into his pocket, Wheeler smiled and told me that he was the best golf player in the world and that I shouldn't feel so bad. Then he sauntered off to the clubhouse to find another victim for the day.

I realized then and there that I had a lot to learn about golf. In fact, what Wheeler did to me may have been one of the most important things that ever happened to me on a golf course. I hated losing, and I realized that the only way I was going to get my money back from Wheeler was to work hard at my game and bring it up to his level. I think that at that moment I became a professional golfer, or at least, a man who was dedicated to playing top-level golf. Until that time I had enjoyed the game and enjoyed the feeling of being able to play it well, and I was stubborn enough to not be turned away from the game by people who didn't want to see a black kid succeed at it. But I had never been truly dedicated to golf up to that point, nor had I realized the inherent deficiencies in my game. Howard Wheeler changed all that in one morning.

Before I left Cobbs Creek that day, I looked up Wheeler and told him that I would be back to challenge him again. He laughed and told me he'd play any time. But I wasn't laughing. I was steamed from losing so much money, and I vowed that the next time would be different.

I realized that if I was going to become a serious golfer, I'd have to buy my own set of clubs. I couldn't depend on Waymon Mack to always let me borrow his sticks, and besides, his clubs were secondhand and not particularly good. That afternoon I went into a department store to price a set of golf clubs. In those days there weren't sporting goods stores or golf specialty stores, and I sure as hell wasn't going to walk into some country club's pro shop. I had to go downtown to one of the big stores.

I found a set of Lawson Little Wright & Ditson golf clubs that came with everything: irons, three woods, and a golf bag. Next to the Ben Hogan Wilson clubs, which I couldn't afford, they were the best clubs you could buy. There was only one catch: the whole set cost $135, and after my defeat by Wheeler, I didn't have but 10 dollars to my name.

I put that $10 down, and the next week I went down there on payday and put down another $50, and the week after that I paid the balance outright. I was 17 years old and had my first set of golf clubs, and believe me, I was one proud cat. I went right down to Cobbs Creek and starting beating balls, and I stayed the whole weekend, hitting balls, putting, and learning my clubs. I figured out how far I could hit each one, how to get the most out of the driver, and how the wedge felt on short, soft chips from the rough.

Two weeks later I was ready for Wheeler. I found him, as usual, lagging around the putting green, and I walked up to him and said, "Remember me?" He smiled big, probably envisioning another big payday, and said, "Let's go."

That time I beat him, and you probably won't be surprised when I tell you that it was one of the most satisfying wins of my career. Although I was still playing mostly from instinct, I was able to play within myself and do what it took to win. I hit the right shots, and I made the chips and the putts, and by the time the afternoon was over, I had won my $20 back.

After that, Wheeler and I became a team, and together, we beat everybody at Cobbs Creek. In those days I didn't know that much about golf. I still had never taken a lesson, and, luckily, the things I had learned naturally, such as my grip and swing, were all correct. They must have been okay, because I've never changed my grip or my swing all these years. But I didn't know anything about strategy. I'd fog the ball down the fairway, lob it onto the green, and then putt out.

Playing with Wheeler at Cobbs Creek, I began to learn about the subtleties of the game. I saw how he sized up the course, and how he knew how to hit every shot to set up his next, depending on everything from the wind and grass conditions to the pin placements on the greens. Because of all of those tricky little sand traps, I got a lot of practice in hitting out of sand, and I started to take time to practice those shots, instead of always hitting my driver and long irons on the range.

Wheeler had always been the man to beat at Cobbs Creek, and now word began to spread about the two of us playing together. I remember one time the famous pro from Wilmington, North Carolina, Ed "Porky" Oliver, came by to play us. Another time we received a challenge from a pair of brothers up in Valley Forge. Their names were Mike and Frank Souchak, and, of course, it was the same Mike Souchak who is still playing with me out on the Senior PGA Tour. Mike was just starting out like I was, and he heard about the good black players at Cobbs Creek. They challenged us and we went up there and beat the hell out of them. We must have won $20 or $30 from the Souchaks, and they were mad as anything. That was a big payday in those days.

As good as Howard Wheeler was — and he and I were always in the 60s or low 70s in those days — he never talked to me about wanting to play professional golf on the white tour. He entered his share of the black tournaments and was regarded as one of the top black golfers in the country, and every year he'd go off to Chicago to play in the famous Tam O'Shanter tournament, but that was the end of it. Howard just didn't have that kind of personality or persistence to push his way into pro golf. He was content to be the local favorite and to take on anyone who wanted to challenge him on his home course.

Wheeler was the next best thing to being a touring pro. He had found a way to play golf nearly every day without having to hold down a full-time job. Because of his golf game, he had made friends with Eddie Mowry, who was married to Ethel Waters, the famous actress and singer. Howard got a gig being Eddie's driver, and that and the money he made hustling on the golf course kept him going. For a black, that was about as far as you could go in golf in those days. I never questioned Wheeler about why he didn't try to match his game up against the Hogans and Sneads and Byron Nelsons of the world. It was still too early for that, and I wasn't looking any farther than Cobbs Creek.

For the next three years I continued working all week at the National Biscuit Company and playing golf all day on the weekends. That is, on the weekends when we weren't called to work overtime for the war effort. Those were good times for a young, single kid from the South turned loose on a big city like Philadelphia. I was all over that city, listening to the big bands play on their national tours, going down to see Connie Mack's Philadelphia Athletics play baseball, and generally dancing up a storm. And brother, back then, I could *dance!*

It was at one such dance that I met the prettiest girl in Philadelphia. I knew that she lived over on 18th Street, because I had seen her around and was trying to figure out a way to ask her out. When I saw her at the dance, I got up the nerve to ask her for a turn. We danced three or four times that night, and then she brought me home to meet her mother. Her name was Rose Crumbley and her mother's name was Amelia. It was your basic love at first sight. We started seeing each other regularly, and I would have married her sooner if it weren't for the war. As it was, we got married in 1947, and now we're going on 45 years together.

Two things happened to me in 1943. My mother died in Charlotte, and I was drafted into the army. Poor Mom, she never did get to see me break out and make my name in the world. I know that if there is a heaven, she's in it, because she was nothing but goodness inside.

I didn't have much time to grieve, because I was drafted into the service, and there was a war raging overseas. I chose the army, and after a hellish basic training in Fort Dix, I was sent to Okinawa with the 79th Signal Heavy Construction team, which meant that I had to scale telephone poles and wire up communications gear right after the first wave of infantry hit the beaches. We went in right behind the 24th Infantry, and I saw my share of men killed and wounded. If you think it's a lonely feeling to be the only black guy in a professional golf tournament, you should try climbing a telephone pole by yourself when bullets are flying. There was nothing to do but hang in there and pray.

When the war ended, I was still in Okinawa, and they gave us the choice of being transferred to Japan, which I definitely didn't want to do, or joining the Army Special Services. I had indicated somewhere that I liked to play golf, and I was allowed to form a golf team right there in Okinawa. There were four white guys and me. One of them was Willie Hunter, Jr., whose father was the pro for years at the Riviera Country Club in California. I had heard of his dad, so I took Willie onto the golf team.

The only golf we played was on a trip to the Philippines, where we got the hell beaten out of us on the course in a couple of matches. Which didn't bother us in the slightest, because it sure beat working for the army.

The only thing I remember about that golf team was an incident that happened off the golf course in Manila. We went downtown to have a few drinks after we got done playing, and we saw this guy sitting in his little buggy on the street with a horse in front. You know, like a horse-drawn taxi. Willie said to me, "Charlie, I heard you were a prizefighter at one time. I'll bet you five dollars that you couldn't knock that horse down."

It's true that I had tried boxing at one time, but I'd never tried it against a horse. So what the hell . . . I walked up to this little horse, took a huge swing, and hit him right between the eyes. Knocked him down, too. And then all these Filipino guys came pouring out of doorways and alleys and beat the living hell out of us. We went back to the barracks that night all bloodied and raggedy. Believe me, it was the last time I ever punched a horse, or any other animal for that matter. Being in the army long enough will make a man try just about anything, I guess.

I served in Okinawa for 18 months and was discharged in 1946. I went back to Philadelphia, where Rose was waiting for me, and resumed my job at the National Biscuit Company. But I had a plan. Those years in the service had given me lots of time to think, and I decided that I wasn't going to be a shipping clerk for the rest of my life. I was going to be a golf professional. I knew that I had the skills and the dedication to make it in golf, and I knew that I owed it to myself to give it a shot.

I worked six more months at the Biscuit Company, which was just long enough to earn vacation pay. The day I got the check, I quit. I was 24 years old, and it was the last time in my life that I've ever had to work a steady, nine-to-five job. I was on my own, with only my Lawson Little golf clubs and my skills to see me through. I headed back to Cobbs Creek and began to practice hard, because I knew that if I was going to be a professional golfer, it would all have to come from within me. I had no teacher, no mentor, and no sponsor, but I had a challenge before me. I knew that it wouldn't be easy, but that was okay. It was the challenge of making it that drove me on.

CHAPTER 4

The National Negro Open

I got a big break in the summer of 1946 when Eddie Mowry invited me to come along with him and Wheeler to Pittsburgh to play in the annual National Negro Open, the biggest black tournament in the country. They were going to drive up there the last week of August in Mowry's big car, and he said he'd foot the bills for my room and board. Eddie was a nice guy, but he was also no fool: He knew that if he got me playing with the pros, I wouldn't be at Cobbs Creek to whip his butt all the time and take his money. I've traveled an awful lot of miles in the last 45 years, but that car ride from Philadelphia to Pittsburgh was the most significant trip I would ever take in my life.

The National Negro Open was sponsored by an organization called the United Golf Association (not to be confused with the United States Golf Association, which continues to oversee amateur golf in the country, as well as the U.S. Open tournament), which ran a kind of minitour for blacks during the summer months. Although it was set up for blacks, whites could play in the UGA events, too, if they wanted, although the prize money and the conditions weren't anything like they were on the all-white PGA Tour. At that time, of course, blacks weren't allowed anywhere near the PGA Tour, so the UGA was our only chance to compete. On our tour, prize money was usually $500 for the winner, and another $500 for the other top finishers to split up, and that was it.

The National Negro Open was played in a different city every year on a tour that typically stuck to northern cities like Cleveland, Dayton, Hartford, Pittsburgh, Philadelphia, and Detroit, although in the fifties we started playing in Dallas, Atlanta, and Greensboro too. The tournaments were always played on public golf courses, which in those days were the only places that blacks could play, and would attract a field of 30 or 40 good players. We're not talking about a manicured golf course here with tents and refreshment booths. We're talking about a scraggly municipal course where they'd give us a half day to hold our tournament on Friday, Saturday, and Sunday.

Still, for black players and black people in general, the annual National Negro Open was a big deal. Anybody with any kind of game would come out to qualify as either a professional or an amateur, with separate tournaments run simultaneously for men and women. All of the biggest black stars in the sports and entertainment worlds came out to play in the open, and they attracted a full contingent of black newspapers to cover the tournaments. Other coverage was pretty slim. We might get a small write-up in the local white newspaper, and occasionally even a mention in the *New York Times* sports section.

Wheeler had already won the open a few times before 1946, and during the drive to Pittsburgh, he warned me that I was going to be overwhelmed by the crowds and the carnival atmosphere of the tournament, not to mention the competition. Of course he and I loved to compete against each other, so I didn't know if he was telling the truth or was just trying to psyche me out to get a competitive edge. I told him that I could handle anything and wouldn't let no crowd get to me, but inside I was already feeling the butterflies start to jump. I'd been talking about becoming a pro golfer, and now it was put-up-or-shut-up time. I was both excited about getting into the competition and fearful of facing my dream head on.

When we got to Pittsburgh, I found out that Wheeler wasn't kidding about the fast environment of a professional tournament.

Within two days of arriving, I met celebrities like Joe Louis, Ike Williams, Sugar Ray Robinson, and Billy Eckstine, a man who very soon would play a big part in my future. The stars were out in full force at the golf course, and I felt like a wide-eyed kid from North Carolina as I sneaked looks at them on the putting green or standing around in circles talking and laughing. Of course, Wheeler knew them all from the tournaments he'd played in, and to them, he was something of a star in his own right since he'd been winning all of the black tournaments. He introduced me as the "other guy at Cobbs Creek who can play," and nobody believed me when I told them that I was beating Wheeler six times out of 10 on our home course. When I started hitting balls, though, they saw that I could back up my talk and word began to get around about the new guy from Philadelphia. Somebody even decided to call me "Charley Horse," because I'm stocky. Thank God that nickname never stuck.

As Wheeler promised, the competition was fierce. For the first time in my life, I found myself surrounded by a whole bunch of black guys who could really play. The National Negro Open was our Masters, and the best players in the country came out to enter it from as far away as Florida and California. In Philadelphia I had developed this cocky attitude that since I could beat Wheeler, then I could beat anybody. Seeing these guys hit the ball, I suddenly wasn't so sure. I had heard about some of the good black players, but now here they were up close, and one look at the way they hit the ball gave me a sinking feeling that I wasn't playing for no dollar bets at Cobbs Creek against businessmen.

They were guys who would become my best friends and my fiercest competition for the next 10 years. Before the week was out, I had played with and befriended three pros who had the skills and the dedication to the game that I myself had. I have no doubt that all of these guys, along with Wheeler, could have made great names for themselves on the tour, but their careers were never allowed to happen. They were Bill Spiller from Los Angeles, Zeke Hartsfield from Atlanta, and to my mind, the best of all, Teddy Rhodes from Nashville. These guys were the Josh

Gibson, Satchel Paige, and Cool Papa Bell of golf, and the UGA Tour was their Negro League. The history of blacks in golf is written around their names, and at that time, in the midforties, they were in their prime, with no place to play but lousy, municipal courses and UGA tournaments where they pretty much always finished in the top 10.

While guys like Ben Hogan and Sam Snead and Lew Worsham were getting headlines every week for dueling at PGA tournaments on the best courses in the country, Spiller and Rhodes and Wheeler were playing for bets on public courses, shooting their 63s and 64s for the benefit of some poor sucker whose money they were taking. I know that given a chance, they could have competed against anyone in the country.

I don't remember how I finished that year in Pittsburgh, but I suspect it wasn't that great. I'm sure that all of the excitement and newness got to me and led to more than a couple of balls hooked into the rough during the competitive rounds, which I believe Wheeler ended up winning again. I don't care how good a player you are or how strong your game is back at your home club: when you go out there and play with the pros, you're looking at a different cat altogether. But I didn't embarrass myself, and I saw that if I worked off some rough edges, I could compete with these guys and I could win, just as I had beaten Wheeler after a couple of tries.

What I remember most about that tournament wasn't the play itself, but the friendships I made. Suddenly I was running in a circle with Joe Louis and Sugar Ray Robinson, alongside black golf legends like Teddy Rhodes and Bill Spiller. In the space of a week I was transformed from a guy who played a pretty good game back in Philadelphia to a professional who could hold his own against the best black pros of my day. I was suddenly surrounded by a group of black guys who loved the game as much as I did, and loved to talk about the shots and the tournaments and the competition. It was exactly what I had always wanted.

At the end of the week I was invited by some guys to travel with them to Detroit and the last stop on the UGA Tour, the annual Joe Louis Invitational. Joe Louis himself was wild about golf, and

it was through his efforts alone that blacks got anywhere at all
in the game in the fifties, which I'll get to later. When I met him
he'd been playing for a few years and had hired Teddy Rhodes
to be his permanent golf instructor, which meant that Teddy
traveled in Joe's entourage and played golf with him every chance
that Joe could get away from training.

Mind you, this was 1946 when Joe Louis was the heavyweight
champion of the world. That year he knocked out Billy Conn
in June and then came right back in September to take out Tami
Mauriello in the first round. But when I met Joe in Pittsburgh,
and afterwards in Detroit, when I spent a lot of time with him,
Joe didn't talk about boxing. He talked about his short game, and
how you line up putts, and the great drive he hit yesterday. He
was totally committed to the game, and after his boxing career
was over, he even entered a few PGA tournaments in California.

Joe Louis was the most big-hearted man I have ever met in
my life. I hated it when he was portrayed as stupid or ignorant
in his later days, and people snickered about him squandering
all the money he made in the ring. Because as far as I'm
concerned, the world has never had a better friend than Joe Louis,
and I don't just mean for the black man. People, white or black,
would walk up to him on the street and say, "Joe, I really need
$100," and Joe Louis would reach into his pocket and give it to
them. On the golf course he would take on anyone that
challenged him, even when the challenger was a far better player
than Joe. You want to bet for $100, or $1,000? Joe would take
the action, and he'd try his damndest on the course, and then
hand over the money with a smile. He just loved the competition,
and he loved to help people out. He didn't care about the money,
and losing a golf match didn't hurt him any. Joe Louis got all the
satisfaction he needed in the ring, and the rest of his life was
meant for pleasure. He was the most generous man I've ever seen,
as well as one of the few black men committed to making things
better for his people. In his day he was a towering symbol of
strength and pride for the black man. He was a true hero.

It was Joe Louis and Teddy Rhodes who got me the biggest
break of my life in Detroit that year, because they convinced Billy

Eckstine, the great singer and bandleader, that he should hire me to be his private golf instructor, just as Teddy was Joe Louis's teacher. Billy had just started getting interested in the game from hanging around Joe Louis and seeing the kind of betting that was done on the golf course. See, Billy had been a softball player and he always thought that golf was kind of slow and stupid, but then he saw Joe Louis out there making all kinds of ridiculous wagers and he thought golf might be interesting. Then Honey Coles, the famous dancer who had been traveling with Billy's band, bought Billy a set of starter golf clubs from Sears & Roebuck, and Billy got hooked. But he was on the road so much that he could never stop for lessons.

Teddy Rhodes had taken a shine to me in Pittsburgh, and in Detroit we played together a couple of times. Without my knowing it, he went to Billy Eckstine and said, "Look here, this young guy is good and he needs some help. Why don't you sponsor him, give him a job with you, and in return he'll teach you how to play. That'll give Charlie a chance to be playing golf all the time and it will give you a good partner."

Billy wasn't too sure about it, but then Joe Louis stepped in. As Billy tells it, he was lounging around his hotel room one morning when Louis calls up and says he wants to play this hot new Philadelphia pro, and he wants Billy to put up the money for the bet. Billy says how much? and Joe says $1,000 a bet. Now, Billy had seen me play and knew that I had a game, and he also knew that Joe's bets had no relationship whatsoever to his ability to win. So he said sure, go ahead.

Later that day, Joe Louis shows up at Billy's hotel room, a beaten man. "Well, the champ got whupped," he told Billy, "but it could have been worse if Charlie hadn't blown up on the 9th hole."

Joe proceeded to tell Billy what had happened. That day I started out by birdying three of the first six holes. On the seventh, a par 5, I eagled. On the eighth I made par. My "blow up," as Joe put it, was missing a birdie putt to make par on the ninth hole. I was 5-under on the front nine, and Joe, who shot a damn good 2-under, had lost three bets and $3,000. "Any time I shoot

2-under and lose three bets, I know I got the wrong company,"
Joe glumly told Billy.

When I showed up later, Billy looked at me and said sternly,
"Joe Louis says you blew up on that last hole," and I could have
killed him. But he hired me to travel with him, and for the next
10 years I was Billy Eckstine's golf teacher, personal valet, and
partner on the golf course. I think it was the most fun a young
man could possibly have.

Teddy Rhodes and I began a great partnership, too, in Detroit
that year. Before the tournament started we were challenged to
a match by Al Besselink, who was one of the white pros who
would come out and play in our tournaments. "Me and my buddy
are going to whup the two best black guys out here," he told
everyone. "Bring me the best you've got."

Besselink was, and continues to be, a hell of a guy, but Teddy
and I took him and his partner apart during a round of golf, and
after that, Bessie didn't come around looking for easy bets. At
least not with us.

My life on the road began at that point. I had left Philadelphia
to play in a tournament in Pittsburgh, and suddenly here I was
in Detroit with a job and a title, Billy Eckstine's Golf Professional.
Hell, I'd never given or taken a golf lesson in my life, but I knew
that I could do it. I called Rose in Philadelphia and told her what
I'd done and she couldn't believe it. She thought the golf part
was pretty neat, but she was wild about the Billy Eckstine gig.
Billy, you know, was like the black Frank Sinatra in those days,
and practically every girl in the country, white or black, was in
love with him.

For the next 10 years I toured with Billy in the winter months,
going from city to city where he played the best theaters to packed
crowds, and in the summer I played golf on the UGA Tour. When
Billy headed to the West Coast for a blow in January, I went with
him and hooked up with my buddies there. Teddy Rhodes lived
in L.A. during the winter, and Spiller, who worked as a redcap
at the train station, made his home there. We'd all play in the
L.A. Open in January, which was one of three white tournaments
that we were allowed to enter (the others were the Tam O'Shanter

in Chicago on the Fourth of July and the Canadian Open in Toronto), and then watch as the white tour headed south to San Diego, Phoenix, and Tucson. We played for fun at the Western Avenue course in L.A. or we'd catch an invitation to the Jewish country club. When Billy moved on, so did I.

In 1947 my sweetheart Rose and I got married in Philadelphia and moved in with her mother, and later that year we had our first son, Charles Sifford, Jr. Thank God for my mother-in-law, Amelia Crumbley, who as far as I'm concerned was the greatest mother-in-law who ever lived. I went to her before I proposed to Rose, and I explained to her that I was working for Billy Eckstine and playing golf, and that I'd be away from home a great deal of the time. She sat me down and asked me if I loved her daughter and told me not to worry, that she'd take care of things at home and I could go off and live my life as I saw fit. When Charles, Jr., came along, she took care of him and Rose, and when I swung into town they were all there to greet me and make me feel right at home.

Those were my cross-country days, when I'd drive from New York to California three or four times a year, stopping in Chicago or Detroit or wherever Billy was gigging, and when there was a spare week or a spare month I'd get in the car and drive back to Philadelphia to be with my family.

In 1947 the National Negro Open was played on my home course, Cobbs Creek in Philadelphia, and that time I knew what to do. I took Howard Wheeler right down to the wire and wound up finishing second after a lousy final round. Wheeler shot a 286 and I had 290. My confidence was building and my game was coming around. I was already rising to the top of the black golf world.

Teddy Rhodes must have missed that tournament for some reason. I don't remember why he wasn't there, but he must not have been, because in those days I could never beat him. It took me six years to beat Teddy Rhodes in a major tournament from the time I first met him, all the way to 1952 when I won my first of six National Negro Open titles. But losing to Teddy Rhodes was nothing to feel bad about, because he was the best. In fact,

I believe he was the best there ever was, and I don't just mean among the black players.

Teddy Rhodes was the black Jack Nicklaus, but you've probably never heard of him because he was black and living in the wrong time. From 1945 to 1950, Teddy was as good a golfer as anyone on the planet. His only fault was that he was far too soft-spoken a person, too much a gentleman, to make waves and try to force his way onto the white tour. Given half a chance, Teddy Rhodes could have put up some numbers in professional golf that would still be standing today.

Instead, he vanished without a trace. His story is one of the great tragedies of golf. Twenty-two years after his death, I still grieve for Teddy Rhodes and a legend that was never allowed to happen.

CHAPTER 5

The Incomparable Teddy Rhodes

Billy Eckstine played a round of golf against Sam Snead once in a celebrity pro-am in the Catskills. Billy was partnered with Jimmy Demaret and Snead was playing with Alan King in the foursome. On a par-3 hole, Billy stepped up to the tee with a 7-iron and knocked a lovely shot about two feet away from the pin. Snead turned to him in mock exasperation, and in that hillbilly accent of his, yelled out, "Who the hell taught you that shot, Teddy Rhodes?"

That was a Teddy Rhodes shot, because within 150 yards of a green, Teddy was the undisputed master. The man could simply pipeline his short irons, and around the fringe and the apron of the green he was deadly. He had the best short game I've ever seen, as well as a beautiful, fluid golf swing. Teddy could flat out play the game. He was so good and so natural that he held his own in the most impossible playing conditions. It didn't matter if he didn't have time to warm up or if he was seeing a golf course for the first time or if you threw a low number at him when you were playing against him. Teddy would rise to the occasion every time and put himself in position to win.

Teddy excelled even in the few white tournaments he was allowed to enter every year. Imagine the pressure and the nervousness he must have felt walking onto a country club course

in L.A. or Toronto or Chicago once a year and facing the likes
of Hogan and Demaret and Snead. In many cases he was the only
black guy out there, and you know that a lot of strange looks
were thrown his way, not to mention a few catcalls. Still, time
and again, he'd finish in the top 20 and frequently make a run
at the leaders. Here's a guy who rarely got to play on the really
good golf courses, and who rarely had to face stiff competition
when he played, yet he was so cool and so good that he could
beat three-quarters of the professional field every time he went
out.

In 1949, for instance, Teddy began the year by shooting a 300
at L.A. and finishing in the money. Two years before in L.A., he
came out with an opening round of 71 that was two strokes back
of the leader and just one stroke behind Hogan and Porky Oliver.
But Teddy didn't have any second chances to make up for a bad
round like the white pros did. If he didn't shoot well at L.A.,
he had to wait a long time to prove himself again, because once
the tournament wrapped, the white pros headed south for San
Diego, Phoenix, and Tucson, and Teddy had to stay where he
was. After L.A., the tournaments weren't open to colored.

So instead of continuing to compete against the best, Teddy
had to hang around and play pickup games on public courses.
He had to wait all the way until the summer to play again. Teddy
began the summer of 1949, which may well have been when his
game was at its peak, by demolishing all of us at the all-black
Ray Robinson Open on Long Island. All he did there was shoot
a 275, with final rounds of 62 and 68, which blew Howard
Wheeler out of the water by six strokes. Teddy won $800 for
that victory. In August he went to Chicago to play in the Tam
O'Shanter and shot a 284 for 14th place against the white pros.
Two weeks later he took the National Negro Open title away from
Wheeler, and he would keep it for the next three years.

God only knows what numbers Teddy would have put up if
he had played on the white tour in those days, or what kind of
influence he might have had on black kids to play golf. They
would have had to write about him in every white newspaper
in the country, because professional golf was becoming a big deal,

and players like Lew Worsham and Chick Harbert and Cary Middlecoff were in the headlines week after week. When Teddy had that spectacular final day to win the Ray Robinson, for example, he got two paragraphs in the *New York Times*. On that same sports page, they gave seven paragraphs to the first round of the Western Open in St. Paul, Minnesota, with glowing descriptions of how Harbert and Lloyd Mangrum shot 67s to take the early lead.

Poor Teddy just came along 20 years too soon to be a black man in professional golf. Although he tried a couple of times to break into the PGA Tour, he was just too nice a guy and too much a gentleman to fight and scratch for his constitutional rights to play. Teddy didn't want any of that pushing and pressing that it took to break into the game. It was contrary to his nature. All he wanted to do was play golf, and when somebody told him that he couldn't play in a certain tournament or on some golf course, he would just turn away and find someplace else to play. It broke my heart even then to see Teddy denied the opportunity to play with the best, because it was obvious that he was made to play golf.

It broke my heart and it chilled me, too, because if someone as good and as good-natured as Teddy couldn't win a spot on the PGA Tour, how was I ever going to get to play? I was still a young guy when I first started playing with Teddy, and I wasn't so sure that golf had more in store for me than it had offered him.

Teddy was born in Nashville in 1916, and like so many of us, he got into the game by caddying at the local country club. He apparently made quite a name for himself on the local scene there, because when Joe Louis came through town — it must have been in the early forties — he heard about Teddy and looked him up. Joe Louis saw what a great golfer Teddy was, and he offered him a job on the spot to travel with the entourage and give Joe golf lessons. Teddy actually took time to think about it; it had never really occurred to him that he could make a living out of golf and play anywhere else but in Nashville.

When I met Teddy he was 30 years old and at the top of his game. He was a handsome guy, tall and light skinned and one of the fanciest dressers on any tour, white or black. In fact, he apparently had a thing with Jimmy Demaret to see who could be the best-dressed guy on the golf course. Teddy was the first guy I ever saw wearing knickers on the course. He looked so elegant that you couldn't laugh at him, and besides, his game was so good that he could have worn a bathing suit out there and not drawn attention away from his swing.

Teddy met Bill Spiller during one of his West Coast swings, and together they tried to break into whites-only tournaments. Spiller was much more of an activist than Teddy or the other blacks. He complained loud and long to anyone who would listen about his rights to play the game, and he was known for picketing professional golf tournaments. He'd stand out there all day with a sign saying that the tournament was unfair for excluding blacks. His attitude rubbed some people the wrong way, but I think he was on the right track. The only way any black men have ever gotten into this game was through being belligerent and adamant about playing. But Spiller turned off a lot of people, and once he got into tournaments, he could never quite deliver the goods to prove that he belonged out there with the best players.

In January of 1948 Teddy and Spiller were turned down from entering the Richmond Open in California because of their race, and that time Spiller talked Teddy into doing something about it. Together (and with a third player named Madison Gunter), they got a lawyer and filed suit against the tournament and the PGA for $325,000, saying that their constitutional rights had been violated.

That was a pretty damn big sum of money in those days, and the PGA had to pay attention. The case was about to go to court when, in September, the PGA formally agreed to stop discriminating against Negroes. They pledged there would be no PGA rules against Negroes in the future and would not refuse tournament-playing privileges to anyone because of color. Satisfied, Teddy and Spiller dropped the suit, eager to get on with their new careers as professional golfers. They didn't even get themselves any money for their trouble.

But instead of suddenly being allowed to play, they were presented with another stone wall. The PGA switched its tournament policy to an "invitation-only" status, claiming that the tournament could invite any professional golfers it wanted and not invite others. In short, the PGA washed its hands of the matter and innocently said that they had no control over whom the tournaments chose. Once again, Teddy was shut out of playing, but only after having invested his time and legal fees towards a lawsuit that got him nothing but a paper victory.

The PGA had lost the battle but won the war. Because it settled the lawsuit, there was no court judgment and the PGA didn't even have to pay anything out. This wouldn't be the last time that the organization pulled a trick out of its sleeve to keep blacks from playing in its tournaments.

No wonder Teddy didn't want to fight. He had tried to fight it through the courts and got nowhere, and Teddy was smart enough to see which way the wind was blowing. Blacks all around the country were trying to play golf, and not only on the professional level. Opposition was so fierce that our pleas had to run all the way to the highest courts to be heard.

In July of that year, a group of blacks in Baltimore went to federal court to enforce a ruling that allowed them to play on the city's public courses. Up to that point they had only been allowed access to one crummy, nine-hole course, when whites had three good 18-hole courses to choose from.

In Miami they made a similar agreement, except they came up with a clever loophole that only allowed blacks to play for a few hours on one day of the week. That case went all the way up to the Supreme Court, and in 1950 they ordered the Florida Supreme Court to give blacks equal access and equal hours on the courses.

If blacks couldn't even play on municipal courses, how the hell were we going to get onto the PGA Tour? No, Teddy Rhodes was before his time, and he knew better than to fight about it. He played where they let him, and when he played, he excelled. By the time things opened up a little bit for me in the early sixties, Teddy was too old and too sick to play. He developed kidney problems in his late forties that hospitalized him several times, and on July 4, 1969, he died in Nashville at the age of 53. He was a fine man, a good friend, and a great golfer.

Teddy was the best of the lot, but there were other black guys out there who could really play this game in the forties and fifties. Howard Wheeler was damn good, and a guy I'll never forget was little Zeke Hartsfield out of Atlanta, Georgia. Zeke had his own unique way of getting back at the golf world for not being allowed to play in the pro tournaments: he was perhaps the world's greatest hustler. Hell, even if they'd let Zeke play on the PGA Tour, he probably couldn't have afforded it, because he made so much money by hustling.

Zeke was a skinny, little guy who looked like he couldn't hit the ball 40 yards. He was friendly as anything and could chat up people all day long. In fact, Zeke really helped me out when I started playing on the tour, because he had introduced me to lots of people in different cities who would let us sleep at their houses. It seemed that anywhere we went, Zeke knew people who liked him well enough to put us up, and it saved us a lot of money in hotel bills, or a lot of nights of not sleeping in the car in towns where there weren't any places that would put up blacks.

When I started to play regularly on the UGA circuit, it was me and Teddy Rhodes traveling together in one car and Zeke and Howard Wheeler in the other. Frequently we all stayed together in some house where Zeke had a friend. The four of us almost always finished in the top five of any tournament we entered, and we pretty much split the pots up between us. If Zeke came out short one week, Teddy or I would give him some of our winnings, and we knew it would come right back to us down the road.

Zeke was good enough as a competitive golfer to win the National Negro Open a few times, but he was far better as a hustler. You always wanted him as a playing partner when there was money on the table, because he always found a way to make the money go into his pocket. At a tournament he could shoot nine birdies and nine bogies for the round, but when the betting started, he always found a way to win.

Zeke was a great hustler because he was so friendly and because he could make it look like he couldn't play a lick. He'd go out to a putting green and practically look like he was cross-eyed as he sprayed balls all over the place. And then some dummy would get interested and suggest a putting contest, and Zeke would knock in 20 balls and take all the guy's money, and he would do it in such a way that it still looked like he didn't know how to play a lick.

Zeke must be going on 100 years old now, and as far as I know, he's still alive and well in Atlanta. He talked to Peter Roisman, my agent, a couple of years ago, and I'll let Zeke tell in his own words how he could take anybody to the cleaners on the golf course: "I used to go down to Akron, Ohio, and sit around and putt a little. Everybody would put up $100 and we'd putt for that, and I was putting that golf ball so bad all day long, they didn't think I could play. They had this guy named Bill there who wanted me to play him, and I said no, I can't play him, but I can out-putt him. Bill was a good putter, and they would bet all the money on him. They had this long putting green and I would hit some long putts, man, they must have been 100 yards, and I was two-putting them all and hitting some of them in. They put up that money and I won it, 12 guys playing at $100 apiece, winner take all. I won it four times in a row!

"So they finally get me onto the golf course. I was hitting some balls on the range and shanking them off into the woods, just for fun. So this guy from Houston, Texas, he says, 'He can't hit the ball: let's get him on the golf course.'

"So we start playing and we start with a par 4. I slice the ball into the woods and then chip it out and I get my par. The next hole is a par 5 coming back, and I tee it up and hit it into a ditch. It's sitting up on the left-hand side of this ditch and I take and hook the ball like crazy and land it right up in the middle of the green. The next hole is a par 3, and I could hit a 9-iron onto the green, but I take a 5-iron and punch it down there and it rolls up to the green. These guys are going crazy, but I'm still calm, just hitting all of those crazy shots and still making par. Now we go to another par 4 hole, and I push my tee shot to the right into the rough and on a hill. So I take out the 5-iron again and let the rough take it off, and the ball rolls up onto the green again. Then another par 3 and I hit the ball into the trap, and then I fly that ball out of that trap right next to the cup. Sometimes I'm way out on the fairway, 30 yards from the green, and I take out my putter and roll it right up to the pin.

"And these guys are saying, 'He doesn't look like he can play; he must be some kind of a genius.' I won all of that money out there. Those guys would probably have killed me if they knew I was a professional."

They don't make 'em like Zeke anymore.

CHAPTER 6

Jazz Age Golf

Zeke wasn't the only guy who knew a thing about hustling. When I was traveling with Billy Eckstine in the early fifties, it was hustle or be hustled, because there were cats out there who stood in line to get a piece of Mr. B. on the golf course. In those days he was the biggest star in America, playing to packed houses every night and staying in the finest hotels, and I was right there with him as his valet, driver, and golf pro. Mr. B. paid me $150 a week, along with all of my expenses on the road.

This was the way it worked with Mr. B. and the hustlers. We'd pull into a town like Chicago or Washington for a week-long engagement on, say, Thursday morning and check into the best downtown hotel. There was a whole bunch of us: the band, the crew, the press agent, the road manager, the personal manager, wives, friends, and the acts who were playing with B.

We're not talking about jugglers and comedians here. Billy Eckstine had assembled the greatest jazz band that ever played. At one time he had guys like Charley Parker, Art Blakey, and a young upstart named Miles Davis playing for him, with guest appearances by Dizzy Gillespie and Sarah Vaughan. On tour with us at any given time were musicians like Duke Ellington, Count Basie, and Louis Armstrong, with all of their fabulous players in tow.

Being around those people was like spending every night in a Disneyland of jazz. Musically it may have been the most exciting time in American history, and Billy Eckstine kept the engine running with his hit songs and immense popularity. He and his bands went out every night exploring new territory to play, and I sat on the side and loved every minute of it.

Man, you want to talk about finding a way to bring white people and black people together. Billy had them all dancing in the aisles and hollering like they were parishioners in a giant Baptist church devoted to jazz. It was the craziest and most wonderful thing I've ever seen.

The press agent would get on the phone and get the newspapers out to write about us and take pictures, and invariably they put in a funny word about how Billy Eckstine traveled with a personal golf pro, Charlie Sifford. I've even got a gag picture in my scrapbook of me helping Mr. B. cut his steak, as the newspaper put it, "utilizing the proper grip on the steak knife."

The stories came out in the paper the next day, and by nine o'clock the phone would ring and some guy would ask Billy Eckstine, "Why don't you boys come around the golf course this morning and show us how you play?"

In Cleveland one time we got a call from a guy who said he'd met Billy at such and such a time, and wouldn't he like to come out and play a friendly round? Billy says, "Sure, but I want to bring along my friend, Charlie." This guy apparently hadn't heard the personal golf pro bit, so he said fine, bring him along. See, we played one way if the hustler knew I was a golf pro, and another way if he'd never heard of me.

We went to the golf course and this guy and his buddy are practically drooling over playing a round with Billy Eckstine. All they see before their eyes are dollar signs. In those days Billy was shooting in the high 70s, so he could hold his own against most players, but a good hustler could always beat him. We started out with even bets, the two of them against the two of us. We were probably playing for $100 a bet. Billy comes out strong, hitting a good drive off the first tee, so I hook mine into the woods. Billy continues to play well through the front nine, so I manage to keep my ball in trouble most of the time. I'll hit a sand trap, take two swings to get it out, top a ball or miss an easy putt, as long as my man isn't too far ahead.

By the turn, Billy is three holes up on his man and I'm even with mine. The hustler decides to make his move. He turns to Billy and says "Hey, man, you're better than I thought, and if we're going to keep playing, you've got to spot me a one-hole lead." Billy agrees, and then I say, "Well how about me? I'm barely keeping up here." The guy looks me over, remembers how bad I've been playing, and says, "Well, you can keep playing us even."

Of course Billy's man then takes off and starts playing great and winning his holes, but they didn't count on me pulling the same trick. I start playing well and beating the daylights out of my man, and by the end of the round, we're five up and they owe us even more. As they're paying us, Billy's man asks my name, and I tell him Charlie Sifford. "I don't know," he says, "but I think you're a better player than you were showing."

As our reputation spread and people began to see how I could play, that kind of scam stopped working. We tried it once on two guys in Seattle. Billy said, "Okay, I'll give you a stroke, but you've got to play my man even." The guy looked at me and said, "I know who you are, Charlie Sifford, so don't even bother trying to play me that way."

One time we were in Chicago to play the Chicago Theatre when a black professional named Howard Brown called up Billy. "I'll play any black professional in the world except for Teddy Rhodes," he said. "Send out your best man." Mr. B. told me to go ahead and play him, and he gave me some money to play with. On the putting green I introduced myself to Brown as Charlie Clifford, and I proceeded to beat him out of four $50 bets on the front nine. He wanted to double the bet on the back, and I knocked him out on number 15.

Walking back to the clubhouse, Brown shook his head and said, "If I didn't know you were Charlie Clifford, I would swear that you were this pro I heard about named Charlie Sifford."

Traveling with Billy Eckstine was so wonderful. We played the hottest theaters in each city, and I still remember what it was like to be backstage at the Paramount Theater and Birdland in New York. On one tour we did 51 one-nighters in a row with Sarah Vaughan, the Count, and Oscar Peterson and his trio. It was nothing but pure enjoyment for me, meeting all those people and listening to such great music night after night. For a country boy from North Carolina, that was surely some fast company.

On those one-nighter tours we were constantly on the move. We'd finish a show in one city, pack up the gear into a big bus and a couple of cars, and drive all night to the next place. We'd check into the hotel, get a little sleep, and then Billy and I would look for a golf course and play all afternoon. Around five o'clock he would head back to the hotel to get ready for the show while I stayed at the golf course and practiced. I'd finish in time to make sure that all of his clothes got into the dressing room at the theater, and then I'd hang around with the other guys and watch the show before packing up and driving off again. When we had the luxury of spending a few days in a row in one place, we'd golf practically all day and take on any action that came our way.

Over the years we made friends at a golf course or country club in nearly every big city in the country. After a while we didn't have to wait for the phone to ring for a game; we could just call our buddies and go out to play. Or we'd just show up at the course and meet the same guys we'd played the year before, and more than likely they were eager for a rematch. It was fun for all of us. They got to hang out with Billy Eckstine, and we got to play competitive golf and make friends. It sure beat waiting around the hotel room all day until showtime.

Golf itself was fun for me in those days. There was no black/white thing, nobody telling us where we could or couldn't play. There wasn't any bullshit about it. We'd show up at the course, be invited to play, and we'd have a good game of it with the local guys. We played against white guys and black guys, and I don't recall a single time when I felt any ugliness on a course. If there was somebody around who didn't want to see blacks on his course, he must have kept his mouth shut, because I don't remember it.

Sometimes we won, sometimes they won, but more likely than not we'd all sit down for a beer after the round and talk golf. If we were still in town the next day, I could go back with or without Billy and find one of the guys we'd met or some of their buddies who had heard about us. After a few days in a town I could meet a dozen or so guys who loved to play and who didn't see me as black, short, smart, stupid, or anything else. They saw me as a golf buddy, they admired my game, and they liked to compete with me as much as I liked to compete with them. Golf was a very easy common ground for friendships, and some of those friendships that I started back in the late forties with Billy Eckstine continue to this day.

But then there is no better game for bringing people together. Man, I've seen it a million times. You can put a black man, a rich man, a Japanese guy, and a poor white man together on a golf course, and they're all going to have a good time. They're going to compare swings, compare shots, match themselves up by handicaps, survey the course, and spend four hours walking around on beautiful green fairways and playing the game together. They all speak the same language on the course; even the people who don't know English know how to say "nice shot"; "good putt"; "bogey, par, birdie."

Golf is such an incredible equalizer. On any given pro-am day, some corporate executive is going to go out there and shoot a better round than me, the touring professional. Or I'll miss a five-foot putt and the worst guy in the group will go out and drill a 20-footer, and I'll admire the shot just as much as he did. We may have different skill levels, but we all struggle with the game equally. When we're together on the course, we're all at the mercy of the winds and the grass and our own frailties, and none of this stuff between people — the racial tensions, the upper/lower class boundaries, the political or religious differences — makes a damn bit of difference.

It was probably in the late forties that this question started popping into my mind from time to time, and I heard it over and over again for so many years that it became like a persistent itch deep inside me that I could never scratch. It would come up after

I played a good round and was sitting around drinking beers with my buddies, and it would come up when I read the newspapers on Monday morning and saw who won the weekend tournament.

"Why can't I play professional golf with the best players in the world?" asked this voice in my head. "Why, in this supposedly free country of ours, am I being denied the right to try to prove myself against the best? More important, why can't I have the chance to go after some of that money that Ben Hogan and Sam Snead and Lew Worsham are making? My wife and baby deserve to eat just as much as theirs do . . . why not?"

It was a question that you'd think a lot of people would have asked of me in those years when my swing was so sweet and I was starting to really get on top of the game. But you know, nobody ever asked me. They knew that there was no way that a black man was going to be out there playing against Ben Hogan, and it didn't even occur to people to question it. It was simply a given: the PGA Tour was for white players, period. I could be this black man way over here on the side winning meaningless little all-black tournaments at public courses. They could accept that. But nobody even asked me if I thought I could play against the white pros. I wasn't even supposed to dream about that, any more than a black man could talk about wanting to marry a white woman.

I had different ways of dealing with the question when it popped into my head. I'd deny any interest in playing on the PGA Tour, tell myself, "What the hell are you thinking about? You're doing fine where you are, and you don't need to be hanging around with a bunch of stuck-up white pros." I'd get mad and get into a foul mood for a day or two. More likely than not I'd just shrug my shoulders and think, "You know that's just the way it is. That PGA constitution says no blacks. It's written right there for all to see, so that must be the way it's going to be. Can't change things you have no control over."

But it always struck me as odd that there I was, sitting in some strange city and drinking a beer with a man, usually white, whom I had just met that morning and befriended over a round of golf; and how easy it had been to get the game together, pay our greens fees, and play; and how we had gotten along fine and learned something about each other from talking and from seeing how we each handled the challenges of the game. It was so easy, but when it came to playing pro golf or joining a country club, it suddenly became hard. Impossibly hard. The most social game in the world had a really nasty ceiling placed on it.

At first, if I really considered it, I knew that my game wasn't good enough to stand up to the rigors of a professional tour. I didn't have the consistency yet and was as likely to shoot an 80 as I was a 68. Shoot, I wasn't even doing too much in those black tournaments to seriously consider making a living as a touring pro. I knew I had something in terms of skill and dedication to the game, but I hadn't learned how to put it all together.

But in the early fifties things started to change for me. All of that golf playing with Billy Eckstine, combined with all of the lessons I was giving him, began to pay off in my own game. For the first time in my life I had the financial backing and the time to really focus on golf, and the results came quickly. God bless him, Teddy Rhodes knew this would happen if I had the chance to concentrate on golf, and through Billy, he had found a way for me to make it.

In July of 1951 I was in Chicago and had a few weeks off when I ran into Bishop Ford, from the Presbyterian Church. He was an old friend whom I had met on the golf course. He told me about a black tournament that was being held later that week in Atlanta and offered me a ride, so I packed up my things and went along. We played at the Lincoln Country Club, which wasn't anything more than a nine-hole municipal course that allowed blacks, but they had put together this tournament called the Southern Open, and there was prize money to chase.

I went into that tournament like a house on fire and didn't stop until I had won. Over four days I shot a blistering 66/62/68/69 and beat Howard Wheeler by three strokes. I won $500, and let me tell you, I never needed $500 worse than I needed it then. It was my first professional win, and it was very sweet indeed.

I sent the money home to Rose in Philadelphia, and she was just as thrilled as me that I had finally won some real money at golf. At the time Rose was working as a saleslady at Woolworth's in downtown Philadelphia, living with her mother and raising our son, Charles, Jr. I'd been sending her most of my $150-a-week salary from Billy Eckstine to keep things together, but we were still pretty poor. That first win was like money from heaven, and it proved to both of us that I might be able to make some money at the game. All the time spent apart wasn't being wasted.

Later that summer Teddy Rhodes won the National Negro Open for the third straight year, but I was gaining on him. By 1952 I put it all together and began to play the best golf of my life. In August of that year I went to the Rackham golf course in Detroit for the National Negro Open, and this time I played shot-for-shot with Teddy over the first three days. On Sunday morning he was ahead by only one stroke, and by the turn we were tied. He and I were playing together in the last group, and instead of fading from the pressure I thrived on it. I shot a 32 on the back nine and beat Teddy. It was my first National Negro championship. I had just turned 30 years old two months before that, and now I was finally the undisputed top dog on the Negro circuit.

It was the beginning of a long run of successes for me. In 1953 I successfully defended my title in Kansas City, and in 1954 I came right back to dust everyone off in Dallas, where I shot a 283 to beat Bill Spiller by nine strokes. That was one of the first times we ever saw a young guy named Lee Elder, who was barely 20 years old. A resident of Dallas, he finished fourth that year. I won the National Negro Open title so many times — every year up to 1956 — that they finally gave me the trophy to keep permanently because I was holding on to it every year anyway. I've still got it at my house.

There were other great matches during those years. At the Seneca golf course in Cleveland, Teddy Rhodes and I fought to a tie in the Sixth City Invitational after 72 holes, and in a nine-hole playoff I beat him with a birdie putt on the last hole, 35 to 36. In 1955 I won four out of six Negro tournaments, including the Gate City Open in Greensboro, North Carolina. They were awfully nice to me in Greensboro when I won that black tournament on the municipal course, but a few years later when I was allowed to enter the white tournament at the country club, it was a different story.

During one of those years I went to the Keney Park golf course in Hartford, Connecticut, and made all of $200 for a win at a UGA Tournament—which was kind of ironic, because in 1967 I earned $20,000 by taking the Greater Hartford Open. Did that mean I played 100 times better at the PGA tournament, or just that the competition was 100 percent whiter? You guess.

I also began to show up well in the few white tournaments I could enter. I was there at Tam O'Shanter in 1953 when Lew Worsham and Chandler Harper hooked up in a magnificent final-day battle that Worsham won. I shot a 300 to finish 22 strokes off the lead and in the money, the same score as my old pal and mentor Clayton Heafner. The following year I improved to 293 and won all of $40 (Bob Toski, the winner, brought home the greatest purse offered in those days—$50,000). In January of 1954 Teddy Rhodes and I both shot 288 at the Los Angeles Open and finished just seven strokes off of Fred Wampler's winning pace.

Given those successes, would I ever get the chance to play on the white tour? I seriously doubted it as the years went by and nothing changed. I was in my prime, but I was winning my $500 victories at lousy municipal golf courses while the whites were shooting for big money at the country clubs. It just wasn't right, and as those years went by I got more and more angry about it.

Why couldn't I play on the tour? We never had any problems or caused any disturbances at the three open tournaments we *could* play. At Los Angeles, the Tam O'Shanter, and the Canadian Open, we were accepted as equals. The white players themselves were generally nice to me and Teddy; they didn't seem to be standing in the way of us playing. Guys like Jimmy Demaret and Porky Oliver and Bob Rosburg went out of their way to talk to us and make us feel comfortable. But the PGA and the tournament sponsors wouldn't budge when it came to letting blacks play.

The only person who could make a dent in the system was the one black athlete whom everyone respected—Joe Louis. After having beaten up practically every fighter, white, black, or brown, who came his way, it made him furious that his beloved sport of golf was so racist. He knew that there were plenty of blacks around in the forties and fifties who could play golf, and he decided to find a way to force them into the game. After Joe's fighting career was over it became his passion to break blacks into golf. It would prove to be his greatest defeat, because even Joe Louis couldn't fight against the corrupt system of golf in America.

CHAPTER 7

Joe Louis Opens Doors

As if he were in the ring with a strong puncher, Joe figured the best way to confront the PGA was head-on. In mid-January of 1952, a week after the Los Angeles Open, he declared his intention to play in the San Diego Open, which had never been open to blacks. He and Bill Spiller and Eural Clark drove from L.A. to San Diego and petitioned the PGA to allow them to enter the tournament, declaring that they wanted to challenge the PGA's ban on blacks. Joe made sure to keep the media informed of what was going on, and the story began to appear in newspapers all over the country.

After a week of heated discussion that was carried almost word for word in the press—(Louis called PGA President Horton Smith "another Hitler" for sticking so unbendingly to his association's bylaws)—Smith came up with a face-saving compromise: Joe could play by dint of a sponsor's exemption. Because of the PGA bylaws, however, neither Spiller nor Clark could play. Neither was a PGA professional, nor had they been granted a sponsor's exemption as Joe Louis had, said Smith. They were therefore ineligible to enter.

Spiller tried to raise more hell about not being able to play and threatened a lawsuit, but his story barely surfaced. Instead, it was Joe who was watched, and that week he became the first black to play in a PGA-sponsored event. He had gotten his foot in the door, and he knew what to do when he had an advantage in a fight. He kept the heat on the PGA and forced a vote that same week by the PGA Tournament Committee that was hailed as a big step for black golfers. In the January 20 issue of the *New York Times*, the headline read, "P.G.A. Committee Votes to Ease Tourney Ban on Negro Players . . . Action [to admit] Effective at Once, Smith Says."

The new rule was voted on affirmatively by six of a seven-member committee that consisted of Smith, Jackie Burke, Jr., my old friend Clayton Heafner, Leland Gibson, Harry Moffitt, and Chick Harbert. Dave Douglas, the seventh committee member was absent. In effect the new rule said that blacks could play in tournaments if, and only if, they were given one of 10 sponsor exemptions or if they were invited to be one of 10 golfers who could compete for open spots in a qualifying round. Because of the PGA's whites-only constitution, we still couldn't qualify by becoming PGA members.

Curiously, the *Times* didn't mention anything about the story it had run four years earlier when the PGA had seemed to pledge not to bar black golfers. That was the time when Spiller and Rhodes filed suit for not being allowed to enter a California tournament, and after a period of legal wrangling, a settlement had been reached whereby the suit was dropped in exchange for a PGA promise of nondiscrimination.

The following week was to be the first test of the PGA's new open policy toward blacks. Joe Louis asked for invitations for seven blacks to enter the tournament, and the Phoenix sponsors agreed to let us all come. That is, they allowed us to attempt to qualify, which meant that we could play a qualifying round on Monday, and if we were good enough, we could earn spots in the tournament field.

There were three professionals — myself, Spiller, and Rhodes — and four amateurs — Joe Louis, Leonard Reed, Joe Roach, and Eural Clark. At the time I was working for Billy Eckstine, but Joe asked him to let me play and Billy said go ahead. On a warm day in late January, we all piled into Joe's and Teddy's cars and drove across the desert to Phoenix. It was to be my first crack at the white tour outside of the three "open" tournaments.

When we got to Phoenix, we realized that no hotel would put us up, but Joe had friends there. He stayed with one black doctor and the rest of us stayed across the street with another (I wish I could remember their names but regret that I can't). One lady whom I definitely remember was a wonderful woman named Mrs. Cross, who used to feed and house all of the black baseball players who came through Phoenix. When Willie Mays and Willie McCovey were coming up and needed a place, they found it at Mrs. Cross's house. Meals were always eaten at her house, because you couldn't find a restaurant in Phoenix that would serve a black in those days. We ate all of our meals at Mrs. Cross's house that week, and the food was probably far superior to anything we could have ordered in a restaurant.

When we got to the Phoenix Country Club for our qualifying round, we saw that there were limits to the club's hospitality. For one thing, they wouldn't let us into the locker room. "You aren't allowed in there," said a country club official. Second, instead of mixing us in with all of the other qualifiers, we were all sent out together as a group, and we were sent out as the first group in the morning, before any of the other professionals arrived at the course and before the gallery started to gather.

It was clearly a get-the-black-guys-out-of-the-way-so-we-can-get-on-with-our-tournament deal. But if that's all they were giving us, that's what we would take. We vowed that if we had to compete to qualify, we'd play our hearts out and force them to enter us in the tournament. They couldn't deny us if we played well on their course. What could they do, try to strongarm us? We had the greatest heavyweight fighter in the world on our side!

We broke up into two groups and hit the first tee. We gave Joe Louis the honor of hitting the first ball, and he put it down the fairway. Teddy and Eural Clark and I then teed up and took a few extra moments to control our excitement before swinging. Yeah! We would show all of those white players and reporters and the country club people who clearly didn't want us around. We'd show them how the black boys did it on the UGA Tour.

Eural and Joe missed the green on their approach shots after Teddy and I put ours within birdie range. We waited for them to chip up, and then, since I was the closest to the pin, I walked up to pull the flagstick out.

Something seemed funny and I glanced down at the cup. I had the flagstick half raised, but I shoved it back into the cup. Somebody had been there before us. The cup was full of human shit, and from the looks and smell of it, it hadn't been too long before we got there that the cup had been filled. Obviously, someone associated with Phoenix's fanciest country club had known who would be the first to reach the green—the black guys.

Do you think that nobody could have known about this? Now how could some guy sneak onto the first fairway of this private golf course, just a few hundred yards from their clubhouse, sneak past all of those groundskeepers and officials who were getting the course ready for their big annual tournament, and get away with filling up the cup with his crap? The flagsticks must have already been in place, or else the guy who put them out there didn't bother to say anything about what he found when he stuck that stick in the ground. Could that be possible?

I was shocked, and then furious. So this was what we'd have to face on the white tour. Eural and I stomped around and screamed until an official came up and innocently asked what the problem was. We held up play for half an hour until they took that filthy cup out of the ground and replaced it, and then we continued our round.

Needless to say, our concentration was shot, which is probably precisely the effect they wanted. I was so angry and tense that I began to whack the ball all over the place, and at that point I didn't care. What a crude, disgusting thing to do to people. Damn, all we were trying to do was play a game of golf and make a little bit of money.

I played so badly I failed to qualify. The others didn't fare much better. I was just starting to cool down when we finished the 18th hole and headed toward the locker room. But then we remembered that we weren't allowed in the locker room, and again that feeling of dread and anger began to rise up. Without saying anything, we started for the parking lot, but Spiller stopped us.

Spiller was always the most militant of the black golfers, and he intended to push this invitation as far as it would go. "I am going into that locker room and I am going to take a shower," he announced. Teddy and the others tried to talk him out of it, arguing that we had to move slowly and not make waves if we were going to play any more white tournaments, but Spiller was adamant. He'd been squelched so many times in the past, and now he was going to seize this opportunity for all to see. He marched into the locker room alone.

Ten minutes later a white guy from the country club walked up to Joe Louis and asked to speak with him. He told Joe that if we didn't get Spiller out of the shower immediately something bad was going to happen. He suggested that somebody might try to drown Bill. Joe shrugged his shoulders and gave us a what-are-you-going-to-do? look. He had to go in there like a big black cop and tell Bill to leave.

The only good thing that happened was that Teddy and Spiller and Clark managed to qualify, but Bill and Eural both played badly in the first round and dropped out. Teddy Rhodes, however, showed once again why he was the best. Despite all of that pressure and harassment, and despite never having played in this kind of tournament or at that course before, he went out and shot a 71 on the first day for fifth place. It was Teddy's way of saying that blacks did belong in the game and could hold their own at any tournament.

A consummate gentleman, Teddy had his own subtle way of telling it like it was. "I haven't been playing too much lately to score too well," he told the newspapers. Hell, he hadn't been playing at all since the L.A. Open, because there was no place of any consequence for him to play. He struggled for the rest of the week, and I don't think he finished in the money.

After that introduction to the white professional golf tour, it's a wonder that we continued to try. But try we did, and the following week we took our show to Tucson, where the Tucson

Open was being played at the El Rio Country Club. Once again
they grudgingly let the black guys try to qualify, and this time
we did a little better. Joe and Teddy and Leonard Reed and I all
qualified and entered the first round together, and Joe and Teddy
both played well until a disastrous, windy third round knocked
them out of the standings. I slipped up and failed to make the
third-round cut, but I had had a taste of the competition and liked
it.

After Tucson, the tour went on to stops in Texas and Louisiana,
but we didn't. In fact there was no other place for the black guys
to play other than the three tournaments that had always been
open to us. Despite their pledges, the PGA didn't really intend
to let us play. There was still a Caucasians-only clause in their
constitution, which meant that we couldn't become PGA
members, and if we weren't PGA members, we were at the mercy
of tournament sponsors and committees, none of whom ever
voted us exemptions. And the PGA certainly didn't lean on anyone
to offer exemptions after the Joe Louis-inspired cloud passed over
Phoenix and Tucson.

Joe got so sick of the exclusion of blacks that he stopped
entering the white tournaments. It was no fun for him to go alone,
and he finally stopped trying. Despite all his efforts, and all of
the press attention, Phoenix and Tucson remained closed to
blacks. I wouldn't be able to play in either place again until 1959.
San Diego did open up a little and I was able to make a few dollars
there beginning in 1954. The press that had written about the
PGA's opening up to blacks forgot all about the story.

Bill Spiller went back to his redcap job at the Los Angeles
train station, Teddy went back to being Joe's professional, and
I went back to Billy Eckstine. For Bill and Teddy, Phoenix and
Tucson were probably their last chances to play white golf. They
were getting old and discouraged after having fought the PGA
twice in four years, winning what seemed to be favorable rulings,
and then watching their chances to play disappear.

I was the young guy coming up, but by 1955 I wasn't so young
anymore. I was 33 years old and at the top of my game, but I
had no place to play. It had taken about eight years to get to the

level that I probably could have reached in a year if I had been given the right opportunities to pursue my sport.

It kept me up at night sometimes, that thought, those nights when I was away from home and sleeping in some boardinghouse or downtown hotel, my wife and baby far away, and not knowing when my next chance to play competitive golf would come. Eight years of struggling to find the game that I knew I had inside of me, with no coach, and no nice practice area, and no money to spend three or four weeks solid on the golf course practicing. How much of me had already been left behind that I would never again get back? How many golf matches had I already missed that I could have won?

Most of the black guys who had come up with me had long since given up the idea of playing golf for a living. They might come out for a Negro tournament here or there, but they'd lost their dedication to the game. The struggle was just too hard and was too obviously a losing battle. They went back to their homes and their jobs at the fertilizer plant or the grocery store or the post office, and golf was just an old memory to them.

The years were going by too fast. I couldn't stop time until the PGA got around to recognizing that black athletes had the same rights to play as whites. Through the rest of the fifties I waited, and that question became like a dull roar in my head: Why, why, WHY am I not allowed to play professional golf?

CHAPTER 8

Forcing My Way

In August of 1955, a week after I'd finished out of the money at Tam O'Shanter, I was sitting around a hotel room in Chicago with Billy Eckstine when Teddy Rhodes showed up. He was on his way to Toronto to enter the 46th annual Canadian Open and wanted to know if I would come along.

"They're giving away $15,000 in prize money up there," he said. "Come on, man, we gotta get some of that."

As usual I didn't have any money, and besides, I was supposed to be driving for Billy. But it never hurt to ask. I went up to Mr. B. and told him what Teddy suggested, and Billy said, "Go right ahead. Win yourself some money." And without my even asking, he reached into his pocket and pulled out a couple of hundred dollars for us, and off we went in Teddy's car.

You know, I'm sure it still happens, but I never seem to hear about how the big, black stars of today help out other blacks the way that Billy Eckstine and Joe Louis took care of a whole bunch of us. Maybe today's black celebrities are too busy or too insulated by their managers and agents and lawyers. Maybe they do their contributing indirectly by donating to organizations like the United Negro College Fund.

But I'll tell you, to have a man like Mr. B. behind me was the most wonderful thing that ever happened to me. In those days when I had a wife and a baby to feed, and only a crazy notion that I could make it at golf, he was the benefactor who made it possible for me to live my dream. I wish that every black kid in the country could have a Billy Eckstine rooting for him.

Teddy played in the Canadian Open frequently, at times driving as far as Vancouver to compete. For one thing, they didn't have any problem with blacks trying to qualify for the tournament, which most of the top PGA pros usually entered. For another, there wasn't ever a problem with finding a hotel or a place to eat in Canada. Hell, I don't know, maybe it was just too cold up there for a Mason-Dixon line to exist.

Teddy and I got to Toronto on Monday, qualified easily, and spent the next couple of days practicing at the Weston Golf Club, where the tournament was being held. We were both rusty and needed time to get used to playing a real golf course. It was getting to be the end of summer, but I had only played in a few tournaments all year.

My year had begun, as it usually did, in California at the Los Angeles Open, where I finished 11 strokes off Gene Littler's winning pace. I tied for 14th place two weeks later in San Diego and pocketed $165, but I wasn't allowed into either of the two tournaments that directly preceded and followed it (the Bing Crosby National Pro-Am and the Palm Springs Desert Golf Classic). I skipped Phoenix — probably still thinking about the reception I'd had there in 1952 — and finished out of the money in Tucson at the end of February.

At that point the tour headed south and I didn't. It was my annual forced layoff from golf, and I spent my time playing with friends at the Western Avenue course in L.A. or traveling with Mr. B. When summer rolled around, the white pros were hitting their stride in top form, but I had to start all over again with learning how to play competition golf.

The summer of 1955 was the first time that I started showing up at several of the northern PGA Tour-sponsored events. Teddy and I would drive out together to play, or I'd just go on my own when my schedule with Billy allowed it. I played in the St. Paul Open in the middle of July, where I won $130 in a tie for 22nd place, the Miller High Life tournament in Milwaukee the following week, where I finished way down in the standings, and the Rubber City Open on the first weekend in August, where I made all of $35. I failed to qualify at Tam O'Shanter a week later. By the time Canada rolled around, I had made a grand total of about $500 from the white tour and about twice that much at black tournaments. Little did I know that I was about to shoot the best competitive round of my life.

Thursday, November 17, was a hot, almost windless day in Toronto, and the Weston golf course was ripe for picking. A full contingent of PGA players had made the trip up there to get their piece of the $15,000 purse, including guys like Tommy Bolt, Art Wall, Jerry Barber, Sam Snead, and Doug Ford. Before the day was done, 40 players would shoot under the par of 72, including Teddy, who racked up a solid 68.

But I was better than any of them on that particular day. I started out by shooting a 31 on the front nine, where I one-putted six of the nine greens. I was crushing my driver, putting the ball out there 280, 290, 300 yards and right where I wanted it, and I was hitting approaches like Teddy himself. Hell, I was putting that ball on the flagstick so much that I didn't even need the hot putter that day, but I surely didn't mind that I had it. I was five under when I made the turn, and suddenly a lot of people began to take notice. Word got out that I was having a hot round, and on the back nine there was a gallery watching every move I made.

By the time I was finished, they had plenty to cheer about. I came in with a 32, shaving four more strokes off par, with another five one-putt greens. I didn't have a bogey the whole round; didn't even have a five on my scorecard. The 63 was a record for the golf course and tied a Canadian Open record that was shared by Bob Rosburg and Porky Oliver.

I should have been four or five strokes up on the field after that performance, but when I went into the clubhouse, I only had a one-stroke lead. Everybody was hot that day it seemed. Fred Hawkins and a Canadian named Stan Leonard both shot 66, and Bolt, Wall, and Barber were right behind them at 67.

Second place belonged to a guy who had shot nearly as phenomenal a round as I had. He was a highly touted young man who was playing in his first season as a professional after having been the U.S. Amateur Champion the year before. He would have tied me had he not made bogey on the 18th hole, where he hooked his drive under a tree and had no shot. His name was Arnold Palmer.

I happened to pass by young Arnie late that afternoon when he was staring at the leaderboard, as if by looking at it long enough he could will himself into the lead. "How on earth did Charlie Sifford shoot a 63?" I heard him say to nobody in particular.

"Same way you shot a 64, chief," I shot back, "except I did you one better."

I had to hand it to Arnold, though. He kept right on going with a magnificent performance for the rest of the weekend, while I fell back. I shot a 74 on the second day to pretty much put me out of the running, and on the last two days all I could manage were a par 72 and a 70. I didn't get to play in many four-round tournaments, and I had a lot to learn about maintaining a high level of play over a period of several days. Arnie had the touch that week, and he'd had enough amateur victories under his belt to teach him how to win. He put together rounds of 67, another 64, and 70 to edge out Jackie Burke, Jr., for the $2,400 first prize.

I won $175 for my 19th-place finish, but I was nonetheless thrilled. For one day I had been the undisputed best golfer in the world, beating the likes of Palmer, Billy Casper, Sam Snead, Porky Oliver, Jimmy Clark, and my old buddies from upstate New York, Mike Souchak and Mike Fetchik.

Teddy Rhodes was also thrilled with my performance, but you wouldn't know it from his joking comment to the press after the first round: "I invited the guy up here. I even drove him up in my car. What does the guy do? He beats me by five strokes."

It doesn't happen very often that you shoot a round of 63, and it's something that I'll cherish for the rest of my life. In this game where something is always breaking down — your backswing, your putting, your draw on the ball — it's a minor miracle when it all flows together and you feel like you have perfect command. I've shot a few 63s since, but that one in Canada was the most satisfying. Damn, that was fun.

I wonder now, more than a quarter-century later, what they must have been thinking down in Augusta, Georgia, that hot August day. Maybe they were sweating a little more than usual, because in those days the winner of the Canadian Open was automatically given an invitation to play in the following Masters tournament. What would they have done if I had held on to win? I took myself out of it that year, but in subsequent appearances in Canada I came close enough to winning to really shake up the Masters committee. I'll tell you later about how they changed their eligibility rules in the middle of a tournament because it looked like I might win.

I was a hot golfer, but after Canada precious little of the season remained. I went to Hartford a couple of weeks later and shot well enough to win $150, followed it up with a big $500 paycheck at the Carlings Open in Massachusetts, and then finished my season with appearances at the Long Island Rotary tournament and the Eastern Open. By the middle of October I was through, as the white tour headed south again.

All told, I made about $1,500 from the white tournaments in 1955, and, more important, I had proven that I could hold my own against the best white players. But what good was it doing me? Here I was, in the prime of my golf career, and all I could do was enter a few tournaments and then watch helplessly as the other players headed off to make their fortunes in places that wouldn't allow me to play. I knew I was better than many of them who were drawing regular winnings checks week after week. I knew that given the chance, I could easily hold my own and make a living on that tour, and that if I tried hard enough I could be at the top.

I was practically starving and trying so hard to hold onto this dream of making my living at golf. I wonder now how I did it. Looking back on all those times when I didn't have a dollar in my pocket, or when I'd call home and hear that note creep into

Rose's voice when she had the rent coming up and didn't know how she was going to pay it. She never once told me I should quit this game and go get a real job, nor did her mother, but there were plenty of times when it seemed like the only reasonable thing to do.

What kept me going? I don't know . . . determination, pride. Sometimes it was just a matter of me not having anything else that I could do, or would rather do, than play golf. There was nothing else I cared about. Other times I vowed that I would not be beaten. I would not give up on this golf dream and let those people win—the white people who controlled the tournaments and the tour and who first told me I couldn't play and then found ways to force me out. I kept coming back, and I kept pushing against those doors. Why? Because I'm a fighter, and it only made me madder when I saw the doors closed.

Shoot, if they'd have let me in to some of those tournaments and if I hadn't played well enough to make any money, I probably would have quit on my own. Because then my pride would have taken over and wouldn't have allowed me to hang around as a loser. Shutting those doors just made me madder. When I was 25 years old and at the height of my game and those doors were shut tight, I was the maddest that I've ever been in my life.

I hear these things said about me these days when I'm nearly 70 years old. I read them in the newspaper: "Bitter Charlie Sifford," "ornery Charlie Sifford," "still angry about what happened to him 35 years ago." Some of these things are still used as justifications for keeping me out of golf tournaments. I hardly ever get invited to play in a pro-am invitational, for instance, where the pros get upwards of $3,000 each for their appearances. Why? Because I'm too old and ornery and bitter. I might somehow upset the businessmen whose company is paying for the pro-am.

Well, you tell me how you'd feel if the best years of your life were spent waiting on the sidelines when you knew — YOU KNEW — that you had a God-given talent for something, but weren't allowed to do it because of the color of your skin. Tell me it wouldn't have an effect on your whole life. Maybe it would make you slightly ornery too. Maybe it would even ruin your life, as it did many of the gifted young black men I knew in my day who eventually gave up their dreams and headed back home, the fires in their bellies extinguished. I've pushed hard to make it this far in golf, and I'm not going to stop pushing, because I know that when I do it will be goodbye, Charlie.

I scrambled through those years in the middle fifties. I did everything I could think of to stay in golf and to get into tournaments. It seemed to me that the minute I stopped pushing, the doors would close for good. There sure as hell wasn't any sponsor, much less the PGA, telling me that with my skills I should keep plugging away. I may have had the raw talent to be a professional golfer, but I'd display my skills only if I made it happen.

I had to find a way to make a living at golf. In 1955 I kept running into a wonderful man named Jack Schram, whose company made Burke golf clubs in Ohio. Of course, Macgregor and Spalding and Wilson made the best golf clubs, but they surely weren't going to sponsor somebody who could only play in a dozen tournaments a year. Jack Schram, however, listened to me carefully when I bugged him about letting me sponsor a line of clubs.

I told him that there was a vast, untapped market in the black community for golf clubs that were sponsored by a black professional, and that he should just see all of the black people who came out to watch us play at the UGA tournaments. He would not only make a lot of money, but he would open his company up to all kinds of sales opportunities to blacks, I reasoned. Of course I didn't really know what I was talking about, but I thought it would be a great thing to have my own personal line of golf clubs. Finally, Jack agreed to manufacture a signature line of Charlie Sifford golf clubs. When the first autographed Burke punch irons and woods rolled off the assembly line, I thought I had finally found the endorsement that would put me over the top.

But Jack ran into problems almost immediately with those clubs. He tried selling them through department stores that had

large black clienteles, but nobody would take them. He advertised
in newspapers and golf publications, with a picture of me
swinging them, and still no luck. I talked about the clubs everywhere I went and begged people to buy them.

Jack finally gave up. "I've got 75 sets of golf clubs with your
name on them here," he told me over the phone one day.
"Nobody will handle them. What are you going to do about it,
Charlie?"

I told him that I would sell them myself, but I had one small
problem. In those days I didn't even own a car. However, I knew
someone who sold them: George Fazio, the golf course architect,
who owned a Ford dealership in Pennsylvania. While I was home
in Philadelphia that year, I went up to see him.

"Sure, we can set you up, Charlie," he told me. "I've got a
nice, new Ford right here. How much money do you have?"

"George," I said, "I've got $900 in my pocket, but I'm not
going to give you $900. I'm going to give you $500."

His face fell. "Charlie, I can't sell you a car for no $500."

I made a deal with him. I would give him the $500 down,
and I would guarantee to pay him $100 a month until the title
was mine. George was a good man. He accepted, and I drove that
car away. Never missed a payment, either.

I went to the factory that made the golf clubs and picked them
all up. I vowed that I would sell every last one of them. I drove
to California, to Texas, to Florida. By the time I was done with
that car, I put 165,000 miles on it, and much of it seemed like
it came on that one selling trip. I went everywhere. I tried to
sell those clubs to the stores, and when they wouldn't buy any,
I tried to sell them door-to-door. I couldn't sell a damn one of
them, and I started to get mad. I was probably the worst salesman
you ever saw, getting all belligerent and demanding that people
look at my personally autographed golf clubs. No takers.

Finally Rose calmed me down during a telephone call when
I was ranting and raving about nobody buying my golf clubs. She
said, "Look, you're not doing yourself any good getting all mad
with those golf clubs. Why don't you put them aside and come
home. Work on your golf game, and then you won't be so crazy."

I hated to give up, and I had one more place to try. A guy in Baltimore said he'd be interested in seeing my golf clubs, so on a spring morning when the roads were all icy from a sudden freeze, I got into the car and slipped and slid from Philadelphia all the way down to Baltimore. I showed this guy my clubs, which I was trying to sell for $135, including woods, irons, putter, bag, and everything. He offered me $40 more than what I asked for them. I drove home, put the clubs in my closet, and forgot all about them. That was the first and last time I've ever tried to be a salesman.

I did anything I could to keep going in those days. I lived in Washington, D.C., for a few months trying to teach some guy how to play golf. His name was Mr. Whitting, and I remember that he paid me well. In 1954 I spent a lot of time in New York City, where there was an indoor driving range set up at 64 East 51st Street. I hit balls and gave lessons too.

People tried to help me out from time to time. In 1955 the Western Golf Association in L.A. sent out a letter on my behalf asking patrons to donate money so that I could travel to more golf tournaments. Of course, it didn't say anything about the fact that I wasn't and couldn't be a PGA member, but no matter. Nothing much came of it.

You might ask why I was able to play in some PGA-sponsored tournaments, such as the Insurance City Open, but not in others. Good question. A lot of it had to do with the local situation, and whether or not the local tournament committee wanted to follow the PGA's rules stringently. In many of the northern cities, qualifications were open to anybody who showed up on the Monday before the tournament started, and I could pretty much always win a spot by qualifying. Other places entered me on the basis of my prior performances in their tournaments, and some places simply knew who I was and how well I could play and entered me as a touring professional.

But there was always this problem of the PGA's reaching up to slap me and the other black players down. We never knew when it would happen that we'd show up at a new tournament and somebody would ask to see our PGA cards, and then inform us that we couldn't play because we weren't PGA members. The flip side of that was when they said that only a few non-PGA members could enter the tournament, and those slots had already been filled by the sponsors.

We knew from talking to people where we could and couldn't play. I sure as hell wasn't going to get into my car and drive to a strange city and try to enter the tournament only to find out that they wouldn't let me in. So for me and Teddy, playing with the white pros meant picking our spots and going only to the places that we knew would allow us to play.

We were in Fort Wayne, Indiana, one year, finishing up a tournament, and were told by a PGA official that we wouldn't be allowed to play in the following week's tournament in San Francisco. There was no point in asking why. They'd have said that it was only open to PGA, but it was really because somebody had decided that no blacks were allowed. They told us the name of the golf course, however, and I realized that it was a course on an army base. I raised hell. How could they hold a tournament that discriminated against blacks on a golf course that was on United States land? Teddy let it go, but I really raised a stink about it, and you know what? They relented and let us play. That was how much their rules meant. If we bitched and hollered and moaned long and loud enough, they could always find a way to put us into the tournament. It's the same way today.

Teddy didn't have the constitution to fight his way into tournaments. He would just let these things go, because he didn't like to get upset or holler for his rights. It was in those years that I realized that if I was going to play white golf, I'd have to fight for every inch and fight to get into every single tournament, and I vowed to do it. I would be the black man who wouldn't keep his mouth shut and just go along; I'd be the one who was in their face all the time until they let me into their tournaments.

I'm glad I didn't know then just how much fight it would take to break me into the game, because I'm not sure that even I would have had the heart to continue. I still thought that if I played well enough there would be no way that they could keep me off the tour. I mean, fair is fair, right? And this was supposedly a gentleman's game that was played with very strong standards of honor and fairness and sportsmanship. If I could just break into that winner's circle in a big tournament, then they'd have to pay attention to me.

But that was easier said than done. There were guys on that tour who had been playing a lot longer than I had and knew more about the game who had never won a tournament. Even Clayton Heafner didn't win many tournaments, and I knew what a fine player he was. Winning was something else entirely. It took a special knack and ability to focus on the game completely for a week's time. It meant practicing long and well and working out the kinks in your game, and it meant having time to study the golf course and map it all out in your mind. You had to put it together to win: hot putter, good course management, making the big shots, and not letting the bad shots take you out of position. One flaw — one double bogey in an early round because you forgot to concentrate — would take you out of the chance to win. Not having your game ready on any given day meant that this whole pack of professional golfers would roar past you. If you just shot par, you'd be lucky to finish in the money. If you had one bad round where you finished one or two over, you were finished.

I knew that I had yet to learn how to win, but by the middle of 1956 I knew that it was coming for me. My round in Canada had done wonders for my confidence, and I was spending as much time as I could on my game. I would spend hours on the driving range, hitting as many buckets of balls as I could afford, and then I'd play 27 or 36 holes on top of that.

In the middle of the summer of 1956 I was driving my car through Rhode Island on the way to meet Billy Eckstine in New York. I pulled into the service station and the attendant recognized me. "Aren't you that golfer, Charlie Sifford?" he asked.

I told him I was, and he asked me if I was going to play in the tournament that week. What tournament? The Rhode Island Open, which was a little, three-round affair that they played every summer. It wasn't a PGA tournament by any means, but nonetheless it was a place to play.

I got on the telephone and called Mr. B., and he said to go ahead and spend a couple of days in Rhode Island. I found out where the tournament was being held, signed up, and started playing the next day. I shot 68, 66, and 70 and breezed to first place in my first victory in a white tournament. Shoot, I probably made $125 for it. As I said, it wasn't much of a tournament, but it sure felt sweet to win. A few weeks later in Hartford I finished tied for third in a strong field and took home $1,116, my biggest paycheck yet.

If I could just hang on, something would happen. I'd make it happen, just as I had been making up this whole dream about playing golf for a living ever since I'd gotten out of the service. Suddenly 1956 had come and gone. My wife was still living in Philadelphia with her mother, and our little boy was growing up while his daddy was chasing all over the country after a golf ball. I had been with Billy Eckstine for several years and the grind of travel was getting to me. Mr. B. didn't really need a golf pro any more. He kept me on his payroll to help me out, but most of the time I was off practicing or trying to get into a tournament, and sometimes we'd go weeks without playing any golf together.

Something was coming, if I could just hang on. They'd have to let me play full-time on the tour if I won a big tournament. Wouldn't they?

CHAPTER 9

Small Victory

I pray to God that I never see another year like 1957. It ended up spectacularly in November when I became the first black golfer to win a PGA co-sponsored tournament, but the rest of it was about as miserable a time as I've seen. I simply couldn't win anything on a golf course, and week after week I came up empty-handed in the tournaments that they let me enter. By the end of the summer I was questioning my resolve to play the game. It may have been the lowest I've ever been in my life, and when I won it was the highest. A weird, roller-coaster year.

At the beginning of the year I had high hopes that '57 would be my breakthrough year, when I would challenge so highly in so many tournaments that the PGA would have to acknowledge my presence. After my showings in Hartford and Rhode Island, I felt like I was on the verge of a major victory, and I couldn't wait to get the new season started. If I could just get off to a fast start, I'd show them once and for all that I could be one of the top players on the tour. If I played well in the L.A. Open, where I had been flirting with the winning circle for years, and followed it up with a strong showing in Phoenix and Tucson, they couldn't possibly ignore me.

I wondered how many chances I'd have. I was going on 35 years old, my game was as solid as it ever would be, and I knew that the one thing you can count on in golf is for things to go out of whack. How long could I remain competitive in that rarified air of professional golf? If I knew then that I would still be competing into my late sixties, I might not have felt so much pressure to do everything that year.

So before the season even started, I had two strikes against me. The first was this pressure that had built up of having to prove myself to the PGA. I couldn't just go out there and establish myself like everyone else. I had to make a major showing in order to be recognized, and I had to do it in the face of all kinds of obstacles. You don't need added pressure when you play golf for a living: the game is hard enough as it is.

The second strike was even more dangerous. It was the fact that I really needed to make some money from golf. My service with Billy Eckstine had come to an amicable close after 10 wonderful years, and I was on my own. I suddenly felt a tremendous pressure to win some money at every tournament I entered, and that pressure got worse and worse with practically every swing of the club.

It didn't help matters at all that I couldn't play in every tournament like the other pros. If they had a bad week in, say, Tucson, they could try to make up for it the next week in Texas. But I couldn't, because more likely than not, I wasn't allowed to play in the next tournament. I had to squeeze money out of every tournament I entered or face several months of making do with next to nothing. Even the best players don't make the cut at every single tournament, but I desperately needed to finish in the money. More pressure.

It was too much to handle. I had taken on far too big a load to be competitive, and it showed in the first tournament of the year. At the L.A. Open, I tried so hard to do everything right that I messed up completely. I overswung my driver and ended up in the rough, and then I tried to make up with great approach shots right at the pin, instead of putting it safely down in the middle of the green. When I missed, I tried to make miraculous chips and sand saves. Hell, I couldn't afford to play conservative golf. I had the whole future of black golf riding on my shoulders at every single turn in the golf course! Needless to say, I didn't even make the cut and left L.A. empty-handed.

The next week was the Crosby tournament at Pebble Beach, to which I wasn't invited, and then I failed to make any money in Phoenix and Tucson. I made a few dollars at a secondary tournament, but suddenly my winter season was over with, and all I had to show for it was $200. I headed home to Rose in Philadelphia, with several long months ahead to think about what I had done wrong.

When the tour turned north I pushed myself to play well, and I practiced endlessly, still to no avail. By midsummer the season was half over and I had finished in the money only twice, for less than $500 total. Tam O'Shanter and the Canadian Open both came and went, and I didn't make a dime at either. I couldn't even hold onto my title at the UGA's National Negro Open, giving it up to Teddy Rhodes in what would be his last big win.

I turned 35 years old that June, and I wondered if I was getting a glimpse of my future, when my game deteriorated to a point where I could no longer compete against the young white pros who came up with polished games and lots of opportunities to succeed. I had no sponsor, no agent, and no bankroll that would pay for all of the transportation and the hotel rooms and the meals eaten in snack bars and restaurants. The only money I made was prize money on the golf course, and even if I succeeded in pushing my way onto the tour, it wouldn't do me any good if I couldn't play well enough to survive. I began to wonder how long I could afford to go on this way: another season, two years? And then what would I do? Go back to Philly and take another job at Nabisco?

It occurred to me that the PGA was watching my terrible year closely and probably with a great deal of satisfaction. I had given them ample reason to award me an Approved Tournament Player's Card, which was the next best thing to a full PGA membership, and they had repeatedly backed off. Maybe they were just waiting for me to disappear, as they had waited for Bill Spiller and Joe Louis and Teddy Rhodes to go away in the late forties and early fifties. The PGA had all the time in the world, but I only had a brief window in which my golf skills could be competitive on a national level. I'm sure they knew that, and since I was really the only black man who could play the game competitively at that point, all they had to do was wait for me to go away.

In those days waiting out black guys seemed to be a favorite game of the golf establishment, particularly the people who ran golf courses in the South. *Brown vs. the Board of Education* may have opened up schools to blacks in 1954, but it took several more years and more Supreme Court rulings to make a dent in golf courses. Even on municipal courses paid for by public dollars, they found ways of keeping us away.

Roy Campanella and Willie Mays were winning MVP honors in the National League in those years, but they wouldn't have been welcomed on a public golf course in the South. In Greensboro, North Carolina, five blacks were convicted of trespassing on a public golf course. When the courts ruled that a public course had to be open to anyone, Greensboro got around the ruling by leasing the operations to a private company, which instituted new rules against blacks. You can imagine how they felt when I showed up to play professionally a couple of years later.

Greensboro wasn't the only place. The same things were going on in Miami, Charleston, Fort Lauderdale, and Jacksonville. In each place they tried to block blacks from public courses by selling the rights to private companies. In Jacksonville, in 1959, the blacks fought the sale. In Miami and Charleston, the NAACP got involved and pushed the cases all the way up to the Supreme Court. It was a long, hard fight, and those guys were just trying to play recreationally! When I heard of those things happening, I felt good that we were working so well within the system to get what we wanted, and at the same time I felt terrible, because I knew that the golf establishment sure as hell would fight before they'd let me in. What kind of chance did one black man have when so many thousands were being denied?

If I thought about it too much, I realized that I didn't have a chance, so I tried not to think about it. All I could do was take it one step at a time, one tournament at a time, and one swing at a time, and let the chips fall where they would. If nothing else, I would show them time and again that I could play golf as well as anyone in the country, and if they continued to deny me my right to play, well then that was their mistake.

That summer of 1957, when nothing was going right for me, I knew that the only thing I could do was work harder at my game and concentrate on relaxing and not pressing at tournaments. I could have given up then. I could have screamed about whitey keeping me out of the game and not giving me a chance. I had every reason on earth to be self-righteous and spend the rest of my days huffing about how the system kept me from playing. But I didn't want to be right, I wanted to play golf. I had to leave all of the pressures behind me and just play better. I enjoyed a brief ray of hope at the Eastern Open at the end of the summer, where I tied for eighth place and made $825. When the tour headed back to California, I was ready to give it my best shot.

I liked California so much that in the winter months I rented an apartment from a man named Jerry Thomas and spent as much of my time on the golf courses as I could. I liked the weather in Los Angeles, Teddy Rhodes was usually there in the winters, and there were plenty of places where we could play. Our favorite hangout was the Western Avenue golf course, where we ran into many black athletes. It was there that I met Jackie Robinson and got some encouragement and advice on breaking into the all-white professional game.

I wanted so badly to move Rose and Charles, Jr., out to L.A. with me, but we just couldn't afford it. Still, it got harder and harder to break away from wherever I was playing to drive all the way to Philly to be with them for a precious few days and then drive out again to the next tournament. So with some of the money that I'd made in Hartford, I brought Rose out to L.A. in the early part of 1957, and she liked it too. We saw a bunch of houses that we wanted to buy, but we couldn't afford one yet. All the same we figured that the first big paycheck I made would go as a down payment on a house. Charles, Jr., was excited about it too. He was nine years old and a huge Dodgers fan, and he had been heartbroken when they left Brooklyn for L.A. When we told him that we wanted to move there for good, he was thrilled.

Some awfully good players were coming out of California in those days, and they made the competiton keen at even the smaller tournaments. Guys like Billy Casper, Gene Littler, Jerry Barber, Ken Venturi, and George Archer all showed up to play, and frequently we'd run into each other at practice. I felt instinctively that I had to be in southern California to have a serious chance at golf.

It was fitting, then, that my big break came at a southern California tournament. They held the Long Beach Open at the Lakewood Golf Course on Carson Street on the second weekend of November. It was a 54-hole tournament that was sanctioned by the PGA, and many touring pros were entered, including Al Besselink, Eric Monti, Billy Casper, and Howie Johnson. Prize money was set at $11,500, with $1,500 going to the winner. How I dearly wanted to get my hands on some of that!

I went into the tournament wondering what to do about my putter. The week before I had played in the San Diego Open and finished out of the money when I three-putted a whole flock of greens. Putting has always been a nemesis with me. I never know when it's going to desert me altogether, and it seemed like that whole year my putter had been on vacation.

After San Diego I decided to switch putters, and a few days later I happened to run into Thelma Cowans, who with Anne Gregory was the top black woman golfer of our day. Thelma had won the National Negro Open title that year, and I was more than appreciative when she pulled me aside and showed me some things I'd been doing badly with the putter. After a couple of days work on the putting green, my stroke came back and I was ready.

Par was 71 at the Lakewood course, which was relatively short, with bumpy greens that were hard to read. I started out the tournament by shooting a 69, which wasn't great, but was a lot better than I had been managing for most of the year. I was in the middle of the pack after the round, and I knew that if I didn't mess up I'd probably make some money. On Saturday, however, after struggling to make a 70, my prospects dimmed and I knew that I would have to come up with a good round on Sunday to make a decent paycheck.

Sunday, November 10, the sun shown down on me. I started out by birdying the first hole, a 412-yard par 4, with a putt that was as sweet and sure as any I'd hit all year. I felt good right away, and I realized that I had nothing to lose and everything to gain. A good round would push me way up in the standings; a great round could put me on top. I parred the second hole, slipped a little by getting only a birdie on the par 5 third, and then put one right on the pin on the next hole, a par 3, for another birdie. I followed it up with yet another birdie, my fourth, and then parred all the way to the turn. I was suddenly 4-under, and my putter was still hot. I began to creep up on the field.

I was playing with Monti, who had begun the day in second place with a three-stroke lead over me. He was shooting well too, but I was better. I birdied three of the first five holes on the back nine, and I was suddenly 7-under and rushing towards the lead. The second-round leader, Dale Andreason, had fallen away, and five other guys faltered who had chances to take the lead. It all came down to me and Monti.

I parred my way up through 16, but on 17, disaster nearly struck. I missed the green on a par 3, left myself long with the chip, and missed the putt. I tapped in for bogey, and suddenly Monti and I were dead even going into the final hole.

The last hole was a 475-yard par 5, and an eagle would have won it. I went for the green with my second shot but missed. Luckily, so did Monti. I put my third within six feet and drilled the putt for a birdie. I was suddenly the leader of this tournament, and there was one man and one putt between me and the win. It was more than a win; it was a giant first step, showing everyone in the world that a black man could hold his own against PGA golfers. As good as he was, Teddy Rhodes had never won a white tournament, nor had Howard Wheeler nor Spiller nor Zeke Hartsfield. I was on the verge of something historic.

It hadn't been easy getting to that point where I was ready to win a golf tournament, and this win wasn't going to come easy either. I watched with my stomach churning as Eric calmly dropped a 10-footer for the tie. I had shot a 64, one of the best rounds of my career, and had leaped over everybody in the field to a first-place tie with Monti. Now I had to win a playoff.

As we walked to the first tee, I took a deep breath to calm the butterflies in my stomach and to remind myself to take it one swing at a time. After all of the practice, and all of the heartache, and all of the doors slammed shut, I was suddenly in a position to win a big golf tournament, and it was a wonderful feeling. But I couldn't dwell on it; I had to continue my hot play and do my best, and if the Lord was willing, I'd come through.

We pushed on the first hole, but on the second I nearly lost it. I missed an easy putt and had to settle for a par, and Eric was three feet away from the cup with a birdie putt that would have won it. He missed it. As I said, the sun was shining down on me that day. The tables were turned on the next hole when he missed the green and had to settle for a par putt. I had hit a perfect drive and put my approach within six feet, and now the tournament was in my hands. I studied that putt from every which angle, and then I dropped it right into the center of the cup.

I was suddenly a winner on the PGA Tour, the first black man ever to achieve that. Even better as far as I was concerned at that moment was the fact that I picked up the $1,500 first prize, plus $500 for shooting the low round of the day. That paycheck would go a long way toward soothing some of the pain and frustration I'd been feeling all year.

The media didn't let my win go unnoticed. A photo sent out on the AP wire the next day was captioned "He's Now in the Big-Time." My win was written up all over the country, although a lot of people sure didn't know my name: *the Washington Post* announced that "Clifford" won a major title. Columns were written about my struggle with the golf tour and the odds I'd faced to overcome the barriers. They suggested that I should be able to join the tour full time.

But I wasn't allowed to enter a PGA tournament the following week. Instead, I played in a satellite tournament in northern California, the Almaden Open, which wasn't a PGA event but still had some damn good golfers. I almost won that one too. It was another 54-hole tournament, and I tied Billy Casper for the lead at the end and entered my second play-off in two weeks. We went 19 extra holes that Sunday and matched each other shot for shot until Billy finally beat me with a birdie on the last hole. That win was like a trigger for Billy Casper, who became one of the brightest lights in professional golf in the early sixties.

I wrote something on my winning scorecard from the last round at Long Beach. I still have it at home. It says, "To my wife and Chas. Jr. This is the one that won the home." The home was the first place we ever bought together, a two-bedroom house in Los Angeles. Rose and Charles, Jr., moved out in the winter of 1958, so I finally had my family with me. We settled down, and Rose got an office job working for the county. It looked like we were on our way.

Did anything change for me by winning the Long Beach Open? Of course not. The PGA had its rules, and one of them said that only Caucasians could be members of the organization. It didn't matter how many newspapers ran that AP photo of me, or how many times someone wrote a column on my behalf. As far as the PGA was concerned, one win in a three-day tournament by a black man didn't mean a damn thing. Nobody contacted me, nobody tried to work me into more tournaments. I just didn't exist as far as they were concerned.

And you know what? I wasn't even surprised. Disappointed, yes; disgusted, sure. But not surprised. Nothing changed very quickly in those Eisenhower years, and golf, the game most tightly controlled by elite white society, wasn't about to bend a little for one black man with a good game. Even with public opinion on my side (never mind about right and wrong), the PGA wouldn't think twice about admitting me.

No, it would take some stronger force to get the PGA to change its mind about admitting a black player to its ranks. It would take something that threatened them where they were most vulnerable—their wallets. The Caucasian clause eventually tumbled, and I was allowed into the game, but not because the rule was so inherently racist and wrong. It tumbled because I happened to meet a bright, liberal, Jewish man who had a real problem with discrimination. I met him on a golf course at, of all places, a country club.

His name was Stanley Mosk, and when he became attorney general of the state of California in 1958, he had a very powerful tool to wield on behalf of people like me. Within two years Stanley accomplished something that no hot putter or public image could ever do. He threatened the PGA, and as the fifties drew to a close, some mighty thick walls began to come tumbling down, with me at the epicenter of what would be golf's biggest earthquake.

CHAPTER 10

The Caucasian Clause Falls

The year is 1960. Jackie Robinson's career has come and gone, but a host of young black athletes are dominating professional sports. Jim Brown is running wild in professional football; Wilt Chamberlain is scoring, well, bucketsfull in the NBA; Bill Russell is leading the Boston Celtics to greatness; the young Cassius Clay is flattening opponents in the Olympics; Hank Aaron, Willie Mays, and Ernie Banks are packing baseball stadiums wherever they go.

But in golf we still have the Caucasian clause. It is located in Article III, section 1, of the PGA's national constitution, which pertains to membership. "Professional golfers of the Caucasian Race, over the age of eighteen (18) years, residing in North or South America, who can qualify under the terms and conditions hereinafter specified, shall be eligible for membership."

No beating around the bush there, huh? The PGA, which was good at hiding behind subterfuges like "invitationals" and qualifying rules, was uncharacteristically direct about proclaiming itself an all-white organization.

Excuse my sarcasm, but it still fries me that a professional sport with such a simon-pure image and such deep connections to corporate America could be so rotten at the core. This is the sport that made national heroes out of Bobby Jones and Ben Hogan and was capturing the heart of America through the

wonderful, inspiring play of Arnold Palmer. Golf was on the verge
of an unprecedented surge in popularity that would see it leap
ahead in everything from purses to charitable contributions. Two
new elements — Jack Nicklaus and television — were about to
blow the game wide open in exposure.

And still the PGA was so goddamned stupid that it threatened
the very existence of the sport by keeping intact something as
mean and wrong-headed and outright ugly as the Caucasian
clause. I don't know what's more disturbing—the fact that the
PGA was so ignorant and arrogant that it thought it could keep
the game alive in modern times while keeping it segregated, or
the fact that it didn't seem to make a damn bit of difference to
the corporate sponsors and general public.

Dr. King was doing his thing all the way to the Kennedys in
those days, but if you wanted to get a real appraisal of the state
of race relations, you needn't have gone any further than a golf
tournament. The players were white, the galleries were white,
the sponsors were white, and the businessmen who paid to play
in the pro-ams were white. Only the caddies were black.

It was all so white and so agreeable to everyone involved that
they could put that rule right there for all to see: "Members of
the Caucasian Race." In that environment, such a statement must
have seemed as natural as saying that players would carry 14 clubs
and only hit approved balls. It is still disturbing to me that of
all the thousands of people involved in professional sports in
those days, and all of the people who flocked to golf, nobody
ever took a hard stand against the Caucasian clause. I don't recall
any sponsors pulling out of tournaments because of race or any
of America's greatest golf courses politely refusing to host a PGA
tournament because of moral objections to the PGA's bylaws.

If I hadn't come around with the kind of skills and personality
I had, when would the Caucasian clause have been lifted? It
outlasted Teddy Rhodes and Bill Spiller and the others. Would
it have held up against Rafe Botts or Pete Brown or Lee Elder,
the black golfers who came in right after me? I truly think that
if I hadn't challenged the PGA as hard as I did, they would have
kept that rule around for another 10 years. If there's one thing

I've learned about golf, it is that nothing changes until somebody
raises a really major stink about it, and I was the only one willing
to do that.

The Caucasian clause itself wasn't added to the PGA constitution until 1943, and, surprisingly, it wasn't the work of the
southern chapters. It was the PGA delegation from Michigan that
proposed the change and then defended it. "Show us some good
golf courses established by Negroes," they challenged. And then
they excluded everyone who wasn't white. Never mind that blacks
had been systematically excluded from having the economic or
social means to establish a country club, not to mention their
being barred from white golf courses. The amendment was voted
in by the PGA membership and it held fast.

But let me back up a bit. There the Caucasian clause stood
as 1957 turned into 1958, and 1958 rolled into 1959, with my
win at Long Beach an old memory of just another three-day
tournament. What could I do, other than to light up another cigar
and play my game? I had my moments: a 65 in the first round
at Tucson, a 64 at Akron to put me near the top. Toward the end
of 1959 I got another win when I took the Gardena Valley Open
Golf tournament in California with a final round of 67. I beat
guys like Jim Ferrier, Jerry Barber, Eric Monti, and Jack Fleck to
win the first-place money of $750, but it wasn't a PGA-sponsored
event.

The tour that week was in Lafayette, Louisiana, where Billy
Casper won $2,000 in the PGA tournament against Arnold Palmer
and Gay Brewer and the rest of them. The guy who finished in
sixth place made more money than I did in my Gardena win,
which made my victory more than a little bittersweet.

I'd have to use that same word to describe what happened
to me in 1959, the year things finally began to turn around. By
the time I won the tournament in Gardena, I had been discovered
by the national media and my cause became known nationwide.
It started when Jackie Robinson devoted his entire column in the
New York Post to the fact that once again I hadn't been invited
to play in either the Bing Crosby tournament at Pebble Beach
or the Palm Springs Desert Golf Classic. Why was it that I could

play everywhere in California, but not at those two tournaments, which were sandwiched around the San Diego Open in late January? "Golf is the one major sport in America today in which rank and open racial prejudice is allowed to reign supreme," wrote Jackie in his column. "Though often called the sport of gentlemen, all too often golf courses, clubs and tournaments apply the ungentlemanly and un-American yardstick of race and color in determining who may or may not compete."

Jackie noted that President Eisenhower was a member of the all-white Augusta National Golf Club, that Bing Crosby had yet to invite a black to his annual event, and that many golfers with records less than mine had been admitted at Palm Springs. "Since Charlie is endeavoring to make a living at his chosen craft, it constitutes a basic denial of economic opportunity when he is barred from membership in the PGA," wrote Jackie. "Not only should court action be considered, but I feel the issue is one for a thorough investigation by the Civil Rights Commission."

Jackie pointed out that a charity golf tournament that was played every year in Miami by professional baseball players had been allowing blacks to play with no problems. He also quoted Teddy Rhodes, who quite correctly noted that Bing Crosby had a large black audience and should be more than a little concerned about alienating a portion of his fans. He closed his piece by mentioning that Joe Louis was so incensed by my exclusion from Palm Springs that he wired Vice President Richard Nixon with a protest. " 'The world is up in arms about swastikas painted on churches and synagogues,' Joe said in his telegram, 'but out in the Vice-President's own home state, similar swastikas are being painted on every green at the Palm Springs course.' "

That summer of 1959 I watched as Teddy Rhodes's game deteriorated to the point where he could hardly compete, and it nearly broke my heart. We started out together in Chicago, where we began the qualification process to play in the U.S. Open. Since we weren't exempt touring professionals, the way we could enter the tournament was by placing at the top of a number of qualifiers that were held around the country. I didn't particularly want to spend three weeks qualifying to get into one tournament, but I'd never played in an open and wanted to give it a try. Teddy had qualified several times for the annual tournament, and he wanted to give it one last shot.

We started out by playing two rounds in May at the tough Medinah courses in Chicago, where Teddy and I finished on top of a group of 21 golfers, who moved on to the next round at Skokie on June 1. We won there too and entered the USGA championship at Winged Foot in New York on June 11.

I played well enough at the open to finish in the top 35, but in a subsequent story about me in *Sports Illustrated,* Dick Schaap noted that if I hadn't shot a 76 on the last day, a decent round would have put me in the top 16, which would have worried a lot of people in Georgia. In those days, the top 16 finishers at the U.S. Open received automatic bids to join the Masters, and there was no way in hell that I was going to get one of those bids. Schaap wrote about the Caucasian clause that was keeping me out of the game, and he pointed out that Teddy Rhodes was 47 years old and had lost his chance. "In simpler language, Charlie Sifford . . . don't feel badly," wrote Schaap. "It doesn't mean that people at Augusta think there's anything wrong with you personally. It's just the curious way the golf ball bounces."

That summer I got my first club and ball endorsements when the Kroydon company signed me to swing their clubs and U.S. Rubber asked me to use their golf balls. Teddy and I were also appointed to serve on the athletic advisory board of the Ballantine beer company, which was largely a ceremonial position, but nevertheless it seemed promising that they'd seek out a couple of black golfers. None of these positions paid anything, but they seemed like the first step in the right direction.

Teddy and I traveled the whole summer in my car, entering tournaments and trying to make a dollar. It wasn't easy. By the time the middle of July had rolled around, I had played in a dozen tournaments and finished in the money only three times. Of those three — the Flint Open, Buick Open, and U.S. Open — my biggest paycheck was the $240 that I won at Winged Foot. That kind of money could buy gas and a room to sleep in and a little bit of food, but it didn't cover much else. Teddy and I split all of our expenses and cut corners wherever we could, but we were still barely scraping by, much less sending any money home to our families.

A guy interviewed me at the Western Open in Pittsburgh that summer, where I was heading for a pretty good paycheck before another bad final round dropped me way down in the prize money. As bad as I was playing, Teddy was doing worse. He didn't make the cut at the Western Open, and for yet another week he came up penniless. "I feel so sorry for that guy I could cry," I told the reporter. "He's been out here six weeks and hasn't won a dime. It's not his game either. His game would be OK if he didn't have to worry so much about where his next meal was coming from."

Poor Teddy. He was pushing 50 years old and was still trying to go out there and scrap hard enough to make a few dollars at golf. That man had been so great in his prime that he should have been riding easy by that time. He should have had automatic sponsor exemptions to any tournament he wanted to play in, and he should have received appearance fees and endorsement contracts just for being Teddy Rhodes, one of the greatest golfers of his time. Golf clubs and country clubs should have been lining up to get him as their club professional. But there was none of that for a black golfer — not in Teddy's day and not in my day. Teddy was allowed to disappear from golf like just another journeyman pro.

I didn't start to make money until the very end of the summer, when I put together some solid golf at the Carling Open and tournaments in Detroit; Portland; and Hesperia, California. I played in 18 tournaments in all in 1959, which just wasn't enough. A PGA Tour player could enter that many tournaments before the end of April. How could I compete financially and athletically against those guys if I could only play in a fraction of the tournaments?

That question finally got the attention of Stanley Mosk, the attorney general of California who had taken office at the beginning of 1959. I had the good fortune of meeting him at his club, the Hillcrest Country Club in Los Angeles, when Billy

Eckstine and I were playing some golf. Hillcrest was a Jewish club, formed when the Jews were barred from joining the older country clubs, and they didn't have any problem with blacks participating.

Billy was acquainted with Attorney General Mosk from lunches and events at Hillcrest, and one day he brought me over and introduced me. Mosk wasn't much of a golfer — tennis was his game — but he seemed to take a genuine interest when he found out that I was a professional golfer who wasn't able to play professional golf because of my color. A passionate advocate of civil rights, Mosk had established a civil rights section in his office and was more than willing to take on any forms of discrimination in his home state.

"Why can't you play on the PGA Tour?" he asked me.

"Because of this Caucasian clause in their constitution that says that only whites can join."

I remember the conversation. He had to think about that one. "You mean to tell me that they actually have that in their organizational bylaws?"

The next time I went to Hillcrest I brought along a copy of the PGA's constitution and left it for him. I followed up with a letter that my lawyer and I drafted that said that I was as qualified as any golfer in the country to be a member of the PGA and that not only was I being excluded from making a living as a golfer, but I was barred from PGA tournaments right there in the state of California.

Mosk — who is now a California Supreme Court justice — got to work. He contacted the PGA and asked them to verify that they practiced open discrimination as a matter of policy. He presented me as a resident of California whose civil rights were being violated and asked them to show reasons other than race why I was being denied membership.

And do you know what? The PGA didn't have any reasons. Of course, they couldn't make me a full-fledged member of the organization, which would still have been in violation of their bylaws, but they quickly found a convenient loophole. In December 1959, roughly three months after my first contact with Stanley Mosk, I got a letter from the PGA offering to make me an approved tournament player, the first black man ever to receive that title. I could officially join the tour in 1960, it said.

To explain what this means, I need to backtrack. Today there are two different organizations in professional golf: the PGA and the PGA Tour. The latter controls most of the tournaments on the professional schedule and sets up eligibility standards for the 125-odd touring professionals. The former organization is mainly concerned with the thousands of club professionals who work in golf shops and give lessons at golf courses all over the country.

In the 1950s there was no PGA Tour, and everything came under the PGA banner. Because their membership was mainly composed of club professionals, a very small percentage of whom played the tour, their membership requirements were set up almost exclusively for club pros. To join the PGA in those days, you had to be sponsored by a club professional and had to either work for five years as a club professional or five years as an assistant to a club professional.

After the war, however, when so many great golfers started coming up, they needed to find a way to let guys play tournament golf who hadn't served for five years in a golf shop. They established the approved tournament player classification and reviewed applications on a case-by-case basis. Guys like Ken Venturi, Doug Sanders, Arnold Palmer, and Bob Rosburg came up as approved tournament players, as well as great foreign players like Gary Player. To get the card, you had to be sponsored by two members and you had to prove that your game was good enough to compete. You also, of course, had to pass the PGA's review.

I got sponsored easily enough by Earl Martin at the Western Avenue golf course in L.A. and Harry Bassler at Fox Hills, but the PGA had refused to recognize me for, oh, a dozen years. In March 1960 I was two months away from turning 38 years old, and I was finally a rookie on the PGA Tour. If I could play in 25 tournaments a year for the next five years, I would become a full-fledged member of the PGA.

But just because I now had a card in my pocket didn't mean that I was any more welcome at many tournaments than I'd been in the past. I still couldn't play in the whole southern and south-western swing of the Tour, and in 1960, approved tournament player or not, I would only enter 20 PGA-sponsored golf tournaments.

For a clear picture of the ironies that year, you need only look at the month of November. The tour went from Tijuana, Mexico (where I had played the year before and had felt as unwelcome as if I'd been playing in Mississippi), to Mexico City, to Alabama. I stayed in California. On the week of November 15, two things happened: the PGA, at its annual meeting, once again voted down a resolution to abolish the Caucasian clause, and I won a satellite golf tournament, the Almaden Open, in California.

Why couldn't the PGA pass the resolution? Because each member state was given two votes, like the U.S. Senate, and the southern states routinely enlisted the aid of the western states to defeat the resolution. Out of 81 votes cast at the 1960 PGA meeting, only 17 were in favor of defeating the resolution.

While I was winning at Almaden against guys like Ken Venturi and Bob Rosburg — I beat Bill Eggers in sudden death with a birdie putt on the first play off hole — Stanley Mosk was active too. To his immense credit, he wouldn't give up with his battle against the PGA, and he stuck with me.

On November 22, just days after the Caucasian clause had been upheld by the PGA, he threw down an icy warning. "We intend to take every step available to us, both in and out of the courts, to force the P.G.A. either to eliminate this obnoxious restriction or to cease all activity of any kind within our state," he declared in a statement that was carried in the national press.

It wasn't an idle threat. Mosk began to work with the attornies general of other states, most notably with Louis Lefkowitz of the state of New York, to pressure the PGA. Lefkowitz began an investigation of the powerful, all-white Metropolitan Golfers Association, and an attorney in his office named Shirley Seigal was able to open a previously all-white tournament to blacks.

That tournament, held on a golf course owned by Cornell University, was opened because, as Jackie Robinson reported, "Lefkowitz pointed out that private groups [such as the PGA] which do discriminate must necessarily forfeit their access to the use of public or tax-exempt facilities unless they refrain from such practices."

The PGA was headed for a showdown, and they got one. They had planned to hold their 1962 PGA Championship tournament — a major event that ranked with the U.S. Open in magnitude — at the Wilshire Country Club in Los Angeles. Mosk wouldn't allow the PGA to use a California course in a discriminatory manner.

He told the PGA that either I be allowed to play in the tournament or they move it out of California. He also got in touch with the Los Angeles Junior Chamber of Commerce and insisted that they not sponsor the tournament. The Chamber of Commerce agreed, but the PGA tried to fight. They said that because of association rules I wasn't eligible to play in the tournament. Mosk said that, if necessary, he would get a court injunction to stop the event. "It was a sporting event, for goodness sakes," said Justice Mosk recently from his offices at the California Supreme Court. "What does color have to do with that?"

He wouldn't let the pressure drop, and on May 17, 1961, the executive committee of the PGA voted to withdraw the tournament and move it to the private Aronimink golf course outside of Philadelphia. They went to all of that trouble just so they wouldn't have to allow one black man — me — to play in their event.

Shortly afterwards the NAACP got involved, blasting the PGA and the Aronimink Golf Course. They charged the PGA with "un-American practices" and branded the whole PGA Championship "an ugly tournament."

Does this sound at all familiar? Isn't this exchange from 1961 practically the same war of words that we heard in 1990 when somebody found out that Shoal Creek in Alabama practiced racial discrimination? Do you understand now what I mean when I say that golf has done nothing to better its record in regard to minorities over the years and that the way they handle any issue of right and wrong is to sweep it under the carpet and hope that it won't appear again?

The PGA was stung by the NAACP criticism and issued this outrageous press release, which I give in its entirety.

DUNEDIN, Fla., June 21 — The Professional Golfers' Association of America today took issue with the National Association for the Advancement of Colored People.

Officials of the NAACP yesterday charged the PGA with what they termed "un-American practices" and branded the PGA Championship as an "ugly tournament."

"There is no truth in the statement that the 1962 PGA Championship was withdrawn from Los Angeles when California's Attorney General asked that a Negro professional, Charles Sifford, be permitted to play," declared Lou Strong, the PGA President, from Rochester, N.Y.

Strong referred to a newspaper article in which that statement was attributed to the NAACP.

"No such request was ever received by the PGA from the Attorney General of California. Moreover, the cancellation of the Championship at Los Angeles had absolutely nothing to do with Charlie Sifford," Strong continued.

"Nor is there any truth in the implication that Negro professional golfers are barred from the PGA Championship.

"The statement that our National Championship is restricted to PGA members is equally untrue. Any PGA Approved Tournament Player is also eligible to qualify for an invitation.

"As for branding one of the world's greatest golf championships 'an ugly tournament', well, that statement hardly calls for an answer. The PGA Championship speaks for itself."

Sifford, a former National Negro Champion from Los Angeles, has been an Approved Tournament Player since March 28, 1960. He was the first Negro to be granted Approved Tournament Player status by the PGA.

Richard I. Thomas of Baltimore was elected an Approved Tournament Player June 19, 1961.

A third Negro professional has applied for playing privileges in tournaments co-sponsored by the PGA and his application is now being processed.

The NAACP criticised the PGA and Aronimink Golf Club of Philadelphia, site of the 1962 PGA Championship July 19-22 of next year, in a letter to W. W. K. Miller, President of Aronimink.

In the letter, the NAACP, after calling the PGA Championship "an ugly tournament", decried the fact that Aronimink has "made itself a party to continuing the un-American practices" of the PGA.

"It is unfortunate that the NAACP did not take the trouble to learn the facts in the case before making these unwarranted charges," said Strong.

"If NAACP officials had taken a moment to ask Charlie Sifford about the PGA and the PGA Championship, he could have given them the facts and cleared the air.

"Charlie knows that he, like any other PGA Approved Tournament Player, had an opportunity to qualify for an invitation to the National Championship this year, as any Approved Tournament Player has any year.

"The fact of the matter is that Charlie simply didn't make the grade this year, on the basis of his playing record."

Approved Tournament Players could qualify for the PGA Championship this year by:

1. Finishing among the 20 TT Point Leaders in tournaments co-sponsored or approved by the PGA in the calendar year 1960.

2. Finishing among the 20 leading money winners in tournaments co-sponsored or approved by the PGA in the calendar year 1961 through the Masters Tournament.

3. Finishing among the 24 low scorers and those tied for 24th place in the 1960 PGA Championship.

Eight Approved Tournament Players won invitations to the 1961 PGA Championship, to be played July 27-30 at Olympia Fields Country Club, Olympia Fields, Ill., through one or more of these avenues.

These eight players are Bob Goalby, Tom Nieporte, Gary Player, Johnny Pott, Dave Ragan Jr., Mason Rudolph, Doug Sanders and Ken Venturi.

Approved Tournament Players have competed in every PGA Championship from 1957 to date. Prior to 1957, the National Championship was restricted to PGA members.

"It is true that the PGA Constitution contains a clause restricting PGA membership to professional golfers of the Caucasian race," said Strong, "as it has for nearly 30 years.

"However, this has nothing to do with participation in the PGA Championship or in any other tournaments.

"The PGA established its Approved Tournament Player classification shortly after the end of World War II to enable those who, for any reason, are not eligible for PGA membership to compete in tournaments."

Shortly thereafter, it also provided for an Approved Tournament Player to gain the experience necessary for PGA membership by playing the PGA Tour for five years, competing in a minimum of 25 PGA co-sponsored or approved tournaments a year.

"One point which many people fail to recognize is that The PGA of America is an Associaton of golf professionals, the vast majority of them club professionals," declared Strong.

"Ours is not an organization of professional golf players only. For nine out of 10 PGA members, playing golf and playing in golf tournaments is only incidental to their principal jobs.

"Even so, our Association has made provisions whereby every PGA member and every other qualified golf professional can participate in golf tournaments on the PGA circuit and in the PGA Championship."

The PGA's powerful 14-man Executive Committee at its Mid-year Meeting May 15-17 in Hollywood, Fla., approved a resolution for reference to the PGA Annual Meeting, which would eliminate the "Caucasian clause" from the PGA Constitution.

"So far as we know, there are at the present time no Negro club professionals who have the necessary qualifications for PGA membership, even if there were no 'Caucasian clause'," said Strong.

"However, if that clause is eliminated from our Constitution at our Annual Meeting November 2-10, it would open the door for Negro playing professionals to qualify for membership, in time."

If the clause is dropped at the 1961 Annual Meeting, a Negro holding an Approved Tournament Player card could become eligible for membership by participating in 25 tournaments a year for five years.

"This would mean that, if they meet all other requirements, Charlie Sifford, Dick Thomas and other Negro players could become PGA members, in time, by playing the PGA Tour regularly," Strong said.

"Many of our outstanding young PGA members, men like Bob Rosburg, Chairman of the PGA Tournament Committee, and Arnold Palmer, PGA Player-of-the-Year in 1960, Dow Finsterwald, former PGA Champion, and Dr. Cary Middlecoff, former USGA Open Champion, among them, came up in this manner.

"If it were not for our Approved Tournament Player status, these men would not be PGA members today. There is no other way by which a man other than a club professional can attain membership.

"Prior to the institution of the Approved Tournament Player arrangement," Strong continued, "a man was required to have served five years as a professional in the employ of a club or as an assistant in the employ of a professional to be eligible for membership.

"Hence, the PGA Approved Tournament Player arrangement is an indication of the manner in which the PGA has endeavored to adjust its requirements to keep pace with changing times.

"It is safe to assume that this process will continue, as it does with all progressive organizations. However, it should be kept in mind that it involves reconciliation of the views of more than 4,800 members and 34 local organizations.

"Thus," Strong concluded, "it cannot be instantaneous, despite the natural impatience of some elements."

That the PGA would issue such a lengthy defense was a sign of the tremendous pressure that was being exerted for it to change. The idea that I had failed to qualify for the PGA Championship because of my playing record was outrageous, and their use of my name in their pathetic defense was slanderous. Of their three qualifying rules, which did they think I had a chance of meeting? I wasn't allowed to play in the 1960 tournament, so that excluded rule 3, finishing among the top-24 low scorers in the previous PGA Championship. Since most of the tournaments before the Masters were held in the South, I couldn't possibly finish among the top-20 money winners on the Tour (rule 2), unless they expected me to win every tournament I entered. And rule 1, finishing in the 20 top point leaders in 1960 tournaments, was equally impossible, since I could play in only a fraction of the tournaments that the other players entered.

Clearly, the ATP rules didn't fit my circumstances in the slightest, but rather than acknowledge this, the PGA chose to discredit me. I had now officially become a "subversive element" to this "progressive organization." Give me a break.

The Caucasian clause finally fell in the November 1961 meeting. The PGA eventually gave me a full year's credit for the 20 tournaments I entered in 1960, and after playing more than 25 tournaments over the next three years and completing a business school course, they awarded me full PGA membership in May 1964.

Don January was one of the players on the executive committee that pushed to ban the clause. He recalled recently that even after it went, there were attempts to segregate golf. "Even after we got the clause out," said January, "a couple of sponsors had a little contention about where [black players] might eat in the clubhouse. Might have a separate dining room for them. The

players said, 'No man! They go where we go or we don't go.'
But there was still a little hangover of that thought."

It was more than a little hangover, Don. When I went out
as the first black man to play on the full PGA Tour, it was one
of the most frightening and dangerous things I've ever faced. It
took a long time for the Caucasian clause to fall. For the black
man in golf, the struggle had just begun.

CHAPTER **11**

The Jackie Robinson of Golf?

I've been called the Jackie Robinson of Golf by many newspaper writers over the years, but to tell you the truth, I'm a little disgusted by the comparison at this point in my life. It's true that I was the first black to break into the all-white PGA Tour, just as Jackie was the first to integrate baseball when Branch Rickey brought him up in 1947 to play for the Brooklyn Dodgers. But that's about as far as the comparison goes.

After the fact of us both being the first blacks in our sport, Jackie Robinson's career and mine — and the games of baseball and golf themselves — have turned out so differently that in racial terms, they're nearly polar opposites. It makes me mad now when some newspaper reporter passes me off to his readers with the simple catchphrase that "Charlie Sifford is the Jackie Robinson of Golf." He's not only missing the real story of what is going on in golf, but he's suggesting that the doors to blacks have been opened as effectively in golf as they have in major league baseball. That is simply not true, and in fact, it is a gross misrepresentation of the state of golf today.

Which is not to say that I don't admire and respect Jackie Robinson and his contributions to sports. God knows he was a brilliant, courageous athlete, and a great man, too. He was a good friend of mine, and we golfed together many times in California during and after Jackie's playing career. In his retirement, Jackie often came to bat for me and for all black golfers in his hard-hitting newspaper column, and he was just as disgusted with the state of professional golf as I am. I would be proud to be compared to Jackie in almost anything, but not in a lie that says that I'm the same symbol of freedom and racial equality in my sport that he was in his.

I'm ashamed and embarrassed for the game of golf itself, because its record on both the professional and amateur levels in regards to minorities has been unspeakable. Blacks have been systematically deprived from playing this game for generations now, and the game of golf hasn't done a damn thing about it. Because of this neglect — because nobody in professional golf has ever had the guts or the foresight to be a Branch Rickey — some of the greatest athletes in the world have effectively been banned from the sport. We are now facing the extinction of the black golfer.

If I was the Jackie Robinson of Golf, I sure didn't do a very good job of it. Whereas Jackie was quickly followed by dozens of great black ballplayers, there are now only two blacks playing on the PGA Tour. One of them, Calvin Peete, is 48 years old and nearly ready to move on to the Senior PGA Tour. The other is Jim Thorpe, who is 42 years old. On the senior tour there are five of us who play regularly. Jim Dent is the youngster at 52, but then you've got Rafe Botts at 54, Lee Elder at 57, Charles Owens at 61 years old, and me, 69.

Out of nearly 400 professional golfers in this country, there are only seven blacks? That's so far out of line that it's ridiculous. Hell, there were nearly as many of us showing up at the Tam O'Shanter in the late fifties. Does this mean that somehow today's blacks inherently can't play this game? Maybe, in the words of Al Campanis, we don't have the correct "faculties" for golf? We excel at just about every other sport there is, but we can't swing a 6-iron to save our lives? No, something is definitely wrong here. It is a national scandal that blacks have not been given the opportunity to play this game, and it is a national tragedy that we might soon be phased out of it altogether.

I'm not ashamed of my career and what I've accomplished. I think I've overcome odds far greater than any other black athlete has ever faced, Jackie Robinson included. I'm proud of what I've achieved in golf despite opposition that has pushed against me for 45 years and continues to hound me to this day. And I'm proud of the accomplishments of other black golfers, because I know that they've had nearly as tough a time out there as I've had. I may have been able to open the door just a tiny crack for guys like Lee Elder and Calvin Peete and Jim Dent, but they still had to be the second, third or fourth black guy to walk through that door. It won't be until the 100th or 300th black player comes along that it will seem normal for us to be a part of this game, and I honestly don't think that that day will ever come.

Look at the difference between what Jackie's breaking the color barrier achieved for his sport, and what my breaking the color barrier has done for mine. Jackie was followed by hundreds of great, black ballplayers who have transformed their sport. I will be followed by nobody.

Jackie retired a hero after 10 years in the big leagues, and a sure lock on the Baseball Hall of Fame. When I retire after nearly 45 years of struggling with this game, the only thing that's going to happen is that there will no longer be a pro golfer who smokes cigars while he plays.

Jackie opened the floodgates for black ballplayers who were ready and able to prove that they could play the game as well as anyone alive. He paved the way for the careers of Willie Mays, Don Newcombe, Roy Campanella, Larry Doby, and Monte Irvin, to name a few. But there are hardly any black kids coming up through the ranks of golf today. They've been excluded from the country clubs and the tournaments and the scholarships and the lessons so long that they don't even know if they have any talent for the game.

Whereas baseball had a second generation of blacks ready to step into the shoes of the black pioneers — guys like Aaron, Clemente, Bob Gibson, Frank Robinson — there has been no such movement in golf. We black golfers haven't been pioneers as far as our sport is concerned. We've been a few oddballs who somehow slipped through the cracks and were grudgingly allowed to play the game in hopes that we'd just disappear under the pressures of the tour. Somehow, through our sheer determination and commitment to making it in golf, a few of us have survived and made a good living off the game. But golf has a history and a sense of tradition that is unlike any other major sport. When they talk about the greatest moments in my game, they go way back to St. Andrews and the feathery ball in the early 1800s, and they proceed through generations of players like Harry Vardon, Frances Ouimet, Walter Hagen, Bobby Jones, Byron Nelson, Ben Hogan, Sam Snead, and Arnold Palmer. When the current crop of black golfers is done with the game, we'll have hardly made a mark on it. Golf will go on without us, and in time our careers will be like an aberrational blip in the sport's archives, an asterisk to hundreds of years of white domination of the sport.

There are many more reasons why I can't be the Jackie Robinson of Golf. For starters, Jackie had a whole team and organization behind him when he took the playing field. Like most other golfers on the tour, I'm on my own when I go out there, and the only way I'm going to earn a check at the end of the week is if I play well enough to beat 60 other guys. Jackie didn't get stiffed by the payroll department when he went zero-for-four, but when I hit a slump, I feel it in my pocketbook.

Jackie didn't play a sport that was accessible to people of all ages and abilities like mine is. He didn't walk out onto their playing field like I walk out onto their private golf course, and his fans didn't play in pro-am tournaments every week with him or stand a few feet away and talk to him while he was trying to compete. Golf is a little too intimate a game for many white people's tastes; they'd prefer their black sports heroes to maintain a respectable distance.

See, in my sport, I'm not traveling from arena to arena to show off my athletic talents like, say, a basketball player. I'm showing up every year at somebody's private country club, and maybe that's a little too much for some people to handle. I'm arriving on Tuesday morning with this traveling circus of a golf tour, and suddenly I'm using their locker room and having a sandwich at their snack bar and practicing on their driving range. And at most of these country clubs, they haven't seen a black guy all year long outside of the gardening staff.

I get the feeling that they think, "We thought it would be really neat to hold a professional golf tournament here at our club, and good for our image and the community and all, but you never told us that we'd have to let *black* guys into the clubhouse. Jeez, next they're gonna want to sit around and play cards in the lounge or let their wives and kids swim in the pool." I get that feeling in many places.

Do you think Isiah Thomas sees the security guard stiffen and people stop what they're doing and stare when he walks into the locker room before a basketball game? I see it all the time in places like Phoenix and Salt Lake City and New Orleans; and the funny thing is, I've been going back to those places for the last 25 years. And they still stop me to ask for credentials, or look at me suspiciously when I head for the putting green.

What has golf missed by shutting out black athletes? Let's imagine for a moment that Branch Rickey never existed, or that in 1947, Jackie Robinson's first year in the big leagues, an incident occurred that got Jackie thrown out of the league. Imagine that he blew up at some racist, filthy-mouthed fan one hot August afternoon in a strange city where he wasn't allowed to sleep in the same hotel as his teammates or eat in the same restaurants, and he lost his head and did something that got him kicked out of the game. It's not so hard to imagine, is it? We all know the stories of what Jackie put up with to integrate baseball.

So just for the sake of argument, let's say that the Jackie Robinson experiment was a failure or worse, a disaster. That means that as great a talent as Willie Mays never gets a chance to play in the big leagues with the whites. Nor does Hank Aaron. Kids like Joe Morgan and Reggie Jackson don't ever pick up a ball and bat, because they don't see any blacks playing the game and have no role models. They're good athletes, so their coaches and relatives steer them to the black sports of running, boxing and basketball. Maybe it would take another 20 years before the sport could right itself and begin producing quality black ballplayers again.

It's a pretty horrible scenario, isn't it? Well, that's exactly what has happened to my game of golf, and you're damn right I'm bitter and ashamed by it. If that had happened in baseball, we would have all been deprived of the great sports moments given to us in the last 30 years by athletes like Lou Brock, Bob Gibson, Roberto Clemente, Juan Marichal, Willie Stargell and many more. Their names are as synonymous with baseball as hot dogs and the seventh-inning stretch, but it really wouldn't have taken much for them to have been deprived from playing the game.

Although nobody calls me a nigger or kicks away my golf ball on the course any more, I can't honestly say that in the last 30 years the game has gotten any easier for a black man to play. In many ways, it has gotten tougher, because the competition is so much more intense and the white players have so many more advantages in terms of financing and access to the game.

If anyone had an insight into how long and how tough the struggle would be, it was Jackie. At the Western Amateur Open golf tournament in Los Angeles in 1948, I ran into him and asked his opinion about something I'd been thinking hard about. "Look here, Jackie, what do you think of this proposition of me becoming a professional golfer?"

Jackie thought about it a minute, and maybe he was reflecting on the abuses that he had suffered the previous year, when he was a rookie in major league baseball. "It's going to be awfully tough to do, Charlie," he said, "but can't nobody do it but you. If you're not going to be dedicated to the task, then don't bother trying it, because you're going to run into lots of bad obstacles."

He warned me that people would call me names and would try to disrupt my game. They would try to make me lose my temper, he said, and they might even try to physically hurt me.

"You've got to be yourself," he emphasized. "Above all, you can't be going after those people who call you names with a golf club."

It would be 13 long years after that conversation before they let me start playing on the PGA Tour. I'm pleased to report, Jackie,

that I still haven't gone after anyone with a golf club. And I'm
still out here plugging away at my game. I haven't done it because
I particularly wanted to force my way into a white man's world.
I did it because playing golf is all I've ever wanted to do, as far
back as I can remember.

Charlie Sifford in 1948—a young man with a great swing!

Charlie's game (and cigar) were hot in the mid fifties.

Charlie receiving the Negro National Open trophy that he won so many times they let him keep it forever.

Billy Eckstein's inscription advises Rose Sifford to keep Charlie ("little horse") cool.

On the road with Mr. B. and jazz greats George Treadwell and Sarah Vaughan —from Charlie's scrapbook.

Life pictures "Billy's Band-wagon"—from Charlie's scrapbook.

Charlie, Sugar Ray Robinson, Teddy Rhodes, and Joe Roach—a rare 1950 photo from Charlie's scrapbook.

WHEN

CONFIDENCE

COUNTS

Charlie Sifford, current National Negro Open Golf Champion.

America's number one Negro golfer, Charlie Sifford, is a
methodical, confident player. Charlie dreams of the day
when he'll carry off top prize in a major tournament.
On or off the golf course, Charlie Sifford is our idea of a
Wildroot Cream-Oil man, a fellow who is neat and
well-groomed with hair that looks handsome and healthy.
Wildroot's exclusive Cream-Oil formula gives hair a
natural sheen without that unpleasant, greasy look.
Softens and conditions stiff, brittle hair. Use it every morning
and have confidence in your appearance all day long.

One of Charlie's few promotional jobs.

(LA9) LOS ANGELES, Nov.11--HE'S NOW IN THE BIG-TIME--Cigar smoking
Charlie Sifford, the first Negro ever to win a big-time golf tournament,
works out at the Western Avenue golf course here today after winning the
$11,500 Long Beach Open yesterday. The 34-year-old golfer shot a 7-under
par 64 in the final round--the best round of the tournament--to tie Eric
Monti and then downed Monti on the third hole of a sudden-death play-off.
The victory was worth $1,200 to Sifford, four-time National Negro champ-
ion. (see story) (APWirephoto) (ew2145 stf-hpm)1957

Charlie wins the 1957 Long Beach Open—AP wirephoto.

Gary Player, always a special friend to
Charlie, when he first arrived in America
in the late fifties.

Teddy Rhodes and Charlie with friends at a municipal golf course—the only places blacks
could usually play—in the early fifties.

In 1958 Charlie waited out the Tour's southern swing with Rose and Charles Jr. in their new Los Angeles home.

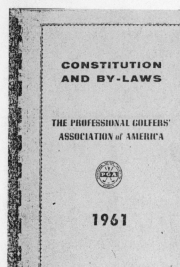

CONSTITUTION
AND BY-LAWS

THE PROFESSIONAL GOLFERS'
ASSOCIATION of AMERICA

1961

ARTICLE III
Members

SECTION 1. Professional golfers of the Caucasian Race, over the age of eighteen (18) years, residing in North or South America, who can qualify under the terms and conditions hereinafter specified, shall be eligible for membership or "H" Apprentice status. However, no Professional Golfer shall be eligible to apply for or to retain membership or "H" Apprentice status in the Association after becoming subject to the jurisdiction of the Government of the United States through affiliation as a member of the Military or Naval Service if it is intended that such affiliation is to be on a

The Caucasians-only rule in the 1961 PGA Constitution and By-Laws.

ARTICLE III
Members

SECTION 1. Professional golfers over the age of eighteen (18) years, who can qualify under the terms and conditions hereinafter specified, shall be eligible for membership. However, no Professional Golfer shall be eligible to apply for or to retain membership or to retain "H" Apprentice status in the Association after becoming subject to the jurisdiction of the Government of the United States (or of the country in which he resides) through affiliation as a member of the Military or Naval Service if it is intended that such affiliation is to be on a "career" or "lifetime" basis or status. Provided that,

CONSTITUTION
AND BY-LAWS

THE PROFESSIONAL GOLFERS'
ASSOCIATION of AMERICA

1962

The rule removed from the 1962 By-laws.

AP Wirephoto from the 1961 Greater Greensboro Open, the day before racists heckled and threatened Charlie the length of the course without interference.

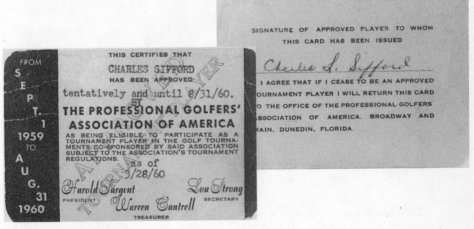

THIS CERTIFIES THAT
CHARLES SIFFORD
HAS BEEN APPROVED

FROM
S
E
P
T.
1
1959
TO
A
U
G.
31
1960

tentatively and until 8/31/60.
THE PROFESSIONAL GOLFERS'
ASSOCIATION OF AMERICA
AS BEING ELIGIBLE TO PARTICIPATE AS A
TOURNAMENT PLAYER IN THE GOLF TOURNA-
MENTS CO-SPONSORED BY SAID ASSOCIATION
SUBJECT TO THE ASSOCIATION'S TOURNAMENT
REGULATIONS.
as of
3/28/60

Harold Sargent
PRESIDENT
Lou Strong
SECRETARY
Warren Cantrell
TREASURER

SIGNATURE OF APPROVED PLAYER TO WHOM
THIS CARD HAS BEEN ISSUED

Charles L. Sifford

I AGREE THAT IF I CEASE TO BE AN APPROVED
TOURNAMENT PLAYER I WILL RETURN THIS CARD
TO THE OFFICE OF THE PROFESSIONAL GOLFERS
ASSOCIATION OF AMERICA, BROADWAY AND
MAIN, DUNEDIN, FLORIDA.

Charlie's first PGA card.

Charlie wins the Greater Hartford Open, the biggest win ever for a black golfer.

Lee Elder on the far left, with his wife, Rose, and Charlie and Rose Sifford,
at a 1969 dinner.

A pro in action.

Lee Trevino jokes with an amateur and Charlie at a tournament dinner during the early sixties.

Rose, Charlie, and young Craig, 1970.

Charlie's birdie putt heads
toward the cup to beat Harold
Henning in a playoff at the
1969 Los Angeles Open.

Charlie and golf professionals from Deerwood Country Club.
Head pro Scott Curiel stands to Charlie's left.

Rose and Charlie happily hold up the 1969 L.A. Open winner's check.

Charlie poses with amateurs at a pro-am event.

Charlie shakes hands with
President George Bush at
the 1986 Doug Sanders
Kingwood Celebrity
Classic.

Charlie and Pope B. Shealy—the man responsible for
Charlie's honorary membership at Deerwood Country Club.

CHAPTER *12*

"Watch Out, Nigger"

Getting the card in 1961 wasn't enough. I had to find a way to play in more tournaments. There was no other way around it. In order to keep my Approved Tournament Player's Card and be automatically qualified for each PGA tournament, I had to finish in the top 60 money winners on the whole tour at the end of every year. Some 200 guys were out there competing on the circuit, and I had to beat two-thirds of them in order to continue playing. If I kept giving away 20 tournaments a year to them, how could I possibly make enough money to keep up?

I had paid my $65 dues to the PGA, but that didn't mean I was automatically entered into every tournament. Like any player I still had to send a written application along with an entry fee to each tournament and then wait for a commitment from the sponsors. From where I sat at the beginning of 1961 it didn't look like anything would open up beyond the usual tournaments I'd been playing in, which led me to wonder just how much I'd gained in my battles. Was this another Teddy Rhodes and Bill Spiller job by the PGA, handing me the ATP card and announcing to the media that they'd let the black guys in, only to find a new way to shut me out of the tournaments and the money list?

The first changes to come my way happened in California, where I was invited for the first time ever to enter the Bing Crosby

115

National Pro-Am Tournament and the Palm Springs Golf Classic. For that I had Jackie Robinson to thank, with his wonderful advocacy on my behalf, with assists from Billy Eckstine and Joe Louis. I also played in a new tournament in San Francisco in January, giving me a full slate of seven events that I could enter in the first two months of the year.

I made the cuts in each one of them except for Phoenix and played well enough to finish in the top 15 four times. In San Francisco and Tucson I led after the first rounds with a sweet pair of 65s. For the first time since I'd started playing professional golf I felt like I had a place to go every week, although it was just for a couple of months.

A note of advice here for future pioneers: when you push open a door, you walk softly through it. I had fought to get into the Crosby and the Palm Springs tournaments, and a lot of people had put the pressure on each tournament to put me in there. Harsh words had been spoken, but I didn't go into either one of those places with a chip on my shoulder. I have always felt that if I could just play in a new place, I'd be happy. I don't go in there with an attitude or with some kind of political agenda, and I don't go in there trying to rub the faces of the sponsors and the tournament directors who resisted me. All I want to do is play and be given a chance to make a living, and when that happens, I'm satisfied. I had nothing but good relations with Bing Crosby and the Palm Springs people when I played in their tournaments, and I went back year after year and enjoyed similar cordial treatment. I'd have been a fool to go in there causing trouble, because that would just give them a reason to shut me out the following year.

As I've said before, the only point that I have tried to make is that a black man can play golf just as well as a white man and be just as much of a gentleman on the golf course. The simple fact of my playing, and playing well, was all the point I needed to make. I have never gone into a place and bad-mouthed the tournament and the sponsors or made inflammatory statements to the press if I was given a fair chance to play golf. It's only when they start stacking the deck against me that I open my mouth.

I actually had quite a nice time going up to Pebble Beach for the Crosby and meeting guys like Bing, Bob Hope, and Dean Martin. Crosby, of course, was the best golfer among them, and he was very serious about his game. For Hope in those days the game seemed like just another opportunity to tell as many jokes as he could shoehorn in. The man loved to entertain, and he was one of these characters who is always on. People asked me back then if I was a little intimidated by being around such big celebrities. Hell, man, I hung out with Billy Eckstine and the greatest jazz musicians in the world for 10 years. No way was I going to get too excited about Dean Martin. I've been around long enough to know that a man is a man, and it doesn't matter how much money he makes or how visible he is. Everyone is entitled to respect.

My game was sharp when I finished fourth at Tucson in the second week of February, but suddenly I was slammed back to reality. The tour went off to the South, and suddenly I was stuck back in California practicing and playing for dollar bets at Western Avenue. The PGA stopped in Baton Rouge; New Orleans; Puerto Rico; Pensacola; St. Petersburg; Palm Beach; and Wilmington, North Carolina, and not one of those places accepted my applications to play.

It looked like I'd be shut out for the entire spring, but unbeknownst to me, something was brewing in Greensboro, North Carolina. The NAACP had taken an interest in my case, and in Greensboro a man named Dr. George Simpson was head of the local chapter and knew the people who ran the Greater Greensboro Open. He worked on them to let me in, and somehow he succeeded. On April 4, a week before the tournament was to start, I got a call: I had been accepted to play at the Sedgefield Country Club as the first black man ever to enter a PGA event in the South.

I can't describe to you the swirling emotions that came over me as I prepared to drive across the country to enter that tournament. I thought about my childhood in Charlotte and about all the white friends I'd made on the golf course. I thought about people like Sutton Alexander, who had helped me out, and the men who had encouraged me to keep playing.

I also thought about the circumstances in which I'd had to leave North Carolina, and about the lynchings. They were killing civil rights workers in the South in those days, and in places like Greensboro they were also fighting bitterly to keep blacks off the public golf courses. How would they feel when I walked into their exclusive country club during the week of their prestigious professional golf event?

The PGA couldn't let anything happen to me out there, could it? I wondered if I might be heading into a very large and dangerous trap: what if something serious happened? Would the PGA and the other golfers come to my defense? Could throwing me to a tipped-off pack of Klansmen be an easy way to get rid of the black man who wouldn't go away?

Everyone in the whole country knew that I was heading to Greensboro. The *New York Times* ran a story about my acceptance to the tournament, and how I had come close to winning in San Francisco and Tucson. Other papers picked up on it. Like Jackie Robinson, I was about to make a very big step for black people, but, unlike Jackle Robinson, I wasn't surrounded by teammates and there were no fences at the golf course to keep back unruly people. Any nut could have decided to make his personal stand against integration by meeting me in Greensboro.

I could envision the headlines: "First Black Golfer Lynched on 14th Tee; PGA Blames Tournament Sponsor." I was alone on this trip, and there is no lonelier feeling than crossing into the Deep South and heading for an all-white country club. Driving across the country I remembered some of the good times with Teddy Rhodes and Zeke Hartsfield and Howard Wheeler when we'd all pile into a car and drive to a new UGA tournament. I'd left all that behind in my pursuit of professional golf, and now I was very much on my own.

I wouldn't have gone at all if it weren't for Rose. When I told her about the invitation, I said that I didn't think I should go. She knew as well as I did that I could be the victim of violence, and I wasn't so sure that I wanted to take that risk. I had just gotten her and Charles, Jr., back with me in California, and now I was going to risk my life for a golf tournament?

But she reassured me. "Nothing's going to happen that you can't handle," she said. "You'll go and you'll do fine. This is what you've been working towards for so many years."

If the good Lord was willing, I'd do fine. All I could do was pray to God that I'd make it, and pray that I'd keep my head if somebody came at me. I remembered what Jackie Robinson had told me several years before. "You can't go after somebody with a golf club if they give you a hard time. If you do that, you'll ruin it for all of the other black players to come."

I hadn't been back in the South for many years. As I drove into North Carolina, it started coming back to me like a bad dream. When I stopped for gas, I couldn't grab a bite to eat in the café. Couldn't use the toilet in some places. In Greensboro, there was no hotel where I could sleep, so Dr. Simpson got me a room at the all-black college, North Carolina A & T. He apologetically said that he'd have put me up in his own house, but it was filled with kids and he didn't have any room. "That's okay," I said in the small, dormitory room. "I'll be fine here."

I was greeted coolly but cordially at the Sedgefield Country Club, and I went about my business signing in and hiring a caddie like I would do at any new tournament. I'm not like Bill Spiller; I didn't have any interest in marching into their locker room to see how far my rights extended. I just wanted to do well on the golf course, and I didn't need any friction or controversy to distract me from my real goal.

The tournament had drawn its usual contingent of top golfers. Sam Snead was there, along with Art Wall, Mike Souchak, Gene Littler, Don Massengale, Jim Ferree, Doug Sanders, and many others. I knew all of them from my years of playing, and to them it was just like any other tournament. They were cordial, too, as they went about the business of hitting balls and putting. Nobody went out of his way to buddy up to me, but that was fine. They were treating me like any other pro, which in itself was a kind of respectful tribute. They were trying to make a living the same as I was, and I didn't expect anyone to pull me aside or make it any easier for me.

The tournament began well for me in the pro-am round, where I tied for third low pro and made $163. My game was sharp and I saw that I could score well on the course. At first I was nervous, wondering if there was trouble brewing, and where it might come from. But as the day wore on it became just another pro-am round with three white businessmen, and I went about my business. A hush would come over groups of people when I walked by, and I heard the whispers ("There's that black player"), but I was used to that. More than anything I think they were curious to see if I could play.

Afterwards I had dinner at Dr. Simpson's house, since I couldn't eat in any local restaurants. The worst thing that day was the college kids in the dormitory. They were so noisy that I didn't get to sleep until past midnight. They were running up and down the halls screaming and yelling so much that I couldn't hear myself think. I decided that the next day I'd accept the offer of a room from George and Betty Lavett, a black family I'd met.

The tournament began the following day, and I had a point to make. I would show them that a black man belonged in that tournament and in every tournament in the country. Many people didn't believe that a black could play as well as Sam Snead and the others, despite my previous accomplishments. A lot was riding on my play that week. If I did well and kept my cool, I could open up the tour a crack for myself and for any other black golfers coming up. If I failed and didn't make the cut, then all of those crackers throughout the South would have an excuse to keep me away from tournaments.

I refused to let the pressure get to me. The course was wet and windy that day, but it didn't bother me any. I went out and put up the best score of the day, a 3 under par 68. My putter came through time and time again, as I one-putted 12 greens and didn't make a bogey the entire round. Suddenly I was the first-round leader of the Greater Greensboro Open. Not bad for a 38-year-old, cigar-chewing black man!

That was the first day that we had any kind of galleries, and once again my nervous early anticipation dissolved as I got into the round. I caught some dirty looks from a few people, but nobody approached me or said anything. I didn't exactly feel embraced by the crowd, but I could handle the little bit of hostility that I felt. This isn't so bad at all, I thought as I was signing my scorecard. If this was as bad as it got, I could play all the time in the South.

At the end of the day I drove over to the Lavetts' house and had dinner. We talked about my playing in the South, and that maybe things had changed enough to allow a black man to make a living at golf without being harassed. I went to bed early in order to be fresh for my morning tee time, but before I fell asleep the phone rang. George knocked on my door and said I had a call.

I thought it was either Rose calling from California or somebody calling to congratulate me for my first round. Instead, it was a voice I'd never heard, but a voice I'll never forget. "Charlie Sifford?" the man asked in a white man's Southern accent.

"That's me."

"You'd better not bring your black ass out to no golf course tomorrow if you know what's good for you, nigger. We don't allow no niggers on our golf course."

The words hit me like a punch in the jaw. I hadn't been called a nigger since I was a kid in Charlotte, and I felt the anger rise up inside me.

"I tee off at 10:15 in the morning," I said. "You do whatever it is you're going to do, because I'll be there."

"You'd just better watch out, nigger," he said, and hung up.

I didn't get much sleep for the rest of that night, and this time I didn't have the college kids to blame. Suddenly things had changed. It wasn't a golf tournament I was in, it was a war zone. I tried to tell myself that it was just some big stupid cracker who gave himself a charge with a crank phone call, but I couldn't shake the fear. I knew how easily black people could disappear in the South, and I knew that if a whole gang of Klansmen were working up the courage at that very moment to pay me a midnight visit, there was nobody around who could stop them.

I thought about not going out there the next day. Maybe I should withdraw from the tournament and go someplace safe.

Obviously the South wasn't ready for me yet, and I wasn't so
sure that I wanted to risk my life to open up the PGA Tour. I called
Rose in Los Angeles and told her what happened. We talked about
it for a long time, and she encouraged me to go out there and
play. "Just keep moving," she said. "They're not going to hurt
you on the golf course, but you make sure that you've got
somebody with you when you go to your car."

The next morning I went out to my car with every nerve in
my body tingling. Someone called out to me and I must have
jumped a foot. It was one of the neighbors wishing me good luck.
On the way to the golf course I kept checking my mirrors,
wondering if anyone was following me.

I got to the country club and changed my shoes in the car,
and as I walked to the practice tee I felt like everyone's eyes were
on me. There are always a few hundred people milling around
at a tournament: players, sponsors, volunteers, caddies, spectators
looking for autographs. Which one of the people who were
brushing past me had made the phone call last night? Would a
group of them suddenly try to drag me off the course? As I hit
my practice balls I tried as hard as I could to calm the butterflies
that were in my stomach. "You can't let them get to you," I hissed
to myself. "You let this shit affect your game, it means that you're
finished with golf."

My tee time was at 10:15, and I stepped to the first tee and
hit my drive. The guy I was paired with hit his, and I started to
walk down the fairway. And then a familiar voice rang out, a voice
that I'd heard over the phone the night before. "Nice shot,
Smokey," he yelled. "How ya going to play the next one?"

I looked over and saw a pack of 12 young white men walking
down the side of the fairway, as close to me as they could get.
They were all taunting me, trying to get my attention by being
loud and unruly. I tried to ignore them as I got to my ball and
selected a club. They were silent for a moment, but as I began
my backswing a voice rang out: "Don't miss it, Darkie."

I pulled the ball to the left of the green and they hooted.
"You can't play for shit."
"Go back to the cotton fields."

"Hey, boy, carry my bag."

They followed me down the fairway again and stood by as I chipped onto the green and putted out, screaming at me with every stroke.

Those creeps followed me from the first tee all the way to the 14th green before the police finally came and took them away. They did everything they could to disrupt my game. They threatened, they shouted, and one time when I went to look for my ball, I found it surrounded by a pile of beer cans. The rest of the gallery fell silent when those drunken rednecks were around, making their taunts all the more audible. They were dragging the Greater Greensboro Open down to the level of a boxing match, and all of those people watching didn't do a damn thing about it. "You are definitely back in the South," I told myself bitterly. "Ain't no doubt about that."

A buzz went up around the golf course about what was happening, and around the third hole I was joined by a PGA official named George Wash. He saw what was going on, and he stayed with me for the rest of the round. He repeatedly asked the unruly gang to quiet down, and he made sure that he was between me and them the whole way.

Why did it take so long to get them off the course? Man, it was the longest round of golf I've ever played. I don't know how I managed to maintain my poise, because I was scared out there. I didn't know if at any minute those guys were going to come after me or if one of them had a gun in his pocket. It took everything I had to concentrate on the game and not let them get to me. They called me every name in the book, and they added a few about my wife and my parents.

There were times when they were only a few feet away from me, screaming at the top of their lungs. I had to watch them out of the corner of my eye, even as I was lining up a shot. At the same time I wondered what it would feel like to take a swing, just one sweet swing, at one of their heads with a 3-iron. That would shut them up quick, wouldn't it.

But I couldn't do that. I knew that if I blew up, it would all be over. I couldn't solve anything by violence. It would just ensure that all blacks, beginning with me, would be permanently barred from the tour. I just had to learn to handle it, because for all I knew this would happen wherever I went to play golf in the South. They rattled me for sure, but I survived it.

I somehow ended up shooting a one over par 72, despite missing seven greens and lots of putts. By the end of the day I had dropped to third place in the standings behind Mike Souchak and Billy Maxwell. When the round was over I went back to the practice tee and hit balls for a long time. I didn't want to talk to anybody or see anybody, and the other players steered clear of me. Inside I was seething with anger and humiliation. What on earth had I done to be treated so rudely, and why wasn't anyone there to stop it? If a gang of black guys had followed Sam Snead off the first tee, would they even have made it to the first green before being hauled off by the police?

I think that I shot one of the greatest rounds of golf in my life that day. Even with that pack of wolves a few feet away from me, I managed to save par on nearly every hole. I'd like to see any other golfer play under those circumstances.

That evening I went to George and Betty Lavetts' house and had dinner. I told them what had happened, and all they could do was shake their heads in disbelief. It had been a long, nerve-wracking day in which I didn't know from one minute to the next if I'd be shot at or punched or met around the next corner by a bunch of rednecks in white hoods.

I realized the magnitude of what I was facing to play golf for a living. This wasn't ever going to get any easier. In fact, it looked like the closer I got to the top, the worse it would get because a lot of people sure didn't seem to want a black man to be successful at golf. My heart was heavy when I went to sleep.

That round of golf at Greensboro became rather notorious as word of it spread among all of the players. Thirty years later many still remember it with a certain amount of sadness. "I remember that I felt very sorry about what happened to Charlie in Greensboro," said Art Wall. "I played there, but I wasn't around that immediate area. I have always had a great feeling about Charlie and I felt very bad about that whole situation."

Don January added, "That's just a shame that someone can voice an opinion that 90 percent of the people there don't agree with, but they all get blamed. Charlie had to have a lot of willpower there."

I went out the next day, but nobody said anything about the incident or apologized on behalf of the country club or the tournament. In fact, as far as the tournament was concerned, nothing had happened. It served to remind me that I was in this alone, and just because they'd given me the card didn't mean that they were going to try in the slightest to be civil with me or accept me as a player. It just made me madder and made me want to try that much harder to do well.

I stayed in third place with a third-round score of 70 and then got touched for a 75 on the last day and finished fourth for a paycheck of $1,300. Although no more people followed me around shouting names at me, little things happened each day — hard looks from security guards, people in the gallery talking while I hit my ball, other people ignoring me when I walked past or made a comment.

By the end of it I was drained; the emotion had been too much. I had a hard enough time as it was keeping my game sharp for four consecutive rounds, but to bring all that baggage along with it made focusing next to impossible.

Going into Greensboro, I had had the somewhat naive notion that after I broke into a few more tournaments I'd be free to live the life of a touring pro and concentrate on my game. But when I left town I realized that the struggle would continue to be as much a part of my career as putting or chipping were. They weren't going to leave me alone: the rules makers, the executive committees, the tournament chairmen, the sponsors, the galleries. If it wasn't one of them getting his piece of the black man's hide, it would be another one.

All I wanted to do was play golf as best I could. Now I realized that would probably never happen. I'd never be able to put all of my focus into my game as long as I had to keep dealing with the shit they threw at me. I was to be the door-opener for the next generation of blacks, and the price I would pay was the unfulfilled potential of my own game.

I still wonder how good I might have been if I had the same opportunities to play and practice as the white pros did in their prime. Nobody has seen my best rounds of golf, because I was never able to play them. I've dedicated my life to being good at golf, and I can't tell you how much it hurts that I never did find out how good I could be.

What could I do? I threw my clubs into the car, thanked the Lavetts for their hospitality, lit up a cigar, and headed down the road for the next tournament. I'll tell you one thing: no PGA rookie ever had a year like I had. And Greensboro was just the beginning, as I was about to find out in a showdown in Texas.

CHAPTER *13*

"You Can't Play Here"

I had two full days to think about what had happened in Greensboro as I drove my car west for Houston and the next stop on the tour. Two days to remember the glares from the gallery, the hateful voice on the telephone, and the faces of the gang that did its best to make sure I wouldn't continue to lead the tournament in the second round. And to remember the weird and incongruous feeling of being afraid for my life on a golf course.

I thought about how it had rattled me enough to throw off my game, and how I had fought to stay within myself. How many black men would have put up with the kind of abuse I had taken on the golf course? How many times can you be called "nigger" and "darkie" before the anger just boils up out of you and you find a way to lash back?

I realized something about that anger that I had squelched inside me; it never went away. It carried over into the third round and the fourth, affecting the way I played and the way I practiced and relaxed. It was still inside me as I drove on through Tennessee and Arkansas.

How many strokes and how many dollars had it cost me to control my temper? Maybe that anger jerked my swing just a hair a few times, just enough to pull the ball off line and turn a birdie opportunity into a par save. Or it welled up just enough to distract me when I was lining up a putt, causing me to miss by an inch. It was just another thing that I'd have to handle if I was going to play professional golf, but it was one more thing that I didn't need.

It struck me that I would probably never play under the same conditions as the other pros. Sure, we'd be on the same golf course under the same weather conditions, but I was dragging along a whole lot more baggage than irons and woods, and people never let me forget it. Greensboro would just be the beginning of the troubles that have plagued me my entire career, almost all of which have had to do with race.

Fans tend to forget that there is more to playing professional golf than hitting shots and putting well during a four-day tournament. Golf is a weeklong occupation that demands constant practice and concentration. It is the most social of sports, where a large part of what you do involves playing with amateurs in pro-ams; dealing with new courses and tournaments every single week; and dealing with the logistics of where to stay, where to eat, where to get your clothes washed and where to find time to make arrangements for the next tournaments.

Under those circumstances, golfers' careers rise and fall on the basis of how well they can adjust to all of the things swirling around them and still play their best games day in and day out on the golf course. They don't give you handicap strokes for being the only guy out there who has to deal with racism. I would have to concentrate doubly hard to succeed if I had to play with people screaming "Nigger!" a few feet away. If that's what it took, that's what I'd do, but by God, they would never stop me from playing.

I hadn't won the tournament in Greensboro, but I felt a larger victory. I had come through my first southern tournament with the worst kind of social pressures and discrimination around me, and I hadn't cracked. I didn't quit. I didn't hit one of those rednecks over the head with a 3-wood. I didn't walk around with a chip on my shoulder or ask anyone for special treatment, and most important, I didn't let my game fall apart. Under the circumstances, I had exceeded my highest hopes while at the same time facing my worst fears.

As I headed south, I began to think of Greensboro as a kind of bizarre initiation that I had had to withstand in order to play on the tour. It was like if I expected to join the PGA's traveling club, then I had to prove that I could handle the pressure and still compete. Okay, I had taken the death threats and the locked doors and the no hotel rooms and the vicious pack of racists. I survived it. Now let me into your club. It seemed to me that nobody could doubt my committment to golf after that, nor could anybody with compassion stop me from playing. As far as I was concerned, I'd done all the proving that anybody could ever need.

I saw the Houston tournament as my first chance to get some payback. It was as if I had qualified to play the whole tour by what I had done at Greensboro, and now this would be my real debut, the one where I went in like all the other pros and played to the best of my abilities. After the way I'd played in Greensboro I felt I could win a golf tournament if I just got a couple of breaks.

The Houston Classic was a fat tournament, with a purse of $40,000 to shoot for. This might not seem like much by today's million-dollar purse standards, but it was among the richest tournaments on the tour in those days. If I could finish in the top five again, I could more than double the money I'd made in North Carolina and put myself near the top of the money list.

Driving by yourself from North Carolina to Houston can be pretty exhausting, particularly if you have to sleep in your car on the side of the road every night with the windows rolled up and the doors locked. I was pretty tired when at last I pulled into town on Tuesday night and looked up my old friend Willie Branch, a nightclub owner who had invited me to stay at his house whenever I was in town.

The tournament was held at the Memorial Park Golf Course, which was a public course, and I drove up on Wednesday morning all set to get in a good day of practice and be ready for the Thursday tee off. But I had no sooner walked into the clubhouse when I was stopped by a man who identified himself as being one of the sponsors of the tournament. "Excuse me, but what are you doing here?" he asked me. Damn, I wish I could remember who this guy was, or for whom he worked.

"I'm here to play golf," I said. "What do you think I'm doing here?"

"Wait a minute. You can't play here. You're not allowed in this tournament."

Inside me I felt the anger rising up and my nerves going on edge. "I'm an approved player on the PGA Tour and I committed to this golf tournament." I reached for my wallet to show him my ATP card, but it had no effect.

"I don't care. You're not allowed here and you'll have to leave."

I looked around for some help in that all-white clubhouse. A PGA official named Joe Black quickly approached. He was one of the guys charged with running the tournament, and I had known him from many of the tournaments I'd entered over the years. "What's this about me not being on the players list?" I asked him. I was still hoping that it was some kind of oversight, but my heart sank when he spoke.

"I'm sorry, Charlie, but you can't play here," said Black.

"What do you mean I can't play here?" I snapped.

"The sponsors of the tournament have not approved your entry, and they are unwilling to allow you to enter at this time," he said. "I'm sorry, but there's nothing I can do about it."

By that time the slimy little white sponsor had walked away, leaving me alone with Black. I bit my lip hard. "I am an approved player of the PGA and I have done everything I was supposed to here," I said hoarsely. "Why isn't the PGA allowing me to play?"

"It's not our decision. It's up to the sponsors, and they don't want you to play here."

He just stood there looking at me, and I felt a wave of nausea roll through me. I didn't know whether I should punch him or start crying or start yelling and screaming for a lawyer. For the first time since I was a little kid in Charlotte, North Carolina, I was being run off of a golf course like some pathetic tramp.

"Is that all there is to it?" I asked.

"That's it, Charlie," he said, looking at me evenly like it would just make me go away. I turned around and got back into my car and drove out of there.

I had come to Texas for payback, and I got it, all right. But it was the PGA's payback for what I had done in Greensboro, and for my role in getting their tournament moved out of California. I don't think they've ever gotten over that one. I not only survived at Greensboro, but nearly won the tournament, and now I was being rewarded by being sent away from a public golf course like a criminal.

It was one thing for the Houston sponsors to exclude me from their golf tournament, but it was another thing entirely for the PGA not only to refuse to defend my rights as a card-carrying member, but to let me drive all the way down there and turn me away at the door.

I had sent in my written committment to enter the tournament and had heard nothing to indicate that there was a problem with my entry. I assumed that since it was a PGA tournament and I had the approved tournament player's card that I was automatically entered in the tournament unless told otherwise. There had been plenty of PGA people hanging around in Greensboro, and nobody said a thing to me about the following week's tour stop.

Hell, I hadn't earned any respect or even a grudging truce from the Professional Golfers Association. If anything, I seemed to have made them more determined to break my spirit. I had been brave enough to drive all the way down there by myself and take my chances with another southern crowd, and they couldn't even be up front about why I couldn't play. It may have been the sponsors' decision to exclude a black man, but the PGA sure didn't try to change their minds.

I had no place to go. I drove around Houston for an hour and then headed back to Willie's house. Thank God for black people like Willie Branch and the Lavetts in North Carolina, because they reminded me that what I was doing wasn't so crazy, and that there was always a place where I was accepted. They understood what I was up against, and they supported me like they were my own family.

If there's one quality that has helped me out above all else in my struggles with golf, it is my ability to make friends with people and get along. People along the way saved me time after time. They invited me into their homes and fed me and befriended me for the weeks I was in their towns, and they invited me to come back the following year. They gave me much more than I've ever been able to give them back. I hope to name every single person who helped along the way in this book, and I hope I remember every last one of them. They were the real heroes of my golfing odyssey, because without them I'd have been sleeping in my car every night in those early years on the tour.

I spent a couple of days at Willie's house, but the tournament began and it nearly drove me crazy to be there when I knew that across town all those golfers were shooting for $40,000 without me. I was stunned by what happened. I called Rose in L.A. and she couldn't believe it, and I talked to my attorney. What could we do, sue the PGA and the Houston tournament? Try to raise a stink in the newspapers? I somehow doubted that they read Jackie Robinson's column in Houston, or that it could have much of an effect. It all seemed an awful lot like what Teddy Rhodes had gone through in 1948, and I vividly remembered that he didn't get a damn thing out of it.

The next tournament was to be held the following week at the Oak Hill Country Club in San Antonio. It was called the Texas Open Invitational, and you can guess for whose benefit it was that they tacked on that last word. I went down there to try to play, and this time I was stopped at the gate by a big, white policeman who wouldn't even let me on the property.

"I'm here to play in this golf tournament," I said.

"No you're not," said the guard. He didn't even look down at his list of players. He didn't have to, because he knew that no black man was going to be a player at his golf course.

Sure enough, I hadn't been invited, nor was I acceptable to the sponsors. For the second time in a week, I was turned away from a golf course.

I headed back to California, and for the rest of the spring I played golf at Western Avenue while the tour that I had fought so hard to join went on to Oklahoma, Las Vegas, back to Texas, Arkansas, and the Sam Snead Festival in West Virginia. "What are you doing out here?'' asked my friends. ''We heard about you doing so well in North Carolina, and we thought you were on that tour for good.''

I thought so too. I had done everything I possibly could have done to play. I had found a way to the California attorney general and fought to have the Caucasian clause removed. I had won tournaments and conducted myself properly and handled everything they could throw at me from death threats to closed clubhouses. I had received national media attention and recognition and the support of everyone from the Ballantine beer company to the NAACP.

But none of it meant crap. The PGA could still find ways to keep me out, and the barriers of golf in the South weren't going to come tumbling down that easily. As far as they were concerned, I had accomplished nothing at Greensboro. The only way I was going to be able to play in those southern tournaments was to fight my way into each one of them individually. At that point, I didn't know if I had that much fight in me.

Can you imagine what might have happened to the game of baseball if when they called Jackie Robinson up to the Brooklyn Dodgers in 1947 they had locked him out in St. Louis or Cincinnati? It could have torn the whole game apart and started a national debate. I didn't even get a mention in the press when I was locked out in Houston and San Antonio. I guess the media thought that everything had been solved when I entered Greensboro, and they didn't bother to follow up on the story.

The sixties were already bringing great changes, but it still looked an awful lot like 1950 to me. Once again, my real golf schedule of 1961 didn't begin until the summer, after I turned 39 years old. I played nearly every week in the northern tournaments in places like Grand Rapids and Huntington, Long Island, and Canada, and once I started playing regularly I only missed two cuts for the rest of the year.

I finished in the top 20 nearly every tournament and managed to stay in the top 60 money winners for the year, which automatically renewed by Approved Tournament Player's Card. That in itself was a small miracle given how many tournaments I missed. But I wasn't allowed to compete in the PGA Championship or the Masters or the British Open, and I wasn't considered for the Ryder Cup team.

As far as golf was concerned, I was an outsider who managed to place well at a few tournaments a year. A freakish black man in an all-white world. Golf may have taken the Caucasian clause out of its consititution at the end of 1961, but it remained as white as could be.

CHAPTER 14

One Door at a Time

Some of those doors took years to open. I guess that when you have a few generations of racism in places like Pensacola, St. Petersburg, New Orleans, and Memphis, it takes a little longer to get through to them. Instead of being isolated incidents, my experiences at Greensboro, Houston, and San Antonio proved to be indicative of what lay ahead.

As I found out as the years went by, this pioneering stuff is never finished. Once you start, you're in it for the long haul. You'd think that it would have gotten easier as the sixties continued, but there was always something new coming up to remind me that I was an unwelcome intrusion in the world of high-society golf.

If it wasn't a pack of jerks following me down a fairway yelling "Miss it!" when I swung, it was some country club official getting his self-righteous thrills by laying down a rule about what I could or couldn't do at his club. Even when they could no longer bar me from playing, the country clubs could still put the black man in his place when it came to using their locker room and snack bar. I saw racism displayed in a dazzling variety of ways. And the PGA never did a damn thing about any of it.

It is 1965 and I'm playing at the Pensacola Country Club for the first time after years of being held away. Once again I am the first black man to ever set foot in those country club doors, and once again I get the evil looks from the old women, rude treatment from the galleries, and the cold shoulder from the businessmen who are fuming that the club allowed this . . . this Negro! . . . into their prized golf tournament.

Before my round of golf I walk into the country club's restaurant to eat breakfast like every other pro, but before I can sit down to eat it, a man is at my side. "Uh, Charlie, excuse me," he stammers, "but you can't eat here. Would you mind taking your breakfast someplace else? This room is, uh, private."

Private to whom? Everybody in the whole golf tournament is eating in there. I look around and everybody in the goddamn room is watching this scenario. I've practically got my eggs half-raised to my mouth and this official is standing over me with a look on his face that says, "Please don't make trouble. Please be a good little black man and get out of the room."

So what do I do? The same thing that I've always done. I wrap up my food, quietly stand up, and walk away, and I try real hard to not think about all of those smug, white faces behind me that are nodding with satisfaction. I go to eat in the locker room.

And do you know what? Five minutes later two or three other guys came down there with their breakfasts and ate with me. Bob Rosburg was one of them, and I think Frank Stranahan and Ken Venturi were there too. That Rosburg was such a good guy; he ate with me in the locker room every day for the rest of the tournament. The other guys knew that something was going on that was wrong and they went out of their way to talk to me and be nice.

It is 1963 and I've finally pushed my way into the tournament in St. Petersburg, Florida, at the Lakewood Country Club. There, I am not only barred from the restaurant, but from the clubhouse, too. I have to change into my golf shoes from the back seat of my car in the parking lot, like you would at a municipal golf course. I change my shoes, pick up my golf bag and walk to the driving range, play my round, and don't get so much as a drink of water before walking back to my car and going home to take a shower and change my shirt.

On the first tee of that golf course, about ten minutes before my starting time, I realized that I'd better go to the bathroom before I began playing. I walked up to the official and told him that I was going to use the john, and he gave me this look and said, "Well, you can't go in the clubhouse, you know."

I looked at him right back and said, "Well if I can't go in the clubhouse then I'll just have to do my business right here on the tee. Would that be more acceptable to the Lakewood Country Club?" I went into the clubhouse and they didn't give me any more trouble about it for the rest of the week.

It's 1964 and I'm getting ready to leave for the New Orleans Open when the phone rings. It's a PGA official calling from Louisiana, and he asks me to hold off another year before playing New Orleans. Why's that? I ask.

"There's a hater in office right now down here," he said, "and we can't guarantee your safety. Wait another year, Charlie, and things will be smoother."

A hater was a guy who hated blacks and did everything he could against integration. He didn't have to tell me another word, because I wasn't about to go down there and be made an example of by some bigot with a high title. I would happily skip the New Orleans Open, I told him. Times haven't changed so much in the last 30 years, have they, when you consider who is running for governor these days in Louisiana.

That same year I worked up the nerve to enter the Mobile, Alabama, tournament despite all of the hatred that was going on in that state with George Wallace and the Klansmen. Before I could leave, though, they canceled the tournament outright. I took that as a sign from above and was grateful.

I never knew where I would run into trouble and where things would go as smoothly as could be. There was just no telling. The week after I went through all of those hassles and meanness at St. Petersburg I headed to Miami to play in my first tournament at the Doral Country Club. I expected much of the same treatment there, but to my surprise, they were as sweet as could be. Nothing was off limits to me, the country club people were gracious, and the only problems I had were on that wicked, long Doral course.

The same thing happened in Dallas and Wilmington, North Carolina. After the treatment I'd received in Houston and San Antonio, I figured that I'd never get into a golf tournament in Dallas. But I went down there in 1962 and was admitted and I ended up finishing in third place and making a couple of thousand dollars.

Sometimes it was harder to go back to a place than it was to break into a new tournament. You can imagine how I felt driving back to Greensboro a year after my debut. I was still the only black man out there, and obviously I was the only black that they saw all year at the Sedgefield Country Club. Would I get the same treatment from the unruly mob as I had received the first time around? Would that anger well back up inside me the minute I set foot on the property?

Nope, I just let it pass. I was there to play golf and make a living, and as long as I was treated civilly I didn't care how they chose to operate their country club. I didn't have to like the tournament people or the sponsors or the community, and I didn't have to like what I saw going on in front of me every single week when there were no black people in the galleries and certainly no black people allowed to join those clubs. I knew what was going on, and I also knew that I couldn't change anything just because I didn't like it. All I could do was my share, and that was to continue to make it on the tour and show that I belonged in that setting.

I got used to the idea that I was on my own out there and that I was going to have to be the one to break it down. Nobody else was going to do it for me. And, certainly, the PGA wasn't going to go out of its way to accommodate me. Do you think they ever exerted any pressure on those tournaments that barred me from playing or threatened to shut down entirely if one of their players wasn't being treated fairly? Just look at the tournament schedules: they played in the same places in Houston and San Antonio and Florida all those years that I was barred. Obviously, nobody raised much of a fuss about the fact that an approved PGA player was continually being shut out.

Here are a couple of hypothetical situations to mull over on a sleepless night: what might have happened if one of those tournaments didn't allow Arnold Palmer or Ken Venturi to use the restaurant at the country club? Or if somebody had said, "Everybody can use the bathroom except for Billy Casper." Would the PGA have shut down the event and demanded an immediate apology, or would they have said, "Arnold, Ken . . . would you mind taking your sandwich down to the locker room? Just this once?"

I honestly don't know, because if there's one thing the PGA proved, it was that it wasn't about to walk away from money. Since the money was at the country clubs, it seems to me that the PGA would have done just about anything that the country club told it to do, even if it was blatantly racist and in fact illegal.

Here's another one: how would Sam Snead have felt if he showed up at a tournament and everyone there was black? Black officials; black players; all-black galleries; soul food in the concession stands; and big, black guards with guns at the door of the clubhouse? Think his swing would be as sweet and his game would be unaffected?

Yes, I had to break it down. They kept me out of the tournament in Houston in 1962, too, and I thought, "God damn, man, this is a public golf course that they're keeping me off." I threatened the tournament committee long and loud and told them if I didn't play the next year they'd be looking at a big lawsuit. They backed down and let me play in '63 and I wound up finishing sixth at that sucker.

It took me yet another year to break into the tournament in San Antonio, which was held at the private Oak Hills Country Club, and they tried to make it as hard for me as they could. They made me eat in the kitchen with the Mexican laborers. Couldn't use the clubhouse to even change my shoes.

The following year I finally got some company when Rafe Botts and Pete Brown joined the tour. We pulled up to the clubhouse at Oak Hills and I just decided that I'd had enough. They had two big, white guards with guns standing on either side of the clubhouse door, but I didn't care. I grabbed my shoes out of the car and marched straight past those guards into the clubhouse and went about my business. Rafe and Pete walked in after me looking a little scared, but nothing happened. I had reached the point by then when I no longer cared what they might do. Let them try to drag me out of the bathroom or refuse to let me take a shower. Let them try to kill me; I just didn't care.

Time after time I had to prove that I was willing to take the heat. In every single one of those towns I had to prove myself over and over again to the country club people, the fans in the galleries, the sponsors, and the tournament officials. The only people I didn't have to prove anything to were the other players, who knew what I could do on the golf course.

There were times when playing the game itself was the least of my worries. If I could just get an even break and go into a tournament like everyone else, I knew that I could make a few dollars. It was just so damn hard at times. Those other guys were driving new cars and staying in nice hotels, and I was nursing my old car along and staying in somebody's guest room. I couldn't go out to eat like the other guys did, and if I had a bad month of playing, I didn't have a sponsor with deep pockets who could bail me out.

Despite the conditions, I cracked the top 25 most of the time, and a half-dozen times a year I'd finish in the top seven or eight. But it cost money to play on that tour and it always seemed like I was struggling to get by. I often wondered how much money I could make if I had the same playing conditions as everyone else, but that was just another hypothetical question. I'd never know that.

The anger that dwelled inside me got bad enough that I had to seek professional help to deal with it. You just can't play golf if you're all tense and angry, and I feared that all of those slights that piled up over the years would eventually either make me burst or make me incapable of playing competitively.

I was afraid of what might happen if I did one day let it all go. I don't think I'm a violent man, but I wondered what I might do to someone if they got in my face over a racial thing right in the middle of a nerve-wracking tournament. My game would not only suffer, but I might find myself behind bars in some penitentiary if I really let myself go. There was more than golf at stake for my keeping my head on straight.

I found a psychologist in L.A. who taught me breathing and mental exercises to relax me, and I frequently used them over the years. I learned the importance of exercise and stretching to reduce stress, and I found some audiotapes that I'd listen to in my car that helped me to relax. I also read *The Power of Positive Thinking* by Norman Vincent Peale and applied its principles.

Other players helped me out when they could. When I had car trouble, Frank Stranahan lent me his wheels at the end of a tournament and I'd drive it to the next town while he flew. Bob Rosburg lent me his pants once when mine got all muddied up and I didn't have another clean pair with me. That was a pretty comical sight, me in chubby old Rosburg's pants with the waist bunched up in my belt.

Having a decent car was like survival for me. That old car that George Fazio had sold me was long since worn out from all the driving I did over the course of a year, and the two or three that followed it ended up dying on the road.

In 1961 I was driving an old Chrysler and I really needed a new car. I wanted to buy a Buick but didn't have the money. It so happened that at the San Diego Open that year they were giving away a brand-new Oldsmobile Toronado to any player who made a hole-in-one on the 18th hole. Well, I stepped up there on the second or third round and I aced it. They gave me the keys to that car on the spot, and I had barely walked off the green when a man approached me and asked if I'd sell the car.

"How much will you give me for it?"

"Fifty-five hundred," he said, and I traded him the keys right then and there. I never even drove that car, but the money I made from it allowed me to buy a new Buick.

Buicks were lucky for me all through the sixties. They had a deal at the annual Buick Open in Michigan where if you finished in the top 10, they'd give you a brand-new car to drive for the whole year. I won one of those cars six years in a row. Man, that was like money in my pocket.

It took me a long time to figure out how to play the tour. In the early years I was scrambling so much just to get into the tournaments and find a place to stay and put up with the bigotry that I hardly had time to concentrate on my game. It got a little easier as the years went by and I would return to the same cities and the same homes.

As I said before, I could never have done it without the network of black families who befriended me and took me in. I stayed at their houses year after year, and even when the hotels opened up to blacks, I'd return to my friends' houses. They are people whom I think about often. Some have passed away, others are still there, and I drop them a card or look them up when I'm in their towns. They fed me and took in my laundry and gave me rides to where I was going. They put up with my weird schedules and kept dinner warm while I was hitting balls until past dark. Some, like the Lavetts in Greensboro, Willie Branch in Houston, and Mr. and Mrs. Harry Jones in San Antonio were there with me during my most difficult times.

All they ever asked for in return was a golf lesson here and there or a story about life on the tour. I owe them all a tremendous debt of gratitude.

In the late forties, when I first started spending time in Los Angeles, I stayed in the home of Olin Marshall, a postal worker whom I had met at a golf tournament. He put me up many times before I moved to Los Angeles permanently, and frequently I'd spend two or three weeks at a time in his house.

In Jacksonville, where I started playing in the late sixties, I was invited into the home of C. C. Richardson, another post office worker who loved golf. He used to play in as many of the black tournaments as he could get to, and he always had a room set aside for me and Rafe Botts when we were coming through town.

One year I gave Larry Mowry a ride to the tournament in Wilmington, North Carolina, in a new Buick that I'd bought. He had a story published in *Golf World* about his wild ride with Charlie Sifford. We got into town, which by the way was where Ed "Porky" Oliver, one of the nicest guys in the world was from, and I dropped Larry off at his hotel. Of course there wasn't a hotel that would take me, so I stayed at the home of Dr. Eaton, a wonderful tennis player who had been instrumental in launching the career of Althea Gibson.

Even when I went into a town where I didn't know anybody, I'd meet someone at the golf course and they'd invite me to stay with them. In Indianapolis it was Mr. and Mrs. Bill Walker. In Portland, I'd stay with Richard McAfee and his wife. My list also includes Mr. and Mrs. Al Parks and Mr. and Mrs. Sunny Duval in Hartford, Mr. and Mrs. Walter Cunningham in Phoenix, John Lewis and Dr. Darrell Wyatt in San Diego, Wiley Wright in Denver, and Mr. and Mrs. Jim Stratton in San Francisco. I will never forget any of these people.

As far as my game was concerned, there were two things that I concentrated on during those years. I had to make my swing as repetitive and consistent as could be, and I had to learn the golf courses. I learned early on in my career to not tinker around with my swing or accept every piece of advice from anyone with an opinion of how I could hit the ball better. Pros are always watching each other hit and offering up little tips if you ask them about correcting flaws. Which is fine. But I didn't need any swing doctor to mess with me and tell me that my grip and my stance were wrong, because all that could do was seriously mess up my head. What I worked on, and perfected over the years, was swinging the same way nearly every single time, and hitting my controlled draw the same way over and over and over. That's my shot, and I'm not about to change it, even if Lee Trevino is winning a million dollars a year hitting that fade of his.

Putting was another story. On the greens it's all about touch and control, and you can work from dawn to dusk and not putt worth a damn if you don't have those things. I worked endlessly in those years on the putting green developing a stroke that I could live with and looking for that elusive touch. The practice helped me become a competent putter, but I've only been a great putter during occasional hot streaks.

You just don't walk onto a course like Doral or Oakmont in Pittsburgh or Medinah in Chicago and tear it up. Especially during those U.S. Opens, when they really make the courses as hard as hell to play. I needed to learn how to handle things like Oakmont's incredibly fast, sloping greens and which holes I could score on at Firestone. The only way to do that was to play every shot on the course and build up a memory bank over the years as to how a certain hole played, what the wind did to the ball, and where the tricky breaks lay in the greens.

I knew that I had the game to be a winner on the PGA Tour, and if I could just put it all together and keep the distractions of race and prejudice aside, I could finish high on the money list, even if I was in my forties. The opportunities to win got better and better, and throughout the year I'd get little glimpses of how it could be to finish near the top and be in that hunt for first place right up to the back nine of the fourth round of golf.

In Tucson in 1962, for example, I finished with a 65 and a 66 on that long, tough El Rio Country Club course and came in third. At the Canadian Open in Montreal that summer I battled Ted Kroll right down to the wire and came in second. In '63 I decided to give the Latin American tour a try and I ended up finishing sixth in Venezuela, eleventh in Panama, second in Jamaica, and first at the little $10,000 tournament in Puerto Rico. I shot 277 over four rounds and beat an unknown local boy named Chi Chi Rodriguez.

Playing in Jamaica was one of the weirdest things I've ever encountered, because the black people there were almost as rude to me as the white people in the South. With their English accents and English ways, they were somehow convinced that they were better than American Negroes, and they did their best to make me feel inferior. I made $1,000 for my second-place finish and gratefully took it the hell out of there and didn't go back.

I also had my first and last encounters with British golf tournaments in the midsixties, when Teddy Rhodes and I went over to play in a couple of Carling opens. Although nothing really overt happened, I had this overwhelming feeling of being unwelcome. The British were so condescending to us, for one thing. Of course we were the only black people out there. They didn't even have black caddies. I hated the golf courses, where the ground was hard as a rock and you had to constantly hit knockdown shots into the wind and you never knew what your ball was going to bounce off of. They looked like big pastures to me.

At one Carling Open there was a cocktail party for all of the players in the late afternoon and the tournament people were picking everybody up in cars. Teddy and I got showered and dressed up to go, and we stood on that corner and watched all of the cars drive right past us to get other people, and then nobody came back for us. We kind of understood the lay of the land at that point, but of course, none of those English people would say anything mean to our faces. We figured that we were better off in Florida, where at least we knew who was out to get us.

There were times when I could have won but beat myself. I should have won the 1963 Western Open at the Beverly Country Club in Chicago. I was right in the thick of it with a 72, 69, and 72 on the first three rounds, and Saturday night I figured I'd do myself a favor and get a manicure. There was a woman whom I knew from my travels with Billy Eckstine. She used to give manicures and pedicures to all of the athletes and musicians who came through town.

I went to her house on Saturday night and had my nails done. The next morning I woke up and my fingers were swollen and bleeding and the nails were peeling off. It turned out that she hadn't sterilized her tools right after giving someone a pedicure before me, and a fungus had gotten into the skin under my nails and just rotted them away.

My hands hurt like hell, but I still managed to shoot a 69 and barely missed forcing a four-way play-off with Julius Boros, Jack Nicklaus, and Arnold Palmer when I bogied the 17th hole. By that time, though, I could hardly hold the golf clubs anymore. My fingernails are still cracked and misshapen from that ill-fated manicure of nearly 30 years ago.

I said before that I was treated fine when I went to play in Dallas for the first time in 1962. I should have added that I was treated fine only up to the point that it looked like I might win the golf tournament. Even in Dallas, that possibility was just too much for at least one spectator to handle.

I was 1-under par and three strokes off the lead when the fourth round began. I was playing in the group right behind Arnold Palmer's, and when he came through, he took over the lead on the first two holes. I was playing well too, and after birdieing the first and eagling the second I was tied for the lead with Palmer. It looked like I would be in a duel with him right down to the finish.

The third hole was a par 3 with a green that was tucked behind a little hill. It was a short hole, where I probably played a 7- or 8-iron. I hit the ball well. From the way it landed, I knew that it would be around the pin somewhere or, at the very worst, on the fringe of the green. The spectators who watched from the tee all applauded and said it looked like it was within birdie range.

But it was nowhere near birdie range. When I walked up to the green, I couldn't find my ball anywhere. There was a whole gallery of people standing on the back side of the green and nobody was saying a word about my ball. I looked around and was shocked to see it about 20 yards away in out-of-bounds territory. It was out of play, but the only way it could have gotten there was if I'd really miscalculated my shot and hit the ball way long.

"Now how in the hell could this ball be out of bounds?" I wondered aloud, but nobody answered. I looked around and got a very sickening feeling. Somebody had moved my ball. That had to be it. It damn near killed me. I was playing my heart out, and I had scrambled to tie for the lead, and now a perfectly good shot was lying out of bounds and costing me two strokes.

What could I do? I picked up the ball, walked all the way back to the tee, plunked one on the green and ended up with a double-bogey that dumped me back into third place. I tried hard to catch up for the whole rest of the round and ended up shooting a 67 for third place. Those two strokes cost me the tournament.

Afterwards a guy I didn't know came up to me. "Your ball wasn't out of bounds, you know," he said. I asked him to tell me what happened, but he wouldn't go into detail. All he would say was that someone had kicked my ball from where it landed to out of bounds, and nobody in the gallery could stop it. He wanted to know if I could do anything about it, but how could I prove that that had happened? I just had to take it was all. When I returned to Dallas the following year the same guy was there to greet me. He followed me around for the entire tournament, standing beside my ball after every shot to make sure that nobody moved it.

I finished in the top 60 money winners in each of those years from 1960 to 1974, and finally became a full-fledged member of the PGA in 1964. But I couldn't say that I was winning at professional golf. I was just barely making it, and people all over the country were doing their damndest to make things extra difficult for me.

I was a pioneer, but all I was getting out of it was more anger and more bitter pills to swallow. When they talk about the American pioneers who built the country and faced incredible hardships doing so, they forget to mention how the pioneering can squeeze so much out of you that you're too exhausted and beat up to enjoy the satisfactions of your journey.

CHAPTER 15

Hartford

I didn't want to be a survivor on the tour my whole career. I wanted to be a winner. As the sixties went by I saw that they were taking my career right along with them and I would have to make my move right away if I was going to take my game up a notch. I had won at Long Beach in 1957 and in a couple of smaller tournaments like the Puerto Rico Open, but I had yet to win a big, four-round tournament against a full field of the PGA's finest. That became my goal.

A very simple line cuts neatly through the roster of touring professionals. It's the line that separates those who win tournaments from those who play well but always come up short. I saw it happen every week out there—one guy would have the will to come out on top. Maybe the greatest example I ever witnessed of this was the 1964 U.S. Open at Congressional when Ken Venturi withstood terrible heat and shot two incredible rounds on the last day to win. I was in the top 15 going into that last day and could have made a run for it, but I wound up shooting a pair of 77s in that blistering sun and humidity. Hell, I just wanted to get out of there without fainting dead away on the golf course.

I realized that I was going to have to rise up over all of the petty bullshit that I encountered as a matter of course and put it out of my mind if I wanted to win. Nobody was going to do it for me or magically make the conditions perfect for me. It became my goal to win a tournament before I was through. I wanted to jump over that line into the elite group of winners. I wanted there to be no doubt in anybody's mind that I belonged with the best golfers, and a win would be something that nobody could take away from me.

I knew a lot was at stake if I won a big one. I wanted it for all of the black kids who didn't know that black men could play pro golf. I wanted them to see a black man holding up that big winner's check, and I wanted it for my wife and family who had stood by me for so long. Most of all I wanted it for myself. Coming out on top would be my personal vindication for all of the miles I'd driven and all of the hardships I'd withstood.

Week after week I saw how hard it was to get that first big win on the tour. I came in second a few times and in the top five many times, but there was a big difference between number two and number one. Winning took something special, an ability to rise up to the challenge of the course and block out all of the distractions on and off the golf course. It took near-perfect concentration down the stretch and mistake-free golf in the clutch moments when the other guys were breathing down your neck.

It also took a winning attitude, which I hadn't allowed myself to have since I stopped playing on the Negro circuit. In order to survive in my early years on the tour I had developed some bad habits. Instead of having a killer instinct when I was within striking distance of the leaders, I made myself play safe time and again. Shooting right at the pins on every hole is the aggressive thing to do, but it's also the road that leads to disaster. You miss a few of those greens and wind up with double-bogies and you're out of there.

I was always too aware that if I messed up and was too aggressive I could put myself out of the tournament and way down in the money. I approached every single shot as if it were the difference between earning enough money to keep me on the tour another week or packing my bags and heading home. That is certainly not a winning attitude, but it was what I needed to survive. It would have crushed me if I had fallen so far down on the money list that I lost my card or had to requalify.

Although I wouldn't say that things exactly softened up out there on the tour, it did seem to get a little easier as the late sixties rolled around. For one thing, I finally had some black friends to share the time with. Pete Brown, who grew up in Jackson, Mississippi, and Rafe Botts, a young guy from Washington, D.C., came onto the tour in 1964 after I signed both of their approved tournament player's applications.

Pete and Rafe were big, strapping guys with terrific games. Pete was good enough to win a satellite tournament, the 1964 Waco Turner Open in Ardmore, Oklahoma. Rafe used to caddy for President Eisenhower in Washington before becoming one of the best amateurs on the black circuit. I met him at a UGA tournament and brought him out to California to play in 1959. By 1964 he was ready to try the tour.

Those guys were as broke and hungry as I was when I started, and they used to drive with me in my car from tournament to tournament. I introduced them to my network of contacts, showed them how things worked on the tour, and tried to smooth the way for them as best I could. If nothing else, we had each other to talk to when some kind of racial crap was thrown at us, and it helped me enormously. Just seeing those guys playing professional golf made me feel that what I had been through was worthwhile and that I had managed to open the doors for them and other black golfers who were coming up.

Which is not to say that their lives were easy and free of prejudice. Pete and Rafe and all the guys who followed them have all gotten their share of bad treatment and meanness from people in tournaments. They played off and on through the seventies and struggled to keep their cards, and they both come out now for senior tournaments. Guards and tournament officials still stop them and ask whom they're caddying for, which continues to be a fact of life if you're a black professional.

Time was helping to break down the resistance to my playing on the white tour, but then I wasn't getting any younger either. I was fast approaching 45 when the 1967 season started, and there

were young guys out there like George Archer and Lee Trevino
to whom I was giving away 15 to 20 years.

You don't bounce back quite as fast from a sore back or a
strained muscle when you're 45, and those golf courses seem
to get a little longer every year when you're out there walking.
You see those young bucks out there hitting 280-yard drives and
practicing all day long and you wonder if the game might be about
to pass you by. I knew that if I didn't win soon it might never
happen. There just aren't a lot of guys pushing 50 who can keep
their game together for four straight days to win tournaments.

But by 1967 at least it didn't feel like I was walking into the
enemy camp every single time I showed up somewhere to play
golf. People were nicer to me and I started to relax and play better.
I also had a brand-new reason to play well—on August 28, 1966,
my wife delivered a baby boy. Craig Leslie Sifford, our second
son, came at a time when Charles, Jr., was 18 years old and about
to move out of the house. I suddenly had my work cut out for
me all over again with this new mouth to feed.

Whatever the factors were, I started to play a lot better and
more confidently as the 1967 season progressed. I was knocking
on the door of the leaders nearly every month, and the money
started falling into place. I made $1,600 in Tucson with an eighth-
place finish in February and followed it up at the end of March
with $5,300 and a fifth-place finish in Greensboro. Every couple
of weeks I would put up a big number like a 67 that would put
me in the running. By the first of August I had made over $22,000,
which was by far the best year I'd ever had on the tour.

For once I didn't have to worry about every penny I might
lose if I made a bad shot, and for the first time in years I found
myself really enjoying the game. I had somehow managed to tame
my savage hook and keep the ball on line. I don't know if I was
playing better because I was more relaxed or was more relaxed
because I was playing better. It's a chicken-and-egg thing, I guess,
but all I knew was that it felt awfully good.

On Monday, August 14, I left from Firestone in Akron, Ohio,
after finishing 18th at the American Golf Classic, and headed for
Hartford. I liked playing in Hartford. I had friends there, the

Duvals, with whom I stayed every year, and I liked the Wethers-
field Country Club course where they played the tournament.
At 6,568 yards, the course wasn't particularly long and was well
suited to my game. I always finished in the money there, and the
way I was playing I knew that I could leave in a week with another
big check in my pocket. The purse was $100,000, with $20,000
of it going to the winner, which in those days was about as good
as the money got on the tour.

They had a good field for the tournament, the brightest name
being Gary Player, who was coming back to the Tour after a
month spent at home in South Africa. Art Wall returned to defend
his championship, and guys like Al Geiberger, Frank Beard, Chi
Chi, Harold Henning, and Julius Boros were touted as having a
shot at the ring. Lee Trevino was a rookie who had finished fifth
at the U.S. Open at Baltusrol in June, and he showed his stuff
by shooting a 31 on the front nine the first day.

Scoring was made even easier that week because they'd been
having trouble with the grass and were allowing free drops
whenever your ball landed in a bad patch of grass. You give a
pro the opportunity to improve his lie and he's going to hit that
green practically every time. We were gonna have a shootout that
week.

Gary Player was true to form on the first day with a sweet
65 that was 6-under par. Right behind him were Terry Dill with
66 and Trevino and another rookie named Bob Lunn with 67s.
I shot a 69 that included an eagle on the 14th hole. I should have
known right then that that hole would be my best friend all week.
It was a reachable 497 yards and I sank about a 20-foot putt to
eagle it. Number 17 was a tough par 3 that I bogied, and then
I came right back to birdie the 18th. I finished tied for fifth place
with about a dozen other guys.

I slipped to a 70 on the second day, and if you had told me
that I was in a position to win the tournament I would have
thought you were nuts, because Dave Hill came out and shot one
of the best competitive rounds of golf ever played. He put up
a 61 that day that could have been a 60 if he had dropped a
10-footer on the 18th green. It was a hot, still day where it was

easy to score on the course and most of the top guys broke 69. Gary Player's 69 kept him in second place, and Terry Dill had a 68 to stay close. Doug Ford put up a 67 that launched him into fourth place, a stroke ahead of Trevino.

I was suddenly six strokes off the lead in about 15th place, and I was going to have to do a lot better than one-under to catch up with those thoroughbreds. Once again I had scored on the 14th hole with a two-putt birdie but got beat up by that long, par-3 17th. I played a 3-iron into it and missed the green and wound up with another bogie.

Saturday was a crucial round for me. I had made the cut easily and was 3-under par, but I had had a tendency in prior years to blow up on either Saturday or Sunday. Maybe I lost my concentration a little after I knew that I would finish in the money but felt that I was so far down that I didn't have a chance at the lead. I would then shoot a high score that would take me out of the tournament for good and leave me no chance for a Sunday comeback.

This time, though, I worked hard to stay on top of my game, and once again I turned in a solid, if unspectacular, round of golf. I shot a 69 on the third day, shaving two more strokes off of par with birdies on the par-5 second and 14th, and pars the rest of the way. By that point I had hit the green on the 14th three straight times and had played it 4-under, which is pretty damn good for one hole.

I was still five strokes off of the lead, which Dill took on that third day, but for the first time in a long while, I had managed to stay within striking distance going into the fourth round. You could see the swings that take place out there. My buddy Dave Hill, for example, followed his incredible round of 61 with an even-par 71 on Saturday, a 10-stroke turnaround. Gary Player and Ray Floyd were lingering a few strokes away from the lead after shooting even par and 3-under, respectively.

What those guys, who were winners, had done was given themselves a shot to win the golf tournament on the last day. They had had their ups and downs over the first three days, but they hadn't done anything disastrous. Now they found themselves a few strokes off the lead going into Sunday, which is the place you wanted to be. A hot round would win the tournament, and that was the best you could ask for.

I was in a group in 12th place that included Trevino and Gene Littler. I knew that if I could put together another solid round I'd finish up high enough to make some decent money. I didn't really think about winning, because it would have taken a really nasty score to make up all those strokes that the leaders had on me. I not only hadn't been making those kinds of shots that week, but I had traditionally had problems on Sunday. Again, it was a concentration thing where I would lapse on the last day and put up a disappointing score that would drop me way down in the money.

I wish I remembered what I did the night before the final round, because I would do it again all the time. As I said earlier, there are times on the golf course when it all comes together and you put together a day of golf that is near perfection. It's a glorious feeling that I had captured a few times in the past with my 63 to beat Arnold Palmer on the first day of the Canadian Open and a few 64s at other tournaments.

But I had never managed to do it on the last day of a tournament, and let me tell you, nothing else compares. If shooting a 64 during a tournament is like throwing a no-hitter, then doing it on Sunday is like throwing a no-hitter in the World Series. I think it was the most thrilling thing I've ever experienced.

My tee time was set for 12:10 PM, and I was paired with Bobby Cole from South Africa and Al Geiberger. We were the sixth group from the end, when Terry Dill, Dave Marr, and Doug Ford would finish play. Gene Littler and Lee Trevino were right behind us, and the group in front of us included Tom Weiskopf and Harold Henning.

I parred the first hole. The second was a 502-yard par 5 that had a slight bend to the left. It worked perfectly with my hook, and for the second day in a row, I reached it in two. I missed the eagle putt by a little, but tapped in for a birdie. One under par.

I went on a run of pars for the next four holes. I was hitting the fairways and reaching the greens in regulation. My putting wasn't great, but it was okay. When I got to the seventh, the putt finally dropped and I had my second birdie. Two under.

I parred the eighth and then came up to the ninth hole, a 234-yard par 3. I hit a two-iron that day and put it on the green. Two putts later I had completed the front nine at 2-under, with no bogies, which wasn't spectacular but kept me in the hunt.

I sneaked a look at the scoreboard when we made the turn. I had picked up two strokes on the leaders, and I saw that Terry Dill and the others were having their troubles. They were playing the front nine even or over par. I said to Bobby Cole, who was also putting together a good round, "You know, if one of us shoots a 31 on the back we're going to win this thing."

Bobby agreed, and then we went out and both birdied number 10. Three-under. I parred 11 and just missed a birdie on 12. On the 13th I hit my approach to within three feet of the cup and tapped it in for another birdie. Four-under for the day, and 7 under for the tournament.

As I said before, number 14 had been my best friend for the whole week, and with an excitement rising in my chest, I knew that if I played it well I would be knocking on the door in the final four holes. I hit a solid drive down the middle of the fairway. As I walked after that ball, the butterflies started inside me and it was all I could do to keep calm. I had been reaching it in two with my 4-wood all week. I pulled out the club, took a deep breath to calm myself, and took aim.

I was a little too fast, and the ball hooked on me. It squirted into a bunker on the left side and then rolled right back out again into heavy rough alongside the green. I was 25 feet away from the cup with no chance to putt. It looked like the best I could do would be to make birdie, but only if I hit a great chip.

I did better than hit a great chip. I hit the chip of my life. The ball came out softly from that grass, bounced about 10 feet from the cup, settled, and rolled straight in. It was my second eagle in four days on the 14th, and suddenly I was 6-under for the day.

I heard a roar from the gallery when my number was posted on the scorecard, but I didn't connect it to me until we got to the 15th tee. Suddenly, thousands of people were running to get into position to watch what I'd do. Word had spread like wildfire that I was putting up some numbers, and by the time we teed off at 15 there must have been 10,000 people standing there watching me. Man, that was a new feeling and I had to work real hard to keep those butterflies from choking me.

I stepped up and drove it down the fairway, and my approach shot landed within 10 feet of the cup. I missed the putt but tapped in for par. I knew at that point that I was in the hunt. Knew it from the way the gallery reacted to my every shot. I dared not look up at the scoreboard, because I knew that there was nothing worse you could do to blow your cool.

Behind me the picture had changed considerably. Terry Dill and Dave Marr were falling away on the back nine, but Steve Opperman was charging with a birdie of his own on the 14th. Ray Floyd, Doug Ford, and Gary Player were still in the hunt, too. This tournament was going to go right down to the wire, and any one of a half-dozen golfers could win it.

The 16th was a long par 5 that I had been unable to reach all week, and I found myself about 50 yards short after my second shot. I chipped it to within eight feet on the third, which got a huge roar from the crowd, and dropped the putt for another birdie. I was 7-under par with two holes to play and had taken the lead.

The 17th had been one of the toughest holes all week. It was a 215-yard par 3 that demanded a perfect shot or the ball would drain off into a trap or heavy rough. All I wanted to do was land the ball safely, and this time my 3-iron was straight and true. I two-putted it for par, and now I had one hole left. Although I knew that there was something going on behind me, I was pretty sure that if I kept the 7-under score intact, I was going to win the tournament. I had to play the 18th even up.

As I said, I wasn't about to look at the scoreboard to see where I stood. I knew that I was on top, and it would only tighten me up to see how close the other guys were. The 18th hole was a long par 4, and by that time it was packed on both sides by a huge gallery. I'll tell you, I had played in hundreds of golf tournaments and seen a lot of galleries, but I never had had the feeling of having that huge gallery waiting to watch what I'd do.

It didn't matter that I wouldn't look at the scoreboard, because on the tee an official came over to me and told me that I was winning. I was so excited that I could barely contain myself, but somehow I took out my driver and knocked one down the middle of the fairway.

I wish I could describe to you that last walk down the fairway. It was like the whole crowd had been funneled into me. They were cheering and yelling my name and encouraging me. I think that a lot of people knew what was at stake and that I had never won a big tournament. They were rooting for me to win, and my heart was flying when I got to my ball.

All I had to do was put it on the green and putt out. I pulled out my 7-iron and looked at the ball. It was sitting in a little rough spot of grass. I could have moved it, but I didn't want to mess around or take any chances on a bad drop. I could hit it from where it lay, so I sized it up and took my stance. I swung, but I was a little fast and again I hooked it. The crowd gasped as the ball settled into a steep bunker on the left side of the green. This wasn't going to be easy. I had my work cut out for me to save par.

I took out my sand wedge and walked into that trap, and a hush came over the huge crowd. Man, I was so nervous that I just about couldn't see. I closed my eyes and prayed to God. "Please just let me make this shot," I said. I swung and the ball came out high and soft and pretty as could be. It thumped down on the green and stopped about four feet from the cup.

Geiberger and Cole marked their balls on the green and let me putt out. I sized that putt up every which way. It was just a regular old, straightaway putt, one that I'd made a thousand times. I took my stance, pointed my cigar down, and stroked it. That dude went right down the center and I had my par and a final-round score of 64.

The crowd roared. I threw up my arms in celebration. I knew that I had just won the tournament, and they knew it, too. Those people were so wonderful. They stood and cheered for me for what must have been 15 minutes. Cole and Geiberger shook my hand and swatted me on the back, and when I moved off the green about 20 other players were waiting to congratulate me.

But the tournament wasn't over. There were still all those guys behind me. Steve Opperman could have tied me and forced a playoff, but he missed a birdie putt on the 16th and bogied the 17th. He needed a birdie on the 18th to tie. My par putt suddenly loomed very large. He missed the birdie and was finished with a round of 67. In the final group only Doug Ford still had a chance, but he needed to birdie the last two holes to tie me. When he parred the 17th, it was all over.

When I realized I had won, I broke down and cried. They handed me that big check for $20,000 and asked me to say something, but I could hardly talk. "If you try hard enough," I said slowly, "anything can happen." And then I was just too shaken up to say more. "Thank you," I said. The crowd roared its approval for another five minutes.

I wish Rose could have been there to see it. I never will forget Hartford, because that's when my dreams came true. It had been my goal to be a winner and I had gone through heaven and earth to find a way to do it. I thanked God for my victory, and for giving me the strength to hang in there all of those years when winning a golf tournament seemed like the unlikeliest thing that would ever happen to me.

If you try hard enough, anything can happen. How long I'd been trying. I was 45 years old and I'd been trying since 1947. When it finally did happen, it was the sweetest thing I've ever known.

CHAPTER 16

A Golden Age for Black Golfers

You know the old saying: the more things change, the more they stay the same. I've learned it the hard way over and over, and never more so than the years following my win at Hartford in 1967.

I always knew that a win would be very important to me personally, but I never realized how much of an overall effect it would have on my life and my game. I was suddenly elevated a notch into a new level of golf, the level of tournament winners and contenders. It was the difference between being one of the perennial guys in the pack and being on the level of the Januarys and the Littlers. I realized that I hadn't felt that way — and people hadn't looked at me in that light — since I was top gun on the black golf circuit. I'd been scrambling so hard to get by that I forgot what it was like to be a winner.

For one thing, that $20,000 first-prize money was like a gold mine. There is an awfully big difference between finishing fifth and making $4,000 and finishing number one with that big check. It pushed my earnings for 1967 to over $47,000, by far the best year I'd ever have on the tour.

That check also put me among the top money winners in golf, a level occupied by the superstars of the game. It did worlds for my confidence to see my name ranked up there with Nicklaus and Palmer and Player, and I definitely liked the view from that ivory tower. It's funny that making $50,000 on the tour in a year was a big deal in those days. Now it would be considered a disaster.

A more subtle change was that people started to treat me like a champion. Everywhere I went they talked to me about the win and had me tell the story of how I chipped in that eagle on the 14th hole on the last day. When I returned to Hartford to defend my championship the next year, the tournament committee gave a big dinner in my honor and flew Rose in from Los Angeles to attend. It all made me feel more confident and important in a way that I'd never felt before, and I began to play better as a result.

I thought for a few fleeting moments back then that maybe I had broken through the final barriers and was on my way to the kind of national recognition that I deserved. Everything on the tour seemed to be more open and friendlier because I won, even in the southern tournaments. The newspapers began to seek me out for stories and quotes on events in golf. It felt an awful lot like all of my hard work had paid off. I had this crazy idea that I might be able to spend my remaining years on the tour as a respected player who could finally enjoy both financial and social rewards for what I'd done. At the very least I thought that I would finally be treated as an important figure in the history of golf.

You know, I saw the respect and reverence that old-timers like Byron Nelson and Ben Hogan had received in the latter stages of their careers. I met and spoke with both men and I respected them too for what they'd accomplished and the level of play that they'd sustained. I didn't expect any special treatment, but I thought that I deserved some recognition for my struggle and that capping off my career with a big win would be the last hurdle to cross.

For example, I thought during the entire year of 1968 that I was bound to be offered a high-level sponsorship or endorsement. It wasn't unreasonable to expect that a big company like Coca-Cola or Oldsmobile might want to parlay all of the press and attention I'd received into an endorsement deal that would help them sell their products. It could happen two ways, either directly through the companies — and big companies have all kinds of promotion executives hanging around at golf tournaments — or through a management company that would sign me and sell me to a number of bidders.

Never happened. People came up to me all of the time and asked if I was available for this or that, but nothing ever came of it. It was all golf course talk that never got to the next level. I tried to push the process along. I personally sent letters to a number of big companies, as did my lawyers, expressing interest in having me endorse their products, and all I got back were letters that said thanks, but no thanks.

The biggest management company in golf was, and continues to be, the International Management Group, headed by Mark McCormack. They handled Palmer, Nicklaus, and Player for a long time before Nicklaus dropped out and started up his own firm to handle the opportunities that came his way. IMG is known for breaking its clients into the highest echelons of advertising with deals that make everyone piles of money.

I looked up Mark McCormack in 1968 after my win and told him that I was looking for someone to handle my business affairs. He turned me down, saying that he didn't take on any clients who couldn't bring in at least $200,000 a year in income for him, which was probably something like $2 million in total billings to the client. I apparently wasn't marketable enough for him.

Some things seemed so natural for me to advertise, such as cigars. I've been smoking cigars on the golf course since I was 12 years old, and I was known wherever I went as the pro golfer who always plays with a cigar in his mouth. When I won at Hartford there were photographs blasted all over the country of me making my final putt with that cigar in my teeth and me accepting the trophy with a stogie. In those days of huge tobacco company advertising, it seemed like somebody would want to sign me up for a commercial.

Again nothing. You know who got a tobacco company endorsement? Sam Snead, who pushed Tiparillo cigars for a couple of years. And Sam doesn't even smoke! Mind you, I think

Sam deserves whatever he can get out there, and he's an old friend of mine from way back. But why would anyone pick him over me to endorse a cigar?

You know the answer and so do I. My black face wasn't going to sell as many cigars to the white consuming public, and there wasn't a big enough black audience to make a difference to the tobacco company. I could have won 14 tournaments and it wouldn't have changed the bottom line of how things sell.

I was also the only player on the tour for many years who wore that floppy kangaroo hat. I liked it because it kept my head cooler than a baseball cap and I used to wear it all the time. Players and fans alike asked me about it on the golf course. But I was never asked to endorse the product and after a while it made me so mad that I stopped wearing the hat.

Most professional golfers get things like balls, shirts, shoes, and so forth handed to them for free. The really successful players move up to another echelon where they get free clubs, and the superelite players, like Tom Watson, get paid a fortune for using the clubs. Other guys get sweet deals with country clubs or resorts where they get paid $30,000, $50,000, $100,000 a year to wear the resort's colors and talk the place up to all of the businessmen they run into at pro-ams.

None of that came my way, either. I had been getting shoes and golf gloves from Foot-Joy, which has stuck with me for the last 25 years whether I was winning or losing, balls and a golf bag from Titleist, and some clothes from Munsingwear. But I was never paid to use any of those products, nor was my name or face used for an advertisement. Those courtesies were still extended to me after the win, of course, but nothing new came around.

About the only real financial windfall I got from the win was the automatic qualification to play in the annual Tournament of Champions, which is open only to the previous year's winners. I don't think I placed very high in the '68 tournament, but as I recall they had a guarantee of $5,000 for entering.

There was another tournament that I should have been able to enter because of my win but couldn't. By 1968 it was the last place in the country that I wasn't allowed to play, nor have I ever been allowed to play there. It was the Masters tournament, America's favorite. One of the great disillusions of my life in golf is that the Masters has become a tournament so revered by golf fans and the media, with all of the fanfare on television every year when it's played. As far as I'm concerned, it has long been the most racist and hateful spot on the golf globe.

I don't want to appear like I'm whining when I say that I didn't get any endorsements or invitations because of my win at Hartford. I didn't want then, and don't want now, anything that isn't due me in the normal course of events. I can hear some critics out there right now saying, "That damn Charlie Sifford won one lousy tournament and thinks he should be making a million dollars a year from Coca-Cola."

That's not what I'm saying at all. The point is that when I won, I had one of the best human-interest stories in professional sports. Practically everybody in the country read about how I had had the hardest time coming up of any golfer in history, and it was well reported how I pushed things aside and hung in there long enough to win a golf tournament.

It just seems to me that if a white player had come back from such odds he would have been courted by any number of companies who wanted to cash in on his celebrity. I got nothing, and I have to think it's because I'm black. It not only hurt me personally, but it was a loss of potentially hundreds of thousands of dollars to me and my family. The bottom line is that like many things associated with golf, it just wasn't fair.

I'll tell you where the greatest source of business advice I've ever received came from: Thelma Cowans, the golfer. She also dabbled in real estate, and in the midsixties she found me a property in L.A. that she insisted I buy. It was a six-unit apartment building on 11th Avenue. I balked at spending the money, but Thelma really twisted my arm, and I think it was the best thing I ever did.

I bought the building and Rose and Charles, Jr., and I moved into one of the units and rented out the other five. We lived rent free and made some money back every month, which was wonderful. It gave me enough peace of mind to know that even if I only made enough money at golf to cover my expenses, at least my family would always have a roof over their heads. Coupled with Rose's job with the county, it gave us enough of a nest egg to live on. When I finally left L.A. in 1975, I sold the building and made a profit.

Although the endorsements never came through after my win at Hartford, something else was happening in golf that was even more gratifying than a fat advertising deal. I was starting to see more black faces on the golf circuit, and for the first time since I'd played the white tour, they didn't all belong to caddies.

By 1968 we had about 10 blacks who had qualified to play on the tour and had their temporary cards. They included Rafe Botts and Pete Brown, my old buddies who had come up in 1964 and gamely hung in there. Pete had a bout with polio in the late sixties that almost ended his career, but he came back strong enough to win another tournament in 1970. Rafe has battled his game up and down for years. In 1968 he only won about $3,400 all year, but he went out and requalified and got into as many tournaments as he could. He's still working hard on the Senior Tour to make a few dollars at golf. Cliff Brown was another guy who got the most out of his talent to stay up there on the tour for a number of years.

Before 1970 rolled around, we saw the emergence of players like Nate Starks, George Johnson, Jimmy Walker, and my nephew, Curtis Sifford, who had a damn fine game. I pulled Curtis out of North Carolina when he was in his twenties and brought him to California to concentrate on his game. He was good enough to break onto the tour in 1969 and play for several years before losing his qualification. He recently turned 50 and I expect to see him out here on the Senior Tour any day.

One thing that a lot of those guys had that I thought was absolutely essential to making it was a sponsor. Curtis was backed by a guy named William Stennis, who owned a bunch of fried-chicken stands in L.A. He paid Curtis's expenses long enough for Curtis to get a foothold on the tour without having to wonder every week if he'd be able to afford to get to the next tournament.

Another wonderful man who helped a lot of the young black golfers out was Mose Stevens, who put up the money to let many young black men pursue their dream of making it in golf. Those guys knew that it was an incredibly long shot to bet on a black golfer doing well enough to make back their investment, but they did it because they wanted to help get blacks into the game.

Of course, the guy who rose to the top and did as much as anyone to put black golfers on the map was Lee Elder. I had been playing with him as far back as 1960, and I knew that he would be a force to contend with when he finally came onto the tour. The year before he joined the white tour, Lee was still making the rounds of the UGA tournaments, and he was so good that he won an amazing 18 out of 22 tournaments that he entered.

Lee came out as a 33-year-old rookie for the 1968 season and he quickly made up for lost time. He played well enough to finish 54th on the money list with $31,000, but more important, he showed in a very direct way that blacks could compete in the game of golf. He grabbed the attention of a national television audience in August of that year by taking Jack Nicklaus to five play-off holes before losing the American Golf Classic at Firestone. That image of the godlike Nicklaus being taken to the wire by an unknown black man was one of the greatest things that could have happened for us.

Once Lee came around I found myself with a powerful ally who could compete at the highest levels of the game. When my career started to wane in the early seventies he came on strong and continued the fight that I had started. He was the first black man to win over a million dollars on the tour, and he also played so well in 1974 that he forced the hand of the Masters people and became the first black man to enter that tournament. If the truth be told, I wished it were me playing, but I've always been proud of Lee for having the determination and the strength to push himself into Augusta. He and his wife Rose have been good friends to us for many years, and I know that he respects me for beginning the fight.

It gave me an awfully good feeling to look around in 1968 and see all of those black men trying to make a living out of golf.

They all knew who I was and what I had done, but they couldn't begin to realize how long and difficult my struggle had been through the forties and fifties to keep knocking on the door long enough to force golf to let me in. I had pushed it open, and I had allowed it to stay open by not killing someone with a golf club when they tried to ruin me. As *Sports Illustrated* put it in a feature about me in 1969, I was in a sense an uncle to all of them.

It was a good feeling, but it was short-lived. Very few of the blacks who came out in the late sixties had the tools to compete in the game and be successful. They would play a few years, struggle to stay on the exempt list, fall off it, and then not have the heart or the skill to get back on. The differences in their backgrounds and the opportunities they had as kids to play golf were just too great to overcome.

Only a couple great players, like Elder and later, Calvin Peete, made names for themselves. The others drifted out of the game and weren't replaced. There was simply no way for the blacks to come up in the midseventies. The country clubs were closed to them, fewer places were hiring them as caddies, and the good white kids were given college scholarships for golf. Our "golden age" didn't last very long, I'm afraid. It sure hasn't carried into the nineties.

All I could do was continue to play and try to set an example. I liked that winning feeling and didn't want to lose it. I knew that I was almost done with the game I'd worked so very hard on, and I wanted to spend a little more time in the limelight. It was very fitting, then, that my second and last win on the regular tour, happened in the place where all of my family and friends lived — Los Angeles.

I almost didn't enter the 1969 L.A. Open because right after New Year's I came down with a bad cold that had me either in bed or feeling miserable for several days. The tournament started on Thursday, January 9, and I was so wheezy that I had to put away my cigars for the whole week. I hate playing golf without a cigar; I get nervous and uncomfortable without that stogie in my mouth. But every time I tried to smoke one that week I started coughing my head off, so I knew I'd have to play without one.

I loved the L.A. Open. I'd been playing in it as far back as the midfifties, back when Ted Rhodes and I would qualify and play together every year. It was a great feeling to play in my home town and go home to my family every night, and I was always looser and more relaxed at that tournament. In 1969 the tournament was being played at the Rancho Park Municipal Golf Course in West L.A., which was a course I had played many times. I knew that I had a good shot to score well going into it, if that cold I had would just allow me to stay on my feet long enough.

Cigar or no cigar, I had something special on the first day of the tournament. It was one of those magic rounds where it all comes together and you start thinking about shooting at the pin on every single hole. I started out with pars on the first two holes, a bogey on the third, and then pars through seven. The eighth and ninth were par 5s, and I reached both of them in two and two-putted for birdies, which put me at one under as I went into the turn.

Those birdies got me started and I came into the back nine hotter than a pistol. Coming in, I shot par, par, birdie, eagle, birdie, birdie, birdie, birdie, and par. That's seven strokes off par on six consecutive holes, which is just about a miracle. On two of those holes I chipped the ball in from off the green, one of which was for the eagle. Man, I shot a 28 out there on a chilly, breezy day, and ended up with a 63 for the round. I raced to the first-round lead past Arnold Palmer, Trevino, Don January, and the rest of them. The closest guy was Dave Hill, with a 66. Those three strokes would loom very large over the following days.

Being ahead of the pack was an unusual place for me, and over the next two days I kept my lead by shooting even par. Very few tournaments are won coast-to-coast by a golfer, and guys like Harold Henning, Billy Casper, Bruce Devlin, and Hill were hot on my trail going into the last round. I had to stay close to par if I was going to go all the way, and hope that nobody put up a crazy number to surge ahead.

There's nothing like being ahead on the last day in your home town. On the final round I had the gallery practically to myself from the first hole. My wife and kids were there, along with practically everybody I knew. Thousands of people followed me the whole way. They cheered me every shot and kept me pumped up the whole way. I've never seen or felt anything like it.

The crowd got really excited when I started out the final round with birdies on the first and third holes, but I missed the fifth and sixth greens and made bogeys. I couldn't manage anything but pars the rest of the way in and made the turn at even par.

Meanwhile Harold Henning, with whom I was paired, was roaring to a final round of 68 after shooting a 66 the day before. Hill, Casper, and Devlin were also all in the running. As we moved into the back nine the whole tournament tightened and became incredibly exciting. Harold finally caught me on the par-3 12th when I missed the green, chipped over it on my second, and took a bogey. Hill, who was ahead of us, made a birdie and tied us. After three-and-a-half days of being out front, I was suddenly fighting for a chance to win the golf tournament on the last six holes. I couldn't let up; the people in the gallery wouldn't have let me even if I wanted to.

On the 14th, Harold took the lead away from me when he drained a 20-footer. Hill had bogied ahead of us and fallen out of the first-place tie, and for a couple of holes the tournament was in Harold's hands. I broke right back in on the par-4 16th with a 20-foot birdie putt that found the center of the cup. The crowd went absolutely nuts over that one.

We were tied going into the last two holes, and we both made par on the 17th, which was a very tough par 3. I saved my par with a tough, scary, six-foot putt. Man, how I made it through that tense day without a cigar, I'll never know.

The crowd was going wild as Harold and I approached the 18th. In front of us, Bruce Devlin had just rolled a 20-foot putt to within two inches of the cup. If it had fallen he would have tied us for the lead, but it stayed out. Hill and Casper had also fallen away on the last holes, so it was down to us, the final twosome. A birdie would definitely win it: a bogey would definitely lose.

I remembered how nervous and scared I'd been at Hartford going into the last hole, but this time was different. Maybe it was the hometown crowd or the fact that I had a win under my belt, but this time I felt more exhilarated than scared. The 18th at Rancho is a 399-yard par 4, and Harold and I both smacked 250-yard drives down the center. The showdown was on.

Harold hit his approach safely onto the green. My approach was a little strong and ended up 40 feet from the pin at the edge of the green. It was an impossibly long putt, and I overhit it. The ball rolled three feet past the cup. Harold sized up his birdie putt, stroked it well, and watched it miss by inches. My heart practically leaped out of my chest when that happened. He dropped it in for a par, and I needed to do the same to keep the tie. I rolled in that three-footer and suddenly we found ourselves in a playoff for the $20,000 first-prize money.

The playoff was to begin on the 15th hole, a 382-yard par 4. It took a few minutes to walk over there and wait for the huge crowd to run over and get settled. I could just feel the energy and support from the gallery; I was the hometown boy and they were all rooting for me to win at that point. Harold and I both swung and put our drives down beautifully in the fairway.

Harold was away and pulled out his 9-iron. He went at the pin but leaked his ball a little and put it down to the right of the green in a ground-under-repair area. That was the chance I needed. I remembered that the day before I'd fallen short of the green from the same spot when I hit a wedge, so this time I called for my 9-iron. I swung and hooked that ball in there, and that sucker landed three-and-a-half feet from the pin and stopped dead. The crowd went wild, and my heart was thumping so loud that I thought it would drown out their noise.

Harold could have moved his ball out of the repair zone, but he liked the lie he had and chose to play it. I watched him and prayed to God that he didn't hole his chip. He gave it a good try, but the ball stopped short of the pin. The opportunity was mine. I only had to sink the birdie putt for the win.

You've never heard it get so quiet as when you're lining up that final putt. I checked it out, took a couple of practice strokes, and stepped up to the ball. I stroked it in there, and I was a two-time winner. The gallery erupted, Harold walked over to shake my hand, and the party had begun.

This time I didn't cry when they handed me that big, oversized check for TV. I laughed. Rose was at my side and she laughed too. It was one of the best times I've ever had. Craig and Charles, Jr., were there to get their pictures taken. I was on top of the world, and I was going to enjoy every minute of it.

After the postround interviews were over in the press tent, someone told me there was a party waiting for me at Willie Davis's Center Field Lounge. Rose and I went down there and we walked in to find all of the black pros waiting to congratulate me. Lee Elder was there, and Rafe Botts and Pete Brown and Curtis was there with his bride. Willie Davis, the great Dodger outfielder, came over to me midway through the party and said, "Hey Charlie, there's someone else wants to see you."

It was Bill Spiller, the L.A. pro who had teamed up with Teddy Rhodes and Joe Louis to break down golf as far back as 1948. He had come with Joe Roach, the amateur player who had accompanied us to Phoenix and Tucson in 1952 when Joe Louis forced them to invite us. Spiller said that he'd watched the whole final round on the television set at the Western Avenue golf course, our old hangout, and everybody there went crazy when I won.

The party went on for a long time, and it was followed by many others. February 3 was proclaimed Charlie Sifford Day in Los Angeles, and they had a little parade for me in Watts on the same street where the riots had raged in 1965. The Watts Chamber of Commerce elected me to its hall of fame, and Mayor Sam Yorty read a proclamation on my behalf.

That night, there was another party for me at a nightclub called the Black Fox. They asked me to say a few words and I was genuinely overcome with emotion over all of the wonderful things that had happened to me. But I was also saddened when I thought of what it had taken to get this far, and that my road in golf was fast coming to an end. "It's just so wonderful to think that a black man can take a golf club and be so famous," I told my friends. "I just wish I could call back 10 years."

The day after I won the tournament, someone sent a telegram to the home of Stanley Mosk, the California attorney general who had fought the PGA on my behalf and forced the end of the Caucasian clause. "Thank you for opening the door for the Charlie Siffords of this world," it said.

There is a postscript to this chapter that took place 15 years after my win in Los Angeles, long after I'd finished playing on the regular tour. On October 7, 1984, I boarded a plane and flew to San Antonio, Texas, to watch the final round of a professional golf tournament, the Texas Open at the Oak Hill Country Club.

I went down there because Calvin Peete was leading the tournament and had a shot at winning, and that was something that I wanted to see. It had been 23 years earlier that I had been run off that golf course and told that I wasn't allowed to play there or even to set foot in their locker room. That was probably the lowest I've ever been in my life. I nearly quit.

When Calvin won the tournament I clearly saw the connection between what I had done and how it had affected the game of golf in America. I had hung in there because I loved the game and because I'm stubborn and willful and because I believed that in America you have opportunities like no other place in the world.

Could anyone have possibly been as thrilled to see Willie Mays play baseball as Jackie Robinson was? Can you imagine the thrill that Jackie might have felt the first time he saw a little black kid play in a little league game, knowing that the kid could possibly make it all the way to the big leagues because of what Jackie had started?

That's the way that I felt when I saw Calvin Peete win in San Antonio. I felt as good about his win as I felt about any of my own wins on the PGA Tour. Despite all of the hurts and slights and meanness that I've faced over the years and will continue to face while I'm in the game, nobody can ever take that away from me.

CHAPTER 17

The Lily-White Masters

Can somebody explain to me how the Masters golf tournament in Augusta, Georgia, became such a revered sporting event? Yes, I know all about the beauties of the Augusta National Golf Club and Amen Corner and the creek and the blooming flowers. I know all about the legendary Bobby Jones and the green jacket that they give the winners and the incredible duels among Nicklaus and Palmer and Watson.

Mind you, I've only *heard* all about this, because I've never been there. They never let me play. To my mind the Masters was the worst redneck tournament in the country, run by people who openly discriminated against blacks. How they could continually deny blacks the opportunity to play in their golf tournament while gaining popularity as the most prestigious tournament in the country is simply unbelievable to me.

Let me give you an alternative vision of the wonderful Masters tournament that somehow became one of the "majors" on the tour schedule despite its invitation-only policy. Call this the minority viewpoint of a player who lived this scenario every year from 1961 through 1974.

If you're black, the Masters marks the week on your calendar when you either take a forced layoff from golf or go play in a little satellite tournament for hardly any money and against

172

second-rate players. It doesn't matter how well you've been playing or what you've accomplished in the past. When that weekend in April rolls around, you sit.

You've fought and struggled your way into tournaments from Greensboro, North Carolina, to New Orleans, Louisiana, to Guadalajara, Mexico, where you took your winning purse in pesos. You've proved to the people in Pensacola and San Antonio and Dallas that you belong in their golf tournaments and in their country clubs, and you've finally become accepted. You win golf tournaments and finish higher on the money list than half of the Masters players. But you're not good enough to play in the Masters, and you're not offered any explanation. Simply, "you didn't qualify."

You read about the upcoming Masters field, hear promos for it on television, hear players talking about it, and somehow it doesn't make a damn bit of sense to you, because you're black and for that reason you can't play. That alone screams of bias and outright discrimination, but somehow the Masters gets away with it. The players love it there, the corporate sponsors love it, the networks adore it, and to hell with the minorities.

President Eisenhower was actually a member of the Augusta National Golf Club! The whole thing is as overt a slap in the face as if once a year in April you got a phone call from the same racist calling you the same ugly name over and over.

I would go so far to say that for a black man, the Masters golf tournament was and maybe still is a symbol for where he really stands in American society. Sure he might get some victories here or there and think that he's finally making it in society, but that one door at the top will never be open to him. And when a door stands firmly closed against you, you really do question the value of what you'd achieved up to that point.

My problems with the Masters didn't start after I'd won my golf tournaments. By then I was positive I would never get an invitation to that tournament no matter what I did. I'd been getting very clear signals for nearly 10 years that I'd never play golf in Augusta, Georgia. I personally opened nearly every golf tournament in the country to blacks, but I could never open the

Masters. They stuck to their invitation-only policy for longer than anyone could possibly have imagined.

Unlike most tournaments that were forced to drop their invitational status, the Masters never had to change. They could, and as far as I know, still can invite whomever they damn well please to play in their tournament. Never mind that the PGA has its own guidelines for which of its members should be eligible for professional tournaments. The Masters always went its own way, and the PGA blindly went along with what they wanted.

The Masters set up different standards for qualification. They usually invited the top 16 finishers from the previous U.S. Open, for example. The top 25 money winners on the previous year's money list were automatically invited (or so they said, as I found out after my Hartford win). They got all kinds of foreign players by issuing automatic exemptions to winners of the British Open and the Canadian Open, and somehow they always had guys from Britain, Germany, Australia, and Japan entered. Any leftover spots in the limited field were filled in by votes of the prior winners of the tournament, which in itself was a pretty exclusive club.

Those were some of the automatic ways of getting into the tournament, but the Masters also could and did change its requirements. I'm positive that they changed their rules more than once to exclude me from playing, because for many years I was the only black man good enough on the PGA Tour to come close to getting an automatic bid. Quite simply, they didn't want a black, specifically me, on their golf course. The most prestigious golf course and tournament in America were also the most conniving and the meannest.

I'm not the only one who thinks so, by the way. Over the years I got a lot of support from many newspaper columnists who voiced similar opinions. Jim Murray of the *L.A. Times* wrote some wonderful things on my behalf, and it became a little game among other writers to chart my progress in relation to where I might fall in the automatic Masters bids. What would happen, they queried in print, if Charlie Sifford qualified for the Masters? Would Augusta change its rules one more time?

I'll tell you why I knew that I'd never get into that tournament: they told me so themselves. In the late fifties, when I was playing a limited PGA Tour schedule and was the perennial champion of the Negro tournaments, it was suggested to Augusta National that I receive a kind of goodwill bid to play.

Word came back from the late Clifford Roberts, long the autocratic chairman of the Masters committee and the driving force for many years behind the tournament. "As long as I live," Roberts said, "there will be nothing at the Masters besides black caddies and white players."

I can't remember now if that quote came from a newspaper or by word of mouth. I wish I did know, because if he said that in the newspaper, I can't believe that it wasn't picked up throughout the whole country. But that was the rule he laid down, and throughout the fifties and the sixties the Masters kept its racial lines clearly defined between caddies and players.

I'll give you another equally outrageous example. In 1962 I went to Montreal to play in the Canadian Open, one of the tournaments where the winner traditionally was given an automatic bid for the Masters. I shot a 67 on the second round to take the lead. That afternoon a call came into the clubhouse. Whoever took the call posted its contents on the clubhouse bulletin board: "The Masters golf tournament has announced that it will not offer an automatic invitation to the winner of this year's Canadian Open." Just like that, in plain English. Could it be just a coincidence that it happened on the day that I was leading the tournament? I don't think so.

Ted Kroll and I went down to the wire in that tournament, and he ended up shooting a 28 or something on the back nine of the last round to win. I finished second. Afterwards Ted, who is a wonderful guy, came up to me and said, "Charlie, you know that I'd do anything to win a golf tournament, but I'm truly sorry that it was you that I had to beat."

My wife Rose had the right attitude about the Masters. "If they don't want you in their golf tournament then forget about them," she said. "It's nothing but another golf tournament. You've got plenty of others to play." Her feeling with stuff like that was if they didn't want us around, then we didn't want to be around them either.

Nevertheless it made me furious that the Masters could be so blatantly discriminatory. I didn't want to play in that golf tournament because I like the way dogwood looks in the spring-time or because I wanted to become a member of the club. I wanted in precisely because they were trying so hard to keep me out. It really got my back up, and I told everyone who was listening that the Masters was discriminating against me because I was black.

I had set certain goals when I started playing on the white tour. I wanted to play a full schedule of tournaments, I wanted to make enough money to feed my family, and I wanted to play up to my potential and win. I also wanted to play in the U.S. Open, the PGA Championship, the Ryder Cup, and the Masters. I did all the other things except play for the Ryder Cup, which was because I never had enough season points to qualify and I never received the at-large invitation. I never made it into the Masters because they wouldn't let me.

In a *Sports Illustrated* article of 1960 Dick Schaap related the following conversation during the final round of the U.S. Open at Winged Foot. " 'If Charlie Sifford has a real hot round,' a golf writer said, 'he can finish among the top 16. Now, that would be interesting. That would mean he'd automatically qualify for the Masters tournament next year.'

" 'Y'all crazy?' said a reporter from Georgia. 'If Sifford makes the top 16, they'll change the rules so only the top 15 qualify. If he finishes 11th, it'll become the top ten. And if he finishes second, then it'll only be the top one.' "

I ended up shooting a 76 that day, which put me down to 31st place. If I had shot a 69, the heat would have been on the Masters. That same scenario was repeated a couple of times during my career.

Another one of the stated requirements for the Masters was to finish among the top 25 money winners the previous year. I flirted with that number many times over the years. Finally, after my win at Hartford I was well up there in prize money. I was practically sure that the last wall would finally come tumbling down and they would have to let me in.

No way. I was told that I hadn't been accepted by the Masters because it was no longer the top 25 money winners who were invited. They had changed the rules. Players were now entered by means of a "points system," whereby points were allocated by the position a player finished in all of the tournaments he entered. Despite finishing first at Hartford and making $47,000 in 1967, I hadn't accumulated enough "points."

They were saying that I wasn't good enough to play in the Masters. But guys got invitations who hadn't won a single tournament or made as much money as I. As Jim Murray wryly noted in his column, "If you come from Formosa, it's easy to get in [to the Masters]. If you come from a cotton patch in Carolina, it's impossible."

"It is a feeling of this 22-handicapper," Murray added, "that the Masters ought to send a car for Charlie and, considering he's the only guy in the field who couldn't get started on his golf career 'til he was 33 years old or his tournament career 'til he was almost 40 because it took democracy so long to catch on in this country, maybe they ought to give him two a side. If they do, I'll guarantee you Charlie will be voting on the invitee next year."

There was finally one other way to get into the Masters and that was by a vote of the past champions. They met every year and offered an invitation to two golfers they liked. I guess they didn't like me too much, even when I was playing my best. The year that I won at Hartford, the champions invited Mike Souchak and Tommy Jacobs. When I won at L.A. two years later, I believe the bids went to Homero Blancas and Bob Murphy.

I know for a fact that Art Wall was the only guy who voted for me to play, but nobody voted along with him. A lot of those past champions came from Texas and the Deep South, and I don't think there's any way in hell that those guys are going to vote in a black man who has been pushing to get into their game. I said so in print, and that pretty much ended any chance I ever had to be voted into the Masters.

I didn't even think twice about the Masters when I won my second tournament in L.A. By that time I knew that it wasn't going to happen, regardless of how much heat Augusta got from the media. Once again I wasn't voted in by the past champions, and I didn't figure in whatever qualification schemes that they had going on. It wasn't much of a surprise.

Mind you, I'm not the only black golfer who was snubbed by the Masters. Pete Brown won a tournament in 1970 and got treated the same way that I got treated in '69. Lee Elder had that marvelous rookie year in 1968 and showed the world that he could play top-drawer golf. Year after year he finished high on the money list and didn't get in. According to the *Wall Street Journal,* 18 U.S. congressmen lobbied the Masters committee to invite Lee after the 1973 season, and they still kept him out.

In 1972, when I was really too old to have a realistic shot at winning a golf tournament, the Masters changed its rules again. They finally acknowledged the pressure and said that anyone who won a golf tournament in the previous year would get an automatic invitation. Of course, that rule wasn't retroactive to guys like me and Pete Brown.

Lee Elder was in a position to win, and finally in 1974 he won the Monsanto Open. The following year he was the first black to play in the Masters. Calvin Peete and Jim Thorpe have since played the Masters, and that's it. Three black golfers in the history of "America's greatest" golf tournament.

I was very proud of Lee for hanging in there and doing what it took to play in the Masters. I also felt for him when he went and actually played, because I remember very well the kind of things that happen to a black player who is breaking the line at a particular country club. I've heard over the years that Lee had some hard times down there using the locker room and such. Lee Trevino had similar troubles and reportedly had to change his shoes in his car at Augusta because people of color weren't allowed into the Augusta locker room.

Many things have changed at the Masters since Cliff Roberts passed away. The caddies aren't all black anymore. That broke down in the seventies when George Archer brought his daughter to caddy for him, and others followed suit by bringing in their white caddies.

They also recently accepted their first black member to Augusta National. Maybe it took them this long to find just the right guy to join the club, but I rather think it was so they could avoid the Shoal Creek fallout and continue to get those breathless television broadcasts every spring. People still come up to me on the golf course and ask what I think about the first black member at Augusta National, as if I'm going to turn backflips over the news. Man, it's going to take a whole lot of black members to make up for what that club has done to black golfers over the years.

What hasn't changed at the Masters is the absence of black players. And there probably won't be any for some time to come. Calvin Peete and Jim Thorpe are at the end of their careers and probably won't qualify again. Nobody else is coming up. And you can be just about positive that old Charlie Sifford is never going to get one of those invitations, or even an acknowledgement of any kind from Augusta National that he has played a role in golf.

That's simply not the way they do things at the Masters.

CHAPTER 18

Jack, Arnie, Gary and a Hundred Other Guys

I've been playing golf for nearly 45 years now with practically the same group of guys week in and week out. So when you ask how I'm treated by the other players, it's a little tough to answer, given that we're talking about a rather extended period of time here. When people ask me, "What's Jack Nicklaus like?" it's like me asking you to describe the guy you've worked next to for the last 30 years. There's a lot of space to fill in there.

Nevertheless, I'll try to share some memories of my fellow golfers. For one thing, many of these guys are my best friends in the world. I've been hanging out at golf tournaments; going to cocktail parties; playing practice rounds; and socializing with guys like Art Wall, Mike Fetchik, Joe Jimenez, and Dave Hill for over a decade now on the Senior Tour and many years before that on the regular tour. Our wives know each other well and spend time together while we're playing golf, and we've all watched each others' kids grow up. They're a wonderful group of people, and I feel lucky that they've been part of my life for so long.

On a purely competitive note, golf has given me a front-row seat to see the greatest players of modern times grow and blossom. Jack Nicklaus, Arnold Palmer, Gary Player, Lee Trevino, Tom Watson . . . they all began their careers while I was playing, and, with the exception of Watson, are still competing against me. I've played many rounds of golf with all of those players and I've been as thrilled as any golf fan by some of the things they could do on a golf course.

It was on the backs of those five players that golf rode to its present-day popularity. I think all of the rest of us who have watched our prize money soar from better purses and TV revenues owe a debt of gratitude to those giants of golf.

Regarding my early years on the tour, people want to know if any players were openly opposed to my being out there. That's a tough one to answer, because again we're talking about a period of many years, and like anyone else, my relationships have changed over the years. For the most part I was treated as cordially as any new player, which doesn't mean that everybody out there was trying to be my buddy, nor does it mean that players tried to make me disappear. Hell, you never know if a new guy coming up is going to be around from one year to the next, and in my case I'm sure that a lot of people thought I'd be gone once the pressure mounted.

There were a few instances when I was treated rudely by other players during a round. I can remember incidents where a player jingled the change in his pocket while I was lining up a putt or was slow to move out of my line of sight. Some players seemed to go out of their way to not speak to me during my early years on the tour or pretended that I was invisible by continuing their conversation and completely ignoring me when I was standing right next to them.

But did another player ever call me a nigger or refuse to play with me during those times when I was breaking in? No way. Man, if that had happened I would have gone right over the top, because there was no way that I could have kept my temper in check if another golfer had been that ugly. If there's one thing that I've always insisted on, it is that I be treated like a gentleman out there. I've never given anyone a reason to doubt that. I think that a lot of guys were aware of the special circumstances that I was facing at many of those golf tournaments, and I earned their respect by handling it and just going out and playing good golf.

In the early sixties my problems arose more from the fact that I was new to playing the whole tour, and since I was the only black guy there weren't other players to whom I naturally gravitated. Life on the tour isn't easy for any rookie, but for me the problems of settling in were probably magnified. I was under so much pressure to perform well and to endure the hardships that I didn't really have the time or the inclination to be real friendly and open. For one thing, I had to concentrate all the time on my game, and it's not my nature to be yakking and joking out there on the golf course when I have a job to do.

For another thing, I'm not going to walk up to a bunch of white strangers and try to be their buddy. I'm a little more reserved than that, and I wait for people to come to me.

In those early days I played a lot of practice rounds by myself. Many were the times when I didn't accept an invitation for a post-round beer because I either couldn't afford it or wasn't sure if some country-club type would have a problem with me drinking in his bar. I had enough things to deal with without facing humiliation in front of a group of players. As I wrote before, players like Bob Rosburg, Frank Stranahan, Ken Venturi, and Porky Oliver went out of their way to help me out.

The golf tour is like a big, traveling corporation where you work alongside the same 150 to 300 people every week. I'm including the tournament officials, the sponsors, the television guys, the reporters you see every week, and the equipment manufacturers, along with the players. Like any business, I suppose, you become closer to some people than to others, but the whole thing works because there are written and unwritten rules of conduct.

I'm sure a few players out there don't like me personally. That's fine: there are several whom I can live without, too. But I'd be hard pressed to say that it's a black-white thing or that they don't think I should be out there. I don't have any enemies in golf. When you've got 72 guys competing for the same prize money, you can't expect to be everybody's best friend.

Jack, Arnie, and Gary: in the sixties they replaced Hogan, Snead, and Nelson as the brightest names in golf. While I was breaking down doors in the South, they were establishing themselves as the Big Three with consistently stellar play. They were the stars who ushered in golf's television era and fueled the modern-day golf boom. I was paired with them many times, and I always felt that I had to be extra sharp on those days. They brought an electric atmosphere to the game, with huge galleries that followed them for the entire round to see what they would do next.

They were fellow competitors to me when I went out there to play, and I tried like hell to beat them whenever I could, but those guys were something special to watch. I admire anyone with a good game and the guts to pull out wins, and those three guys had all the tools.

Their games were as different as could be. Nicklaus was the bear who could outmuscle practically every golf shot and had the keenest concentration of anyone I've ever seen. Man, that guy was strong. When he first came out on the tour he looked like a little weightlifter or something. He hit some shots from situations like deep rough that none of us could believe. You'd see his lie and figure that he'd do well to just get the ball back to the fairway, and the next thing you knew, Jack was slashing away with a 3-iron and putting it on the green.

Palmer was an inspiring, streaky player who hated to hold a lead but staged awesome comeback charges to win tournaments. He was always a very charismatic man, with that rabid gallery of his that would follow him right out to the parking lot to watch him put his clubs in the car.

Player had a smooth, all-around game and nerves of steel, particularly in the major tournaments. You know from the minute you lay eyes on him that he's a fierce competitor. He's also a gentleman and a man who commands respect wherever he goes.

Jack Nicklaus and I have always gotten along well. I was paired with him in the very first professional tournament he ever entered, the 1958 Rubber City Open at the Firestone Country Club in Akron. Jack was a big, hefty kid with a crewcut, an 18-year-old amateur who was testing his game against the pros. I shot a 65 on the first day to his 70, and he turned around the next day and shot a 64. I remember him as being friendly, likeable, and intense, with an unbeatable game.

He was the closest thing you'll ever see to a can't-miss amateur. He had everything—the mechanics, the determination, big driver, good with the irons. And that kid could putt like a lion. In his prime he was the greatest putter I've ever seen.

I met Jack's father at that tournament, and we became good friends. He and I shared a fondness for good cigars, and he used to send me boxes of cigars from his drugstores. He was a really nice guy, and Jack looked just like him.

My son Craig was five years old when I brought my family down to Fort Worth to play in the Colonial in 1972, and we happened to rent a condo right next door to Jack and Barbara. One day Jack walked by on his way to the golf course, and Craig called out, "Hey Fat Jack, where you going?" Fat Jack. God knows where he got that from. And Jack said, "I'm going to play golf, Craig." Well, for the rest of the week Craig called him Fat Jack so much that he had *me* calling Jack Nicklaus that. It was pretty funny, and Jack still brings it up sometimes when I see him.

Jack did something for me a few years ago that was very touching. I happened to be down in Florida in January of 1985 when he was about to dedicate a new golf course, the Bear Lakes Country Club in West Palm Beach. They had invited a group of people down to watch Jack give a clinic and play an exhibition round. For some reason I was invited, although I was the only pro there and I hadn't had much contact with Jack for several years.

I was standing in the crowd watching Jack warm up when he spotted me. He stopped what he was doing and announced to everyone who I was and what I had done for the game of golf. He remembered the first rounds of golf that we had played together (and he made a point of reminding me that he'd won by a stroke). He told them that I had always been a gentleman to him and that he appreciated the way I'd made him feel comfortable in his early days on the tour. It was a very nice thing for him to do, and I appreciated it immensely.

Of all the white players on the tour, I think that Gary Player has done the most for blacks. Some people might say that it's a reaction to his being from South Africa, but I say that it's just the kind of man he is. I have as much respect for Gary Player as I do for anyone alive. He was the first guy to bring his black caddie, Rabbit, to England for the British Open, and he used to bring Rabbit back to South Africa every year for a tournament. He also invited me and Lee Elder to join him back in the early seventies. I couldn't make it, but Lee has played over there a couple of times, I think. On his ranch in South Africa, Gary has a school for black children that is one of the best private schools in the country.

Gary has helped me out many times, but the one I'll never forget came after I'd retired from the regular tour and was working at a public golf course outside of Cleveland. To most of the players I was ancient history, but Gary never forgot about me. He gave me a call out of the blue one day and said that he was passing through Cleveland the following week and was there anything he could do for me.

I said sure, you could come by my golf course and give a clinic, which is a thing that a lot of pros do where they come out to the golf course and give a demonstration for spectators. They'll hit a few balls, tell some stories, and give tips on swinging correctly. Gary agreed, and I put up signs announcing his visit the following weekend. When he arrived we had 1,500 people out there to watch him, and Gary hit balls and talked for an hour.

When he finished, I gingerly asked him what I owed him, because guys of Player's caliber could get as much as $15,000 for a public appearance. "You don't owe me anything," he said. "Just keep being a man." Class guy, Gary Player.

I really haven't had that much contact with Arnold Palmer over the years. We're paired together from time to time and we have a cordial relationship on and off the golf course, but from the very early days Arnie has traveled in a class all his own. Of course I was there when he won his first PGA tournament, the 1955 Canadian Open, where I set the course record of 63 on the day that he shot a 64. I wish I could have stayed that close to him all the time, because Arnie's career took off like a rocket after that.

Palmer's charges to victory were astounding to watch in the early days. He would capture the attention of the entire golf course as he pounded into contention with that cranky swing of his and that putter that could get incredibly hot. Of course the way he could blow leads was equally astounding. He just never seemed to like being the front runner. Instead of shepherding his lead, he'd keep trying crazy things like shooting right at pins and watching four-five-six-stroke leads disappear on the back nine.

Jack, Arnie, and Gary undoubtedly have had a great deal of influence over the game. They were the top names on the marquee for many years, and they still attract big crowds wherever they go. Jack and Arnie became whole corporations unto themselves, and they're just as busy these days with their many business interests as they are playing golf itself. Their star status gives them access to the highest levels of the game, and their attendance can make or break a tournament.

Because of their celebrity, questions regarding the Big Three have been posed to me over the years, and frankly they're questions that I almost hate to bring up in this book. I think they're unfair questions and I generally don't answer them. But to put the matter to rest, I will discuss it here.

The questions are, "Did any of those guys ever exert any influence to get you into tournaments or take you under their wing or make that road any easier for you? Did they ever come out publicly on behalf of blacks playing the game in general, and for you to get your fair share?"

My feeling is this: no, I don't think Jack Nicklaus or Arnold Palmer ever tried to change anything for me, and I wouldn't have wanted them to. I am not someone who goes begging for help or a shoulder to cry on. I don't want Jack or Arnie or Gary or Lee Trevino or anybody else to inconvenience themselves for my sake, because it's just not their job.

Those guys are golfers — the best in the world — but they're not politicians or civil rights activists or newspaper columnists. It's not their job to stump for the black man to get into the game, any more than it's their job to pop off about the state of the economy or the proliferation of nuclear weapons.

They are players, and they have to play within the system that has been set up. For one thing, I don't believe that they would have any real influence over the game if they popped off in the newspapers over playing conditions for blacks, especially not in those early years of the sixties, when they were struggling to be the best they could be.

If they had started voicing their opinions, it might have just gotten them into trouble with the powers that be—the sponsors, the country clubs, the tournaments, and the PGA itself. Why should those guys, who had the potential of being the finest to ever play the game, jeopardize their careers one iota for Charlie Sifford? Why should they take time away from their games to work some kind of inside ropes for me? Nope, I don't believe in it, and I wouldn't have appreciated it if they had said something.

Look at Gary Player. He leads by example, and he isn't bringing his black caddie all over the world because he wants everyone to see what a hero he is. He does it for his own reasons, and I respect him for it.

It's also unfair to single those three players out as being the ones who should carry the torch for black players. Nobody ever asked me if Al Geiberger or Doug Sanders were doing enough for black players. My answer would be the same: why should they?

Look, my whole career in golf has been about being accepted on the basis of what I do. Yes, the system was patently unfair from the beginning and stacked against me. But I didn't get to where I am by complaining or whining or getting celebrity golfers to stump for me or bitching to every newspaper reporter who walked onto the golf course. I got to where I am because I could play as well as anyone else out there, and if I had had a few more chances early in my career, I could probably have played better than 95 percent of them.

It's not the players who need to change that system, it's the tournaments and the country clubs and the PGA itself. I don't think it's Jack Nicklaus who needs to get more involved, I think it's corporate America itself. The people who bankroll these tours and the sponsors who pay for the TV time and are making a great deal of money out of golf . . . it's in their best interests to make the game healthy and whole.

It would have been a hollow victory for me if, say, Arnold Palmer pushed the Masters committee into inviting me to their tournament. That rings an awful lot like Shoal Creek dropping one black guy onto its membership list to keep the hounds at bay. I was more than qualified to play in the Masters, and if they couldn't recognize that on their own and change their attitude toward black golfers, then it wouldn't have meant a damn thing if I'd gotten in there from some pressure by a star golfer.

Jack, Arnie, and Gary did their part. They treated me with the same respect they afforded any professional golfer, and they played just as hard against me when I was paired with them as they would have if they were paired together. And that's the way I want it.

Some thoughts on other golfers: Lee Trevino has become known for his nonstop talking and sense of humor, but that man has more competitive fire in him than practically everyone else put together. For him, and for Chi Chi, who is another world-class joker, the talking is the release that allows them to stay calm and collected out there.

Trevino doesn't talk about it much, but he went through some of his own hell when he broke into this game. He changed his shoes in the car more than a few times because he wasn't allowed into the clubhouse door because of his color, and he keeps some of that anger deep down inside. Contrary to his public image, he's an intensely private man. You never see him at the cocktail parties or pro-am parties, nor does he ever go out to dinner with the other players or pal around. He's all business out there, and joking is part of the way he plays.

He is also probably the most gifted golfer that any of us is likely to see for quite some time. The man can hit every shot in the book with that flat swing of his, and his chipping is three steps above anyone else's. He didn't win $1.2 million in his first year on the Senior Tour because he was lucky. The guy can just flat out play the game.

I feel at times that I've been competing against Don January, Miller Barber, Gene Littler, and Mike Souchak ever since I was old enough to walk. They're fine men, all, and have been good friends and good competitors through the years. In various combinations we've pushed each other through more tournaments than any of us care to remember.

Dave Hill and I became fast friends in 1966 when we went down to PGA National in Florida for the PGA Team Championships. Neither of us had a partner when we got there, and I saw him sitting around looking forlorn because nobody had picked him to play. I went up to him and said let's go, and we became a team. We shot 65/68/65/66 and could have won it if we hadn't messed up on the last two holes on Saturday and Sunday. We've been teaming up together ever since.

The same goes for me and Roberto De Vicenzo, my teammate at the annual Legends of Golf tournament. We play with the old guys, the over sixties, and despite the fact that I turned 69 in 1991 and Roberto turned 70, we've won it three out of the last four years. See, our secret is that we don't feel that we're really that old, so we play younger. Those 60-year-olds don't stand a chance.

I have many fine memories from golf, both on and off the golf course. I've seen hundreds of players come and go and have witnessed golf careers that rose to great heights or plunged into failure. The guys whom I'm playing with now on the Senior Tour have hung in there year after year for decades, playing at a level that few athletes can match in any sport. They are my opponents and my competition for prize money and standing, but most of all they are my friends. My hat is off to them, and tonight I'll light a cigar in their honor!

CHAPTER 19

End of the Road

I knew that I wasn't going to play on the PGA Tour forever. In 1971 I started to think about what I would do when I couldn't play competitively any more. I began to put out feelers for the kinds of things I might be able to do after my playing days were over. I wanted to stay in golf in some capacity, but I found out the hard way that there weren't any more golf opportunities for a black man than there had been when I began to play. The same doors that I had worked so hard to push open were about to swing back shut in my face.

If I had a wish in those days, it was that I could keep on playing forever. It seemed like I had just learned how to win and how to enjoy myself in my profession when my game went into decline and I found myself too old to respond. In 1971 I won a small satellite tournament called the Sea Pines Open at Hilton Head, South Carolina, but after that the pickings got awfully slim. I turned 50 in 1972, and although I was still fit and strong, it got harder to keep my game razor sharp through a four-day tournament. By 1973 I was spending more money on travel expenses than I made in prize money, and I knew that I couldn't continue that way for long.

The game of golf itself was going through some changes that didn't make things any easier for the older guys like me. For one

190

thing, there was a whole army of talented young white guys who had come straight out of college to join the tour, and those kids could play. Guys like Hale Irwin, Tom Weiskopf, Tom Watson, and Johnny Miller pushed the older fellows for their share of the pie from practically the minute they turned pro.

The financial structure of the game changed in the early seventies too, making it harder for me to hang on. The purses were bigger than ever, particularly for the winners. It was no longer enough to finish consistently among the top 25 to 40 every week. If you didn't vie for the lead at least a few times during the year, you'd finish way down in the prize money. A case in point for me was the midsummer tournament at Westchester in 1974, where Johnny Miller took home the winning check of $50,000. I finished about 15th and made $494.

As I saw my opportunities to play on the tour slipping away, I mourned more than ever those years that I'd lost. I had given away more than a dozen years to Jim Crow, and I wanted them back. I didn't mind playing against guys who were 15, 20, 25 years younger than I. I'd gotten used to that. In my mind I was a 40-year-old man who could still compete against the 25-year-olds, but my body thought differently.

I couldn't tack those dozen years onto the back end of my career. There wasn't a jury that could order me exempt from qualifying because my career had started so late. That wall of finishing among the top 60 money winners every year loomed ever larger and became increasingly more difficult to climb as the seventies wore on.

Where had all my time gone? They had finally let me play full time in 1961, but I figure that it wasn't until 1966 that I really broke in all over the country and could settle down to lead a reasonably normal life as a touring professional. Some golfers enjoy careers of 20 to 25 years; my real career didn't last 10 years. Of all the things I lost during those years of waiting, time was the most precious.

In 1974 Johnny Miller broke loose and won a huge number of tournaments. He broke the record for prize money that year, raking in $353,000, which was more than I had earned in my

entire career. By that year the list of young stars included Lanny
Wadkins; Tom Kite; Ed Sneed; and Ben Crenshaw, who came out
of college in Texas with as smooth and confident a game as I had
seen since Arnold Palmer broke in. You just knew that with his
skills and his level head, he was going to be a successful
professional.

Kite and Crenshaw were the new breed of golf professional,
and their success coincided with the imminent extinction of black
golfers on the tour. The new players had come up through
colleges where they were given full scholarships to play golf and
spent years perfecting their games. They played dozens of
tournaments against stiff competition, learned their way around
top golf courses, and had sponsors who were more than eager
to back them once they'd graduated. When they turned pro they
knew a lot of things about playing golf that I never knew at their
age. They hit the ground running and were successful right away.

Contrast that to a black kid growing up at the same time in
the late sixties. He not only didn't have the opportunities to learn
the game as a child, but he couldn't even caddy any more because
electric carts had replaced the need for caddies on most courses.
He still had little or no access to the game outside of crowded
public courses, and even if he was pretty good, there was no way
in hell that he was going to get a college scholarship to play golf.

The only way a black could make it was if he were a miracle,
like Calvin Peete, who never touched a golf club until he was
23 years old. And miracles don't happen very often. I've got
nothing against Tom Kite or Ben Crenshaw or Greg Norman or
any other white golfer. They had the sense and the skill to take
what was offered them and make the most of it. I just wish that
the golf establishment had made some of those opportunities
available to everybody.

Two nice things happened to me in 1974, which was my last
year on the tour. In April I was honored by the Cleveland Chapter
of the National Negro Golf Association, which wanted to make
a point on my behalf. They scheduled a testimonial dinner for
me at the Cleveland Plaza Hotel during the weekend of the Masters
tournament, and they invited many of the top touring profes-

sionals to attend. Of course most of the top golfers were already headed to the Masters. The point of the evening was that I should have been there too.

A lot of players sent letters and telegrams on my behalf. "The only sad thing about Charlie's career is that no one really will ever know how great he could have been had he had a chance to play on the PGA when he was in his prime and at his best," wrote Chi Chi Rodriguez to Clarence Rogers, the Cleveland attorney who chaired the testimonial. Chi Chi also enclosed a check for $125 "for ten tickets I would appreciate your giving to ten black caddies."

Arnold Palmer wrote, "By your perseverance and talent you have added an extra dimension to tournament golf that was long overdue. . . .The game is much the better for this." Jack Nicklaus sent a telegram, and more letters came in from Lee Elder, Tom Weiskopf, and even the White House, which sent acknowledgments from Vice President Gerald Ford and President Nixon. "The new rise to national prominence of black golfers is in large part due to your pioneering efforts," wrote the president. "I welcome this opportunity to congratulate you on your consistently fine play and exemplary conduct during all your years on the pro golf circuit."

I rather doubt that Augusta National paid much attention to any of that, or to the newspaper articles that came out about me being in Cleveland and not in Georgia that week. The story of how the Masters continued to exclude blacks had become old news by that time anyway. The press and even the government had been trying to open the Masters for years, to no avail.

All that changed, however, a few months later when Lee Elder won the Monsanto Open in Pensacola, his first win on the tour. The next day the Masters announced that he'd receive an invitation for the 1975 tournament. That was the second good thing that happened.

I played at Pensacola that year and finished in 11th place, but I couldn't have been happier if I had shot straight 67s. I was so proud of Lee and the way he had come through. He knew that the only way a black man was going to get into Augusta was to win a tournament, and he had dedicated himself to that task. I was also tickled that his win came in a city where less than 10 years earlier I'd had to eat in the locker room with Bob Rosburg because they wouldn't let me in the restaurant. Things changed slowly, but they did change.

I needed more than a testimonial dinner that year. I needed a job. As 1974 wore on, I saw that I was headed for a low finish on the money list and I'd be doing something else for a living the following year. It was great that the National Negro Golf Association had seen fit to honor me, but golf was and still is a white game, and nobody in the white golf establishment seemed too intent on capitalizing on my imminent retirement.

I put out feelers for a job at the golf courses in Los Angeles, where I had lived for so many years and gotten a hero's welcome when I won the open. I talked to the powers that be at Western Avenue, which had practically been my home course for 20 years, and at Rancho Park, where I had won the tournament. They politely told me that there were no openings, which wasn't such a big surprise. Even then, they didn't have any black golf professionals or assistants. In fact, at the two dozen public courses in the city, none had a black on the professional staff. I obviously wasn't going to become the first.

I asked around in all of the cities that we played on the tour. I would have done practically anything—give lessons, run the golf shop, appear at outings as a kind of public relations man and celebrity golfer. One year I talked to the Coors Brewing Company about such a position. At that time they held upwards of 10 tournaments a year for all of their customers and regional salespeople, and they wanted a name professional who would go out and play in them and keep the top clients happy. I didn't get that job either.

I talked to country clubs, private clubs, public golf courses — all with the same results. I needed a job to feed my family, and suddenly golf had nothing to offer me. It was more than discouraging. It made me feel that all I had done to open the game for blacks hadn't been enough. Here I was, the recognized pioneer of my race, and even I couldn't get a job. Where did that leave another black man who loved the game but didn't even have the qualifications I had? It sure didn't look like golf had opened up much more than to allow a few top black men to play the tour.

When I needed golf to do something back for me I realized that it was the same old story. The day had finally come when Charlie Sifford couldn't play golf on the tour any more, and they were going to let me slip away. It had just been a matter of time before I would disappear from the game with hardly a trace, and maybe a lot of people in the golf establishment had been waiting for this moment for 13 years, when I stood up against the Caucasian clause and put the heat on the PGA.

At first I couldn't believe that there was no place left for me in the game, and then I got mad as hell. I knew in my heart that I had contributed a great deal to golf, but apparently it wasn't enough to sway even one country club or the PGA or a big corporate sponsor. They all were finally rid of the angry, old black man who had hollered long and loud about his rights to play.

The year ended, and sure enough, I didn't finish high enough on the money list. The only way that I could enter golf tournaments in 1975 was to either receive an exemption directly from the tournament sponsor or go out on Monday and play a round against all of the local guys and the club pros and the wanna-bes for one of the two or three open spots.

I must be an eternal optimist, because I thought that the tournaments would give me a break and issue me sponsor exemptions. After all, I had been returning year after year to those places and always had cordial relations with the sponsors and the tournament committees. I let it be known at the outset that I'd like to continue playing, and I found out right away where I stood. I wasn't invited to either the Crosby or the Palm Springs tournaments at the beginning of the year, and I wasn't going to go around the country begging for an exemption and being turned down. Likewise, nobody came looking for me that year to ask me to play in their tournament.

The only way I could enter was if I qualified on Monday morning. I got into a couple of tournaments that way and then said the hell with that. I was too old to be chasing around the country trying to qualify like a 20-year-old rookie. A scant six years after I had been on top of the golf world by winning the L.A. Open, I was out of the game. My total tour earnings were $341,345 for a lifetime of work.

In the middle of 1975 a job in golf finally did present itself, and, in a kind of reverse discrimination scenario, I got it because of my race. In the suburbs of Cleveland, Ohio, there were two private country clubs that had been closed to blacks and Jews for a number of years. As I understand it, these clubs got on the wrong side of politics when they refused admission to Ohio senator Howard Metzenbaum because he is Jewish. He got so mad about it that he took the clubs to court and forced them to become public golf courses.

One of the clubs, the Sleepy Hollow Country Club in Brecksville, Ohio, needed to change their all-white, all-Gentile image quickly when they were forced to go public. They decided to hire a black professional to help attract blacks to the course. Up to then, no blacks had ever been allowed near the place, and there was a stigma that had to be broken down if the club was to survive. Through my friend Clarence Rogers, the attorney who set up my testimonial dinner, I was offered the position.

To be honest, Cleveland was about the last place I wanted to move to. I liked living in California, and my wife and sons were happy there. We hadn't lived in cold weather for over 15 years and had no desire to move to a place where the wind howled for three months out of the year. Furthermore, the job that they offered me wasn't exactly a bonanza. Although many club professional jobs at country clubs and big courses offer a touring professional a big salary and a cut of what he sells in the pro shop, Sleepy Hollow didn't have the budget or the means to pay for my experience. I didn't go in as a celebrity professional, but as a small-time businessman.

They offered me a straight commission deal where the only money I could make was off the sale of golf paraphernalia in the pro shop, cart rentals, and lessons. There was no salary, no perks, and I had to put up the money for the inventory myself. I was basically offered the right to lease the pro shop and the cart concession, and my money would only come from the profits of those two operations.

What choice did I have? Nothing else was coming my way, and I had to do something to make money for my family. We packed up and left our friends and home in L.A. for a place where we hardly knew anybody. Neither I nor Rose, who came to work with me in the pro shop, were business people, yet we had to figure out how to run a pro shop profitably. For the next 13 years we were stuck in little Brecksville, and I think they were among the most difficult years of my life.

From March through November we were slaves to that golf course. We opened at six in the morning and stayed open until eight at night or later, depending on the time of year. Whatever the season was, we could count on a line of people waiting to get on the golf course an hour before sunrise and the last stragglers bringing in the carts a half hour after it was totally dark outside. We had a few people working for us, but it was always tough to find good people who would keep the job for long. Man, I didn't get into golf to be an administrator, but that's what I became.

I tried to give lessons, which was an utterly frustrating experience. People would come in there who had never touched a golf club in their life and didn't know if they swung right- or left-handed, and they expected me to teach them how to play in an hour's time. They would sign up for lessons and not show up, or quit after one or two times.

We stocked everything in the pro shop from balls and gloves to new sets of clubs. It cost us over $25,000 to bring in the inventory, and then we found out that most people shopped down the street at the discount golf shop. We couldn't afford to buy carts, so we leased them from the cart company in exchange for part of our profits. It was a very, very tough way to make a living, but Rose and I stuck with it.

The hardest thing for me was to be nice all the time. I had made my living out of concentrating and taking golf very seriously, and now I was supposed to joke around and pretend that golf didn't mean anything to me. I had to be nice to the jokers

who came by at 6 PM and rented carts, which meant that I would
still be waiting after dark for them to come back. I had to be nice
to the people who complained to me about not getting the tee
time they wanted, even though we had nothing to do with
reservations or scheduling, and I had to be nice when people
bitched about spending $20 for one golf lesson, "and I still don't
know how to play golf!" I have a lot of patience, but those people
practically wore me out.

I played as much as I could. Every winter I went down to
Florida and qualified for a couple of satellite PGA tournaments.
In the summer I competed in the Ohio tournaments and qualified
for the U.S. Open. I was really just playing for the fun of it,
because I knew that realistically I didn't have a chance for a high
finish if I only played in a few PGA tournaments all year. I guess
I hoped that somebody would notice me out there and offer me
a job that would take us out of Sleepy Hollow to a better and
more lucrative place.

I had a few golfing tricks left up my sleeve. At one tournament
in Ohio for local pros they were offering the use of a brand-new
Chevy for a year if a golfer shot a hole-in-one on the 17th hole.
I was the first golfer on that particular tee on the first day of the
tournament, and I promptly put a 6-iron into the cup for my sixth
career ace. It reminded me of the days when I had to play well
at the Buick Open in order to win the use of a free car for another
year. Man, that was some pressure.

Even when I was by all intents and purposes out of the pro
game, the PGA found ways to throw me. In 1975 they held a
tournament called the PGA Seniors Championship for guys like
me who had played the tour and were over 50. It was a kind
of precursor to today's senior tour, but it was only one tournament that they held in Orlando. I think they expected Sam Snead
or Tommy Bolt to win the thing and give the PGA lots of good
publicity, but I crossed them up and won it in a playoff.

But the PGA had a real curve to throw me. They had a deal
going that whoever won the seniors championship would play
the winner of the British Senior Championship in a one-on-one,
match-play tournament. I was to play a guy named Kel Nagle in

a 36-hole match that was to be contested on an American course of the PGA's choice.

This is something that I will never, ever understand, nor will I ever forgive the PGA. They chose a country club course called Bideawee in Portsmouth, Virginia, where Chandler Harper was the pro. Kel Nagle and I were to play two rounds in one day, winner take all.

I drove down to the course with my friend Charles Ashley from Cleveland. I had never been there before, and I was surprised to see that the course was located right in the middle of a black section of town. Inside the gates it looked like any white country club and I didn't think anything about it. But I should have known something was up because somebody mentioned that the blacks didn't even caddy at Bideawee and I didn't stop to ask why.

Kel Nagle and I teed off and played the first 18 holes and he beat me one up. We were to stop for lunch and then go out and play the final 18 for the championship. We walked into the country club for lunch and everybody was looking at me funny. My friend Charles came up to me and said that he'd just met the mayor of Portsmouth, a member of the club, who had told him that I was the first black man ever to play the course. They not only didn't have any black members, but they didn't even allow black caddies at Bideawee! Charles and I were about as welcome there as if we'd been mass murderers.

"I don't know why they brought Charlie down here to play," the mayor said, meaning the PGA.

I didn't know why either, and right then and there I started to raise hell. I found Chandler Harper and I asked him, "Chandler, explain something to me. Why did you have to accept this tournament here at your club when you knew that no blacks have ever played here and I would be so out of place?"

"Well, Charlie," he said, "I had nothing to do with it. The PGA suggested that you play the match here."

Now why on earth, of all the golf courses in the country that had opened to blacks or had been places where I'd played in the past, why would the PGA choose a segregated golf course in the middle of Virginia for me to play a match where I'd be representing the United States of America? Wouldn't it occur to them that I might be just a little uncomfortable in a place that practically had whites-only signs posted on every tee? I just didn't get it. I raised hell for that entire lunch break with the tournament representatives, and I considered not going out for the second round. But that wasn't my style. I went out and played the last 18 holes of the match and got beat one up again. When it was over I got in my car and drove out of there, so mad I couldn't see straight.

I have always believed that if you work hard and do your best, you'll get ahead in life. My father told me a long time ago that if you think you're right, then stand up and be counted. During my career on the PGA Tour, I tried as hard as I could and when things weren't right, I stood up and demanded to be counted. I showed that blacks belonged in the game and, given equal circumstances, could play golf just as well as whites. Through sheer persistence I opened doors that fine men like Teddy Rhodes and Bill Spiller couldn't budge.

I think I did golf a great service, but the PGA seemed to think otherwise. Instead of lauding my accomplishments and bringing me into the fold as a champion of the game, they tried to humiliate me and keep me out of golf.

The battle wasn't over. When the PGA saw that they could make good money from their senior stars, I found myself right back where I had started from in 1947 — pushing to get into a game that didn't want me. Round two was about to begin with the Senior PGA Tour in what were supposed to be the enlightened eighties. But it was the same old discrimination in a shiny new suit. My fight for equal opportunity in golf wasn't over. In fact, the next few years would see more clashes than ever with the golf establishment, with me in the middle.

You know, I would have been more than happy with a peaceful retirement where I could make a few dollars and enjoy playing and receive some recognition for what I'd accomplished in golf. But fighting back is a lifelong occupation, and I wasn't to have any peace. At 58 years old I'd have to go out and start all over again. It wasn't right, it wasn't fair, but then, what had been right and fair in my career to that point?

CHAPTER 20

No Room for a Legend

I'm an avid sports fan. Over the years I've watched as intently as anyone else the rise of sports like boxing, football, and basketball. I keep an eye on baseball, too, but I like boxing, football, and basketball the best. I've seen how those three sports have pulled themselves up over the last 20 years and become an important part of American life. Well, maybe not boxing, although the big stars like Larry Holmes and Marvin Hagler and Sugar Ray Leonard certainly captured the attention of the public during their spectacular careers.

If you want to see a sport that should be a model for all of professional athletics, look at basketball, which was on the decline in the sixties and was literally pulled up into the stratosphere by an aggressive commissioner, a healthy relationship between players and management, and a clean image. It wasn't so long ago when basketball had a big problem. It was too black. It was played in inner-city arenas, and its best players were black men.

The NBA solved that problem by doing two things extremely well: they came down hard on the issue of drug use, which was the biggest potential threat to the sport, and they made stars out of deserving black ballplayers like Julius Erving, Kareem Abdul-Jabbar, and Michael Jordan. The stars got the huge dollars and the national celebrity that they deserved and the sport used some of its newfound profits to take care of the average ballplayers, giving them the highest minimum salary in sports.

Basketball saw that it had to be progressive in the seventies to succeed. At that time, however, golf got meaner than it had ever been. When golf had the opportunity, with the advent of the Senior PGA Tour, to really straighten itself out and clear up its biggest problems — the elitism, the polarization between whites and blacks, the disparity between stars and average players — golf did what it had always done. It ignored the moral stance and went for the cash.

If there was ever a doubt that professional golf was motivated solely by greed and the almighty buck, that doubt should have been burst like an old balloon when they set up the Senior Tour. You might have given the game the benefit of the doubt in the forties and fifties when I was coming up. After all, it was a game that had come out of a long tradition of elitism and segregation, a game played almost exclusively in country clubs by people with means. Maybe it came as a surprise when blacks took up the game and liked it, and we couldn't expect the old rules to break down quickly just because of issues like legality and morality.

But you'd think that by the midseventies, golf would have gotten itself ready to face the modern world. And if it had taken a long look at itself and thought about what it needed to do to truly become a sport for all Americans, it could have begun right there with the senior tour.

Here's what I'm talking about. In 1978 a country club in Austin, Texas, called Onion Creek had a great concept for a golf tournament. They had seen that events like the PGA Seniors Championship, the annual tournament that I had won in 1975, were popular and that the public and the media liked to see the old stars go out and compete.

Onion Creek decided to gather all of the great "legends" of the game and hold a 54-hole tournament called the Legends of Golf. Golfers over 50 would team up in twosomes and play an exciting best-ball format that would keep scores low and make for a unique competition.

The club put together a fat purse of $400,000 and sought out name professionals who were 50 and older. They hoped to get all of the guys who had won the major tournaments: former champions of the Masters, U.S. Open, British Open, and PGA Championship. They planned to attract the Sam Sneads, Art Walls, Tommy Bolts, and Ben Hogans. Then they would round out the field by inviting other pros who had been in the limelight during their PGA careers. With that kind of purse, they figured correctly, they could lure a whole bunch of top over-50 players.

Did you happen to catch a key word in there? Invitation. The Legends of Golf was to be an invitational tournament, where they could invite anyone they pleased and also not invite anyone they didn't like.

Guess who they didn't invite. I wasn't legend enough to be asked to play in the Legends of Golf in 1978. They invited players who hadn't won as many golf tournaments as I had won and hadn't finished as high on the all-time money list as I had finished. There were many slots open for players who hadn't won a major championship, and I didn't get any of them.

Bob Toski, for example, was invited. When a newspaper reporter from Cleveland called the Legends director, he was told that Toski was invited "because of the contributions he has made to golf." I don't doubt that Bob Toski has made contributions to the game, but what about Charlie Sifford?

I suddenly got that old creepy feeling that I had felt before I got my approved tournament player's card in 1960. Here was a fat golf tournament for which I was obviously qualified but wasn't allowed to play. They had set up a qualification system that was unfair to me, since I was never allowed to play in the Masters and had limited access to the other championships, and then went out of their way to ignore me when they handpicked players to round out the field.

I thought I had gotten past all that crap 20 years earlier, but it was coming back. And nobody at the PGA did anything about it. I got the same kind of responses that Ted Rhodes got in the forties: "Sorry, but they didn't invite you and there's nothing we can do about it."

Then the golf tournament added insult to injury by stating publicly that I wasn't qualified to play in their tournament. In order to justify their decision not to invite me, they had to discredit me. Fred Raphael, the Legends director, told the reporter from Cleveland, "They compare Charlie to Jackie Robinson. Heck, Jackie was a great player. They aren't comparable. Charlie isn't in any of the golf halls of fame. The rules for entry have not been changed."

I couldn't believe it. Suddenly I was the bad guy for speaking up and asking why I wasn't invited to a golf tournament. I didn't call them names or go down there waving a banner. I didn't even sue them, although I probably had grounds to do so. When the reporters started calling them up, asking why I wasn't invited, they made me out to be some crackpot who didn't have the slightest qualification for a tournament with the top senior pros. And this was after I had won the 1975 PGA Senior Championship against most of the guys who were entered in that Legends.

Damn, it made me furious, and it also made me sick to my stomach. I was 56 years old, and I didn't want to carry the banner any longer. I had had enough of breaking down the walls of golf. I just wanted to enjoy the game and continue to play as long as God allowed me to have the strength to swing a club. After a few years off the circuit, I missed those matches against Art Wall and Don January. I wasn't trying to force the issue for blacks to get into the game; I just wanted to be allowed to play.

You might say, as the Legends people did, that it was their tournament and they could set it up any way they wanted. It was my sour grapes that I hadn't won the damn U.S. Open and didn't automatically qualify. But that doesn't cut it. Golf has always had an arbitrary standard that it followed to determine selection at its tournaments and on its tour, and that standard was the money list. When I finished playing in 1975 I was among the top 20 money winners on the tour, and when the Legends tournament started I was among the top 20 money winners of the golfers over 50 years old. The PGA should have insisted that its standard be followed if the Legends was going to be a recognized tournament.

It's like holding an NBA all-star game and saying that the players won't be chosen by the amount of points and rebounds they've had, but by how many NBA championships they've won. Call it the Legends of the NBA, but don't invite Dominique Wilkins or Karl Malone to play.

What made things worse as far as I was concerned was that tournaments like the Legends changed their eligibility requirements to gloss over complaints like mine. It made their requirements seem awfully arbitrary when, a year after the first tournament, they amended their qualification list to include previous members of the Ryder Cup team. Of course, I was never on that team — another place where team members were chosen both by points standing and special invitation — and I don't doubt that the Legends knew that.

I raised hell about the Legends for four years before they finally let me in. At one point I figured that it would be another Masters that I'd never be allowed to play, and I felt my advocacy would only serve to open things up for guys like Lee Elder and Jim Dent when they turned 50. It was a role that I knew all too well. If that was my lot in life, I'd accept it, but I never understood why it had to be that way.

What was the real reason that I had been overlooked by the Legends? You never know in golf, but I suspect that the tournament people got together with the sponsors and went over the whole list of available players. They handpicked the ones whom they thought were the most popular and the most likely to sell tickets. They had a field of, I don't know, 50 or more golfers, and every one of them was picked not by his standing in the game but by the strength of his "legend" and his recognition factor among fans.

When my name comes up on those kind of lists, I'm pretty sure that the first reactions by the tournament and the sponsor go something like this: "Who's Charlie Sifford?"

"He's the black guy. The one who made so much trouble with the PGA that they had to let him onto the tour."

"Well we don't need any trouble at our tournament. Let's forget about him."

Where was the PGA to defend the rights of its players? They were probably at the next chair, nodding their heads, because they didn't want any trouble either, and I had been labeled a troublemaker. The PGA isn't a players' union, they'd tell you. They don't have any control over who does and doesn't get picked. But in governing our sport, how could they let tournaments and sponsors dictate how its competitors are chosen? It just doesn't seem right to me.

Sure, I complained about it. I didn't get into the first Legends, or the second. Every year like clockwork my phone would ring and reporters would ask me why I wasn't playing in Austin that week. My answer was that I didn't have any idea why and that I thought it was unfair. They'd run the story in their newspaper and there I was again, Charlie Sifford, the bitter black man. And every year the Legends would respond by saying that I had no business in their golf tournament.

They finally gave up justifying their system by once again changing the rules. In 1981 the Legends announced that they'd invite past winners of the PGA Seniors Championship, and suddenly I was a Legend of Golf. Why they couldn't have done that in the first place, I'll never know. I teamed up with Mike Souchak and played the tournament, won a few dollars, and enjoyed myself.

I've gone back to the Legends practically every year since, and in fact Roberto de Vicenzo and I have won the Legendary Champions portion of the tournament for players over 60 in three of the last four years. I have a great time, and I enjoy the team format immensely. I've never had any problems playing there, and there's no reason why I should have a problem. It's just another game of golf.

I think I started getting that bitterness tag when the problems with the Legends came up. I know that I had already been branded a troublemaker by the PGA because of all I'd fought against over the years, and now it was easy to label me a bitter old man. I don't think I've ever been bitter. I'm thrilled with the opportunities that golf has provided me, but I know that I've had to stand up and fight every step of the way. I think it's made me wary of what really goes on behind the scenes.

Man, when the senior tour began in 1980, I was absolutely thrilled. It started out for players over 55 years old, and there I was, 58 and playing against guys my own age for the first time in my career. It was wonderful to see that fans would still come out to watch us play, and that guys like me and Roberto and Ted Kroll could still put that charge of excitement into a gallery.

I celebrated the beginning of senior golf by finishing third at the U.S. Senior Open at Winged Foot behind Roberto and Bill Campbell, and sixth at the Atlantic City Senior International, where I shot a 63 on the last day. I then won the Suntree Classic in Melbourne, Florida.

That win was just as thrilling for me as my victory at the L.A. Open. There I was on the last day of a four-day tournament with a newfound hot putter and a shot at the lead. I blew past Don January with five birdies in a row, beginning on the fifth hole, and then put him out with another birdie on 13. Boy, that was fun, and it didn't hurt any when they handed me the winner's check of $20,000.

When the senior tour looked like it might be around to stay, the PGA changed the rules again and made the age limit 50 years old instead of 55. Somebody looked at a roster of players and realized that if they made it 50, guys like Arnold Palmer, Billy Casper, Gene Littler, and Miller Barber would come out sooner rather than later. It suddenly meant that I was giving away the years again to those younger guys, but that was okay. I was used to it.

Golf became fun again on the senior tour. It was challenging, it was competitive, and it was fun. I still had my job at Sleepy Hollow to return to if I needed it, and that freed me up to play with as much confidence and security as I ever had. In a way the senior tour has given me back some of those years that I lost, and I thank God for it. I've made more money and had a better time in the last 10 years than I ever had on the regular tour.

I got sick in 1981 and didn't play too well or too often, but I still made enough money to finish among the top seniors. And then things really got great. Over the next three years I made nearly $180,000 on the senior tour, and in 1985 I had my best season ever. I made $104,294 in prize money at the age of 63. All told, I've earned over $800,000 on the senior tour, which is nearly triple what I made on the regular tour. In 1990 I reached a milestone that few golfers can claim: I went over a million dollars in combined official earnings at golf.

For that I am both proud and grateful. Who would have thought so many years ago when I was lugging bags at the country club in Charlotte, North Carolina, that the son of a laborer could go so far in his chosen field? I had picked a tough occupation, but I had stuck with it and stayed healthy long enough to reap the benefits.

Rose and I stayed in Cleveland through the 1988 season and then we left Sleepy Hollow for a brand-new home in a fashionable suburb of Houston, where I'm a member of the Deerwood Country Club. I got a very nice endorsement deal from Toyota over the last few years, and I'm still playing as well as anybody my age in the whole country.

Many of the guys on the senior tour describe it as a second life and a rejuvenation. I promise you that nobody benefited more or appreciated the new tour more than I did. It gave me the chance to play and to continue to show that I could do as well on the golf course as anybody my age. It gave many black players new opportunities to become part of the game. Jim Dent has excelled on the senior tour, as has Charles Owens, who is a remarkable athlete despite severely damaged knees. Lee Elder turned 50 in 1984 and promptly won two tournaments, and my old pals and traveling companions Rafe Botts and Pete Brown play at many tournaments during the year.

It would all have been practically perfect if they gave us the same opportunities that they give the white players. And if I hadn't had to threaten to sue for equal rights on two different occasions. As I was to learn, the Legends of Golf wasn't the last tournament that didn't think enough of me to invite me. When the same thing came up again a couple of years later, I finally stopped being a nice guy about it. I found a lawyer. As much opportunity as there was on the senior tour, there still seemed to be a line drawn that I couldn't cross because I was black. At 65 years old, I got tired of asking nicely and being patient. I thought it was high time I demanded to be treated equally.

CHAPTER 21

Suing to Play

Three more times in the eighties golf tried to turn its back on me and I had to resort to legal pressure to be allowed to play. It happened at different times during the decade, which goes to show how things never really change much over the years.

The first instance was the Vintage Tournament at Indian Wells, California, on a course that was redesigned by George and Tom Fazio in 1980. George, you will recall, was my old friend, who had sold me my first car so many years earlier. He has designed a number of excellent golf courses, and the Vintage was reported to be a beauty. They officially opened the course in March of 1981 with a $300,000 seniors tournament.

Just like the Legends, the Vintage planned to pull in the top senior tour players and get itself some national recognition with a first-class tournament attended by all of the older stars of golf. Getting a professional tournament is quite a plum for any golf course, and for a new course it can practically ensure its success. The excitement and activity that a major golf tournament brings to a place can be used by the sales and marketing people for years to put a development over the top. It suddenly becomes more than a golf course in the eyes of the wealthy public who come to buy memberships or homes at the golf course. It becomes a place that has captured a bit of golf history. If it's an annual tournament, it gives the community a repeating jolt of excitement and attention.

Consequently, holding a major golf tournament becomes an important part of the total marketing plan for any golf course that can put up the money and capture a slot on the schedule of the regular or Senior PGA Tour. It is a resource that has to be managed carefully to maximize the return on the investment. When business gets involved to that extent, the club becomes very careful about how the tournament is run.

Just like the Legends in its early years, the Vintage wanted to control exactly who came to their fancy new golf tournament. They made the tournament an invitational, with restricted entry. Once again, I didn't qualify for an automatic invitation, and once again I didn't get a special sponsor's invitation to play.

It was much the same story as before. By that time I had won at Suntree, finished high on the senior money list, and was still among the top 20 all-time money winners among the seniors. Yet none of that mattered to the Vintage. I somehow wasn't a marketable enough name for them and their participants, and I was denied the right to play, despite the fact that they billed themselves as a Senior PGA Tournament. Typically, the Senior PGA Tour didn't say a thing about it.

It made me mad that all of my fellow pros were playing for all of that loot without me, and it made me furious that the tournament was being held in the state of California. Hell, 20 years earlier I had received protection straight from the attorney general of California against discriminatory golf tournaments in the state. We had now come full circle with a tournament for which I was qualified but wasn't allowed to enter.

I didn't do anything about it the first year, but when they didn't invite me to the Vintage again in 1982, I went straight to the office of Attorney General John Van De Kamp and filed a complaint. The attorney general's office began an investigation, and for the first time I was contacted by the Vintage.

They didn't call to invite me, though. They wrote to tell me to stop pressuring and threatening them. A letter from Mick Humphries, the director of the tournament, said, "Those invitations that are discretionary are given to persons who show a sincere interest in assisting us in our growth. You have certainly not gone out of your way to do that and future consideration of you as an invited player will be on that basis and not as a result of pressure tactics.''

I'm not quite sure how I was supposed to assist their growth when I wasn't allowed to play in their tournament, and I wonder how much thought the Vintage gave to my personal growth when it excluded me from the right to earn my living at its golf tournament. Besides, it wasn't my job to make the tournament grow. I'm a golfer, not a marketing consultant, and if they wanted to put on a professional tournament to make the golf course look good, than they should have invited qualified professional golfers whether they liked them or not.

I found out later that as far as the Vintage was concerned I didn't get along with amateurs, and therefore I wasn't desirable for the tournament. Like most events on the Senior PGA Tour, the Vintage had several days of pro-am play during the professional event, and for some reason they thought that their amateurs were different and less likely to get along with a black man than all of the other amateurs I played with on the rest of the circuit.

Hell, I had been playing pro-ams for 30 years. I never had a problem with them when I played the Hope and Crosby tournaments in California for so many years. I'm not saying that I'm all smiles and chatter when I'm out there playing with amateurs, because that's not who I am or how I approach the game of golf. But neither am I rude or arrogant, and you can't say that about every professional golfer. I think maybe the Vintage thought its amateurs would be offended by being paired with a black man and that rather than face any potential grief over it, they simply excluded me. It was a standard corporate decision that didn't have anything to do with what was fair or what my accomplishments had been.

Right is right, and the attorney general saw it my way, just as Stanley Mosk had seen it my way in 1960. The state of California threatened to close down the Vintage for discriminatory practices, and in the middle of 1984, just weeks before the tournament, they completed a memorandum of understanding with the Vintage which expanded the criteria for choosing players.

I still didn't receive an invitation to play, despite the fact that the Vintage became a recognized stop on the Senior PGA Tour that year. They should have been following the PGA's guidelines for qualifying, but they didn't. It wasn't until the following winter, when the then California assemblyman Art Agnos got involved and put more pressure on the Tournament, that I was given an invitation to play the Vintage.

At that time Deane Beman, the commissioner of the PGA and the Senior PGA Tour, swore to me that he would force tournaments to uphold the 20/20 rule of selecting players who either fell within the top 20 all-time money list or the top 20 from the previous senior tour season. But I don't know why he waited so long, and I'm not even sure what he could have done had the Vintage not gone along with his ruling.

By the way, do you know why Deane Beman finally got around to forcing the Vintage's hand? Do you suppose it was because he felt strongly that a PGA member was being denied equal rights to play? Could be, but a funny coincidence was that the television show "60 Minutes" had gotten wind of the story and wanted to interview me. It was while I was deciding whether or not to spill the beans on national TV that I got a call from Deane begging me to not say a word and everything would be fixed. And it was.

It seems to me that sponsors have far too much power over the golf circuit on matters such as eligibility. Yes, I know that the Senior PGA Tour couldn't operate without the big corporate sponsors and the broadcasting fees, but I don't think that should give them the power to disregard a player's merits just because they don't like him personally. It was bad enough when I didn't get invitations and exemptions to tournaments based on what I'd done for the game. When I was qualified by means of my earnings and still didn't get into tournaments, it was downright discriminatory. Golf bends way too far to accommodate the wishes of its corporate sponsors, and I think that this attitude of raking in the dollars in the short term can only be destructive to the game in the long run.

Given all of the things that have happened to me in golf, this next one is so crazy that it's almost funny. But I can laugh about it only because I won after a long lawsuit. It amply illustrates how little protection a PGA player has if he crosses wires with a tournament.

It also shows that no Buick is safe from me when they put it up as a prize at a golf tournament. I'd been winning them since the midsixties, but this one was the toughest of them all to drive away.

This story could have happened to any guy on the tour, but it figures that it happened to me. Call it my destiny, but I always seem to get in the middle of situations in golf that aren't right, and then I have to fight like hell to make them right.

Okay, it's the first round of the 1986 Johnny Mathis Seniors Classic golf tournament at the Mountain Gate Country Club in Los Angeles. It's a nice day, and I begin play in the 10th group to start off on the 10th tee. We get to number 15, a par 3 that goes 168 yards, and I pull out my 5-iron and tee it up. Sitting alongside the tee is a brand-new Buick Riviera, which I assume is a prize for a hole in one. I promptly knock my ball into the hole for an ace, maybe the eighth of my career.

Great. I've won another Buick on the golf course. I continue to play the round and end up with a 73, which isn't too spectacular, but is okay. But when I get done, all of the media guys rush up to me and say that I won a $100,000 jackpot for the ace. My first thought is they're putting me on.

The story slowly comes together. Apparently, when the round of golf began that day the first guys who came to the 15th hole saw a sign announcing that the first player to shoot an ace would be rewarded with the Buick and a check for $100,000. The car was put up by Buick and the cash was to come from Fremont Insurance Group, a co-sponsor of the tournament.

Lots of players saw the sign. Not only that, the first groups of players were handed flyers at the tee that announced the prizes and said the competition would be in effect on Friday, Saturday, and Sunday. A similar flyer was posted in our locker room throughout the week. Lots of players swung for the ace before I got there. Nobody made it.

When my group got to the tee, the sign was partially torn and the volunteer wasn't there with the flyers. The sign that I saw was ripped in half, with something about the Buick being awarded for an ace still readable. We later learned that the tournament officials who were playing directly in front of my group nearly went crazy when they saw the sign. They claimed that they had talked about offering such a prize during the week but something had fallen out of place and they had withdrawn the offer. Somebody from their staff had put up the sign erroneously, they said. When they got to the tee they tore it down and figured that that canceled the promotion.

But it's not like nobody knew about the prize. They had talked it up to all of the golfers who came through in the morning. Furthermore, their PR person sent out a press release announcing the jackpot prize and the Buick. The *Los Angeles Times* reported the next day that they received the press release via fax two hours after the tournament had begun play.

But they still wouldn't pay me the money, and they even denied me the Buick at first. They said that the jackpot prize was off because they'd withdrawn the offer before I got there. In fact, the tournament promoter and a guy from the sponsoring insurance company had watched from the 16th tee as I aced the 15th, only minutes after they'd torn down the sign.

The players all felt that I'd been royally shafted, except for one curious exception. Jerry Barber made a point of writing to the sponsors and declaring that I shouldn't get the money because the sign had been torn down. I guess Jerry would have walked away quietly from the $100,000 if he were in my shoes.

I got on the phone and called Jerry Roisman, my attorney from Hartford, Connecticut, and told him to get the hell out to Los Angeles on the next plane.

Jerry arrived that night and we spent the next two days arguing with the tournament officials and the PGA people. I thought the PGA should intercede on my behalf, but they refused to even talk about it. They sided with the tournament. Damn, it made me furious. I had been shafted out of $100,000, everyone in Los Angeles knew about it thanks to the article in the *Los Angeles Times,* and the PGA wouldn't even investigate the issue. Whatever the tournament said, went.

It was clear that the tournament wouldn't budge and the senior PGA wouldn't intercede on my behalf, so we sued. We joined the tournament directors and the sponsors, including Buick, in the lawsuit, and I thought seriously about adding the senior PGA but didn't. They handed over the Buick before trial began, but the money took a while longer. We won a jury verdict in the United States District Court of California, and in February 1988, nearly two years after I had sunk the ace, I received a check for $100,934.00. The greatest irony of all is that it was the single largest paycheck I've ever gotten out of golf. It was like winning the L.A. Open five times, with a Buick thrown in to boot. Not bad for one swing of the club.

It was a little tough to believe that the senior PGA would ever intercede on my behalf against a tournament when the senior PGA itself was making rules internally that directly affected my ability to compete on an equal basis. It got so bad that I almost sued the organization itself in 1988 after they made a rule that would have literally taken hundreds of thousands of dollars out of my pocket.

The situation had to do with a kind of bonus package called the Super Seniors, which was established in 1987 by the Senior PGA Tour and sponsored by Vantage cigarettes. The Super Seniors is an incentive for golfers on the senior tour who are over 60 years old whereby at several tournaments during the year the older guys compete against each other for additional prize money.

For example, at a tournament like the GTE Northwest Classic in Seattle I would play three rounds of golf between Friday and Sunday in the regular senior tournament. All three of those rounds would count for prize money and standing in the regular tournament purse, but the first two rounds would also count toward this tournament within the tournament, the Super Seniors money. They'd compare all of the scores of the guys over 60 and award money based on best score. If two guys were tied at the end of Saturday's round, they'd play a sudden-death playoff to see who took home the first-prize pot.

Now this was a wonderful thing when they announced it at the beginning of the 1987 season. It meant that not only would I compete against the 50-year-old guys, but I'd frequently also be competing against the 60-year-old guys for the Super Seniors money, and I could beat most of them on any given week. With pots of $35,000 a week in that first year, I could stand to make as much as $100,000 extra from the Super Seniors purses over the course of a year.

To make things fair, the Senior PGA and RJR/Nabisco, the sponsor and parent company of Vantage, agreed to set up qualifying based on the all-time money list. Only 12 players were allowed to compete for the Super Seniors purse, and of those dozen they picked the top-10 guys over 60 who had earned the most money, another guy from a sponsor's exemption, and a final guy from the previous year's senior tour money list.

I qualified easily under those requirements, and by the middle of the first year I was near the top of the Super Seniors money list, with over $30,000. I was competing against guys like Roberto De Vicenzo, Joe Jimenez, and Art Wall, and it was a wonderful added battle that both the players and the fans loved. The galleries paid attention to which super seniors were leading each tournament, and the whole thing seemed to be a big success.

But then RJR/Nabisco and the Senior PGA abruptly changed their stance on the Super Seniors in the middle of the first season. Goaded by a Senior PGA advisory council that consisted of several players who had promotional connections with RJR, the tobacco company wrote to the Senior PGA at the end of August and said that it wasn't getting what it wanted out of the Super Seniors. RJR said that it wanted more "name" players competing for Super Seniors money, and it urged a change in qualification rules so that more "name" players would make the 12-player roster each week.

I don't want to name the "name" players because I don't think they're such big names to begin with. Suffice it to say that we're not talking about Arnold Palmer or Gene Littler or Don January here, none of whom were 60 in 1987. There aren't a whole lot of great players who could have won a number of tournaments and still not finish in the top 10 combined money earnings, so I don't know what their problem was.

In a meeting in September the Senior PGA rammed through the change. Beginning a month later super seniors would only be chosen based on the number of all-time wins that they had on the regular and senior tours. Since I only had four official wins to my credit, I was suddenly far down the list and stood the chance of not being able to enter future Super Seniors events if 10 other guys with more wins showed up at a given tournament.

Something was awfully fishy about the sudden rule change. Obviously nobody had stopped to consider that in the first place it wasn't fair to me to base eligibility on all-time wins. How on earth was I supposed to have as many wins to my credit as a guy who had been playing on the tour since he was 25 years old? Some of those guys had turned pro before 1950 and were winning their tournaments when I was still playing for $500 at the National Negro Opens. Most of the guys my own age had at least a 10-year head start in their opportunity to win tournaments.

Why go off the money list for eligibility? As far as I'm concerned, the reason was targeted directly at me and a couple of other guys. Apparently, some of the "name" golfers didn't like to see other names ahead of theirs in Super Seniors earnings, and they tried to tailor things so that we wouldn't have a chance to shoot for the top Super Seniors dollars.

At the time of that rule change, the top five Super Seniors money winners were a black man (myself); two Hispanics (Roberto De Vicenzo and Joe Jimenez, who had never played on the regular PGA Tour); a guy who had seen limited time on the regular tour (Mike Fetchick); and a guy who had won only twice on the regular tour (Howie Johnson). That must have rubbed some people the wrong way, and they bullied through a change to push us down.

Well, the hell with that. We were out there trying to make a living just like everybody else, and if we played better in the over-60 circle, so be it. We weren't in a popularity contest out there, we were playing professional golf. And if RJR/Nabisco was going to set up this minitour for guys over 60, then they should have had to stick to rules that were fair to everyone, whether or not they'd won the Masters or any other damn tournament.

I got together with my lawyers immediately after the ruling came down, and Howie Johnson and I joined forces to fight it. We heard from Bill Johnston, a member of the players advisory committee that recommended the change, that the rule had been pushed through by a group of players with close ties to RJR/Nabisco. They had refused to consider any suggestions that would have made the Super Seniors fair to everyone. Johnston ended up walking out of the meeting because the deck was so obviously stacked.

In December, our lawyers fired a warning shot over the Senior PGA's bow. We demanded that the Senior PGA cease and desist its discriminatory practices regarding Super Seniors eligibility and suggested that keeping Howie and myself out of the tournaments amounted to bias based on age and race. Going to an all-time win system merely persisted in perpetuating the racial injustices of the past, they suggested, and choosing players based on former feats discriminated against the present-day players who were performing better on the golf course than the old "name" golfers. If the Senior PGA didn't change the rule, we would sue for real and punitive damages.

We waited to hear if the Senior PGA would back down, and in the meantime Howie and I continued to enter all of the Super Seniors tournaments through the end of 1987 because all of those "name" golfers weren't showing up to the tournaments. We ended up finishing first and third, respectively, in earnings. Howie took home over $84,000 in prize money in addition to what he won in the senior tournaments, and I finished with over $60,000. The prize money for Super Seniors was to go up in coming years, and combined with the number of golfers who would turn 60 in coming years, I could stand to lose a fortune if they kept the new, unfair rule in effect.

In an attempt to appease us Deane Beman wrote to the Senior PGA Tour sponsors at the beginning of the 1988 season and suggested that I should receive the sponsor's exemption at every Super Senior tournament. "While it is impossible to credit Charlie with more victories than he actually won, it is possible for sponsors to take this information into account — along with Charlie's career money-winning record and other factors — when evaluating their choice of a Super Seniors sponsor's exemption," he wrote.

"I have never requested or recommended a particular player for a sponsor's exemption and am not doing that now. Each sponsor's exemption is up to the individual sponsor who may have many different reasons for his ultimate selection.

"I do think, however, that it is a valid request to pass this information on to sponsors and to ask them to consider it when making their decision."

For the next year and a half, Deane Beman personally saw to it that I got the sponsor's exemption for each Super Seniors tournament. When a tournament in Utah refused his request, Beman called me in my hotel room and asked that I refrain from taking any legal action. Jerry and Peter Roisman, my lawyers, had spoken repeatedly to the Senior PGA Tour over the prior year and a half about the situation and had not received any remedies. It looked like we would have to sue.

Finally, though, Beman must have gotten tired of the whole situation and realized that I wasn't going to go away. In a senior board meeting in October 1989 he pushed through a resolution that changed Super Seniors eligibility to every golfer who was over 60 years old and qualified for the senior tournament, with prize money divided among the top dozen finishers. Which is exactly how it should have been set up two years earlier, regardless of what the "name" players wanted. RJR/Nabisco, by the way, didn't seem to have any objections to the latest change.

The Super Seniors continues to be an exciting diversion within the tournament, and many different players have taken home the $9,000 first prize money, including some of the "names." The field has gotten stronger in recent years with the arrival of guys like Littler and January, and it's tougher to come out on top, but I still manage. Joe Jimenez and I have been vying for the season-high prize money practically every year. I finished second to him in 1989 and 1990, with earnings of over $100,000 each year. Which isn't bad for a guy pushing 70 who isn't enough of a "name" golfer.

If I hadn't stood up to fight with both cannons firing when they slipped in that rule change, I'd have been just another black man who got dumped on because the Senior PGA Tour found a way to keep him down. And if it wasn't the Senior PGA Tour doing the dumping, it was the Vintage golf tournament or the Legends of Golf or anybody else who decided that I wasn't good enough or marketable enough to enter their golf tournament. But I don't stay down, I fight back. Does this sound familiar? Don't you think they would have learned by now?

CHAPTER 22

The Black Jack Nicklaus

Where then, are the black Jack Nicklaus and Arnold Palmer? Where are the stirring black golfers who can pick the sport up to new levels and provide new thrills? I'll tell you where. . . they're playing college basketball or struggling in baseball's minor leagues or holding down a steady job somewhere. Golf was simply never an option for them, and we've been deprived of the pleasures of watching them play the game, just as surely as we would have been deprived if Sugar Ray Leonard hadn't been steered toward boxing, or Jerry Rice had been taught that only whites can play wide receiver.

Wait just a minute, people might say. Blacks have been able to play on public golf courses throughout the country for at least the last 30 years. The PGA qualifying school is open to anyone. Nobody's standing at the doorway to golf tournaments saying "You can't come in here, boy," like they did in 1961. If your black Jack Nicklaus wants to play golf so badly, Charlie, where is he? Haven't blacks simply chosen to not play golf?

Sorry, but it doesn't work that way in golf. This isn't baseball, where you can find a vacant sandlot and start working on your skills before being brought up slowly through the ranks of college ball, the minors, and then the pros.

The competition in professional golf is so extraordinary, and the player's life is so solitary, depending on earning his own way

222

week after week on the tour, that it takes more than talent to succeed. We see guys all the time at the pro-am outings who know how to play golf and can shoot scratch. Every club pro at every golf course in the country can play a decent round of golf. But that doesn't make them professional golfers.

In order to make it in this game you have to have tremendous discipline and focus to go with your talent, and you have to be given every opportunity to succeed. You need to practice endlessly on every part of your game, and you need to have the right equipment and the right facilities to practice well, as well as enough of a financial backing to allow you to spend 8 hours a day at the golf course until you get it right.

Do you think that hitting balls off a mat at a public driving range is the same as hitting off grass at a country club? Can a round of golf on a rinky-dink public course, with its flat fairways and thin sand traps and bumpy greens, prepare you for the challenge of playing at a first-class golf course against the best golfers in the world? No way. It's like taking the kid directly from the sandlot and putting him in Yankee Stadium and expecting him to perform at his peak level right away. It just isn't done.

It is because of the way the game of golf has been set up in this country that we may never see the black Jack Nicklaus. We may not even see any more black golfers, period, for a long, long time. And yes, I do know about Tiger Woods, the young black golfing phenomenom, and I pray to God that he be given the opportunities to get his education and come up slowly so that his talent won't be wasted.

It is because of the country clubs that don't allow blacks, and because of the winner-take-all attitude that shifts all of the attention of the sport onto a few (white) names, and because of the corporate sponsors who are only interested in securing those few names, and because of the networks and the press that never seem to lay a glove on lily-white golf.

It is because you have to start playing this game as a kid in order to ever get skillful enough to compete on a professional level, and black kids don't have role models in golf, or teachers, or decent courses to play, or the $500 to buy a set of clubs.

Why aren't I a role model? Because as far as my press clippings are concerned, I'm bitter, irascible old Charlie. The one with the cigar. Calvin Peete is the sharecropper's son with the diamond in his tooth. Charlie Owens had the bad legs, Jim Dent is the big hitter, Lee Elder is in his twilight. Right now the only black role model in golf is Michael Jordan, and God bless him, I hope he overcomes all of the hype and keeps improving his game.

With all of the stone walls facing black kids who were interested in the game, there was one little loophole over the years that allowed them to be around golf. And now, even that has been pulled away. The one opportunity that young black kids had to learn this game was the caddy system. Just about every black professional golfer came up that way, carrying bags as a kid at the local country club and doing his damndest to find the time and the opportunity to hit balls and learn the game. We may have been chased off the course nearly every day, and we may have had to learn how to swing so quickly that we were forever stuck with a short, compact movement to the ball, but we knew that as long as they needed us as caddies, we could find a way to practice our golf.

The collapse of the caddy system pretty much will spell an end to black professional golfers, because that little back door was the only way most of us could ever worm our way into this game. Now that country clubs have golf carts, they don't need to have poor black kids around to tarnish their images. Now they hire young, white golf pros to man the pro shop and give out golf carts. The opportunities for black kids to be around the game are slim or none.

If a black kid is athletic, he will be steered toward the black sports of football, baseball, and basketball. Even if he shows considerable promise at golf, he knows that he's going to have a hell of a time getting a college scholarship to play the game, so why not stick to a bread-and-butter sport? And if somehow he overcomes all that and gets his game to an acceptable level, he then has to find a sponsor willing to foot the enormous bills of PGA qualifying school and traveling on the tour.

I don't know about you, but I haven't seen many white sponsors who are willing to hand a black kid — even a black kid with promise — the $60,000 a year it takes to travel the PGA Tour. That's not racism, it's business, they'll tell you. Even if the black kid overcomes impossible odds and makes it on the tour, he's not going to get the endorsement income or the appearance fees that a comparable white player can expect. The black kid simply isn't as profitable in the long run, hence he's a bigger risk.

This isn't bitterness talking, it's experience. Calvin Peete was one of the top golfers in the world in the late seventies, but he didn't get endorsements. The only money he earned was what he won on the course. Curtis Strange, on the other hand, had a couple of good years recently and reportedly makes $1.5 million a year now on appearance fees and endorsements.

Lee Elder has won over $2 million at golf and was the first black to play in the Masters in 1975. But he never modeled clothes or did an American Express ad or was asked to be a guest commentator on a golf broadcast or was paid $10,000 to appear at some big corporation's annual golf outing. He was never made a star by the sport, and now that he's older and his game has faded a little, he's just Lee Elder, the first black guy to play in the Masters.

It seems to me that the only way a black golfer is going to receive those kinds of things is if he's simply a phenomenal player, a Michael Jordan of golf. He'll have to be a superstar to get the kind of recognition that even players like Ben Crenshaw and Tom Kite receive. But if he's a regular old black touring pro, forget it. Bad investment. If that isn't some kind of pressure to put on a young player, on top of the pressures of trying to compete in this extremely competitive game, then I don't know what is.

Hell, I wouldn't advise any young black kid to take up the game of golf with a thought of making a living from it. The odds are just too stacked against him at this point. I wouldn't wish this kind of pressure and disappointment on anyone.

It seemed to come as a surprise to the national media that many country clubs still don't allow black members, and that frequently, PGA tournaments, including the United States Open, are played on courses that are in effect segregated. Of course, the clubs usually don't come right out and say that they have a policy that excludes blacks. And Jews. And women. And everyone else who isn't a white male. They say that they simply have never had a black/Jewish/female member apply who was acceptable to the membership, but they'd keep on looking.

By the way, I've never been refused a game of golf at a Jewish country club. Back in the fifties, when the only places I could play on were municipal and public golf courses, they let me play all the time at the Hillcrest Country Club in L.A. In fact, it was there that I met Stanley Mosk. It was never a problem or a big deal that I was black at the Jewish country clubs, but across town at the WASP clubs, I was definitely not welcome, even when I was invited to play with members.

It was no secret to me or the other black golfers on the tour that most of the courses we played were owned by private clubs that didn't have any black members. We could tell just by walking in on the first day and seeing the suspicious looks. It's like that at Medinah in Chicago, Merion near Philadelphia, Pine Valley in New Jersey, and it's most definitely like that at Augusta National, that shrine to golf in Georgia. In fact, I'd venture to say that most of the top country club courses in America are segregated.

Why it took until 1990 for the PGA to take notice of this is way beyond me. It is a distinct sign of the arrogance of that organization and the utter disregard thay have for minorities that they would have allowed tournaments over the years on courses that they knew were deliberately segregated. It was only when a determined band of black people in Alabama stood up and raised a stink about Shoal Creek, and with it a national uproar where practically everybody decried the existence of segregated country clubs, that the PGA took a stand and stated that in the future, the membership policies of clubs would be taken into consideration when choosing tournament sites. Now those country clubs are scrambling to find one single black man to whom they can extend membership privileges so they can say they're integrated.

Of course the PGA knew that the sites of its tournaments were segregated. They just didn't give a damn. "Why make waves at the most prestigious golf courses in America, just so a few black guys will be happy?'' is their attitude. ''If they don't like playing at a segregated country club, they can just choose to not enter the tournament.''

Well that attitude stinks, as far as I'm concerned. The governing body of professional golf should be exerting its powers for the benefit of all its players, and to the betterment of the sport. It shouldn't be sitting back waiting for the inevitable public challenges to the game. It should be at the forefront of change to make sure that golf is available to anyone with the skill and desire to play it.

The PGA is run by a bunch of white men who want nothing more than to make a pile of money. They are not treating the sport of professional golf as an institution that needs to have a firm moral and ethical stance in order to withstand the rigors of time. In their glee to bring in bigger purses, bigger TV contracts, and bigger corporate sponsorship, they have mistaken profit for character and financial statements for identity. They are running the sport of golf as if it were a corporation that eventually might be taken over or broken up into assets to sell off one at a time.

In this game, the players are just pawns in the corporate scheme. You qualify to play on the tour, you play as long as you can finish in the top-125 money winners, and then you disappear. Nobody helps you look for a job when you're done, or seeks special exemptions to get you into selected tournaments. When you have no further use to the business, you're gone. And when you have a grievance against a tournament or a sponsor, or you want to know why you never get invited to the special outings where they pay a pro upwards of $5,000 to play, the PGA simply says that it can't help you.

''We have no control over what the sponsors or the individual tournaments decide,'' they tell the players. ''We can't tell them whom to invite.'' It's back to that invitation-only crap that they used 40 years ago to get rid of Bill Spiller and Teddy Rhodes.

This helpless, there's-nothing-we-can-do-about-it attitude is always the PGA's excuse. ''We'll look into it, Charlie,'' they promise. ''We'll try to talk to the sponsors.'' What they should be doing is running their sport, not reacting to it.

I realize how angry and bitter this all sounds, and I know that a lot of people are going to say that this is all a big bunch of sour grapes from an old, sour, black man. I've won over a million dollars at my sport and made a good living for myself and my family, and what the hell am I complaining about.

To tell you the truth, it feels funny to voice my frustrations with the game. I've never been a whiner or a complainer. I've made it a point during my golf career to conduct myself with dignity on and off the golf course, because I damn sure never wanted anyone to have the excuse to call me a slovenly, lazy black man who was looking for a handout. I've never asked anyone for anything other than the opportunity to be able to play, and when I got those opportunities, I shut up and took what I could get on the golf course. I'm proud to say that I earned every nickel that I made on my own merits, and nobody ever threw me a token appearance or a commercial endorsement because I bitched and moaned my way into it.

It is just that now, at the end of my career, I am so overehelmingly disappointed and frustrated with the opportunities that golf has wasted to reach out to all people. This is an utterly wonderful game that we play for a living. Show me another sport where a guy off the street can pay his money and play on the same field with the same equipment as the pros. Anybody can play golf, from eight-year-old kids to grandmothers, and they can all play on the same course and try the same shots. With the handicap system, they can figure out ways to compete and make the game exciting.

On the PGA and senior tours we raise millions of dollars a year for charity, and we sponsor junior golf programs throughout the country. We travel from city to city all year long, and thousands of fans come out to see us at each stop and enjoy the sight of watching a professional hit the ball and compete against their home course. We're the cleanest sport in terms of drugs and crime, and we're known for the personal ethics that players keep that will have them call penalty strokes on themselves and even give up their winnings if they find out they did something like sign a scorecard wrong. Golf has a unique way of reaching people that no other sport has.

But underlying all of golf's generosity and good manners and traditions is an ugliness and an elitism that is hard to shake. I saw it forty-five years ago when I started getting into tournaments, and I see it today. I can't believe that with all of the changes that have gone on in the world that golf has adjusted so little. As far as this game is concerned, Martin Luther King, Jr., was no more than a guy with a high handicap. Nelson Mandela never existed. The elaborate manners and country club snobbishness that were part of this game when Ike was playing it are just as much the rule today.

From my perspective as a guy who lives within that world but is always seen as an outsider, it seems like golf is the last stronghold of some peculiar kind of whiteness that goes along with big business and fancy country clubs and the way people with money choose to spend their leisure time. It is a kind of whiteness that is not easily integrated, as if they're saying, "We've given the black man desegregation in schools and housing, and we've (grudgingly) given him some semblance of equal opportunity in employment, but that's as far as we'll go. Don't even think about coming into our private clubhouse, buddy, because we're not giving any more."

If the world of golf is any barometer, we've got a long way to go before achieving any kind of racial equality in this country. I just thought that things would be different after some of those initial obstacles were pushed away, and now I'm old and almost through with the game, and I don't believe I'm ever going to see things really change. It's really too bad, because golf could bring a lot of people together from different backgrounds and provide some kind of framework for understanding. It could, but it hasn't. I wish it could be different.

In the early days I was just too busy trying to scratch out a living on the golf course to think much about my place in history. Now I'm trying to enjoy my last years in the game and trying to give a little something back. I think what golf needs is not a Jackie Robinson, but a Julius Erving or an O.J. Simpson: a black man with a great deal of personal magnetism and a whale of a game who can demonstrate that blacks can fit into the game in a way that everyone can appreciate and enjoy. Maybe when the black Jack Nicklaus comes along and beats the pants off of everybody and does it with a smile and a clear speaking voice and a sound awareness of the media. . .maybe then we other black guys will get the recognition and acceptance that we've always thought we deserved.

CHAPTER 23

Just Let Us Play

I have a simple barometer that tells me nearly every week on the tour that golf isn't ready for blacks. I call it the Lee Elder test. I'll be standing on a putting green or walking to the driving range or coming off a round of golf and a fan will walk up to me, stick a piece of paper in front of me and say, "Hey, Mr. Elder, will you sign this please?"

A variation goes like this: "How's your game going, Mr. Dent?"

Or, "Hey, Charles Owens, where's that long putter of yours? That putter been pretty hot for you, Mr. Owens?"

Lee Elder gets the same thing with my name attached to it: "Hey, Charlie Sifford, where's that famous cigar of yours?" In fact, all of the black players share in this round robin of names, whether they're a guy like Pete Brown who plays occasionally or someone like Lee who plays every week.

Mind you, this happens continuously, and it hasn't changed in the 11 years that I've been on the senior tour. Not a big deal? Maybe, but it indicates to me that despite what we've accomplished, the handful of black pros are still generic, anonymous players in the mind of the golfing public. We're one man, "the black guy," with one name, Lee/Charlie/Rafe/Charles/Jim.

As often as it happens, I still don't understand it. I'm five feet seven, and I've had a cigar in my mouth since I was 12 years old. How can somebody mistake me for Jim Dent, who is 16 years younger and about five inches and 40 pounds bigger than me? Charles Owens is six feet tall and lean as a fence post. He doesn't look like Charlie Sifford any more than he looks like Gay Brewer.

It indicates to me that golf still doesn't have much use for its black players if it can keep us so anonymous that we're interchangeable to the viewing public. What do you need to do to get some recognition and fame from the sport? Lee Elder has won nearly two million dollars in his illustrious career. Jim Dent and Charles Owens have won many tournaments as seniors, and I'm probably the best golfer my age in the country. You might read about us and hear our quotes when a racial issue comes up in golf, but how often do you read a straight feature story about us as golfers? How often do you see us on television or see our pictures in the magazines?

It's not enough that they let us play in the tournaments. I opened that door 30 years ago. We want to come into the mainstream of golf because we deserve it by virtue of our play. I think all of us on the senior tour, and Calvin Peete and Jim Thorpe on the regular tour, have played well enough, and long enough, to deserve some recognition.

Irritating things go on every week on the tour, and at times the irritation spills out into something worse. I can't tell you how many times I or my fellow black pros are asked if we're caddies in the course of a season. I'm 69 years old and I wear the Toyota logo on my golf shirts and I'm pretty confident that I don't look like a damn caddy. But I can promise you that every other week I'll get a caddy reference thrown my way. "Caddies can't go into that locker room," a guard will say before I walk into the clubhouse.

Or, "Excuse me, but aren't you looking for the caddy registration?" a woman will ask when I approach the players' registration tent. If you want to see Charlie Sifford in a foul mood, just catch me on one of those days when people have been asking me if I'm a caddy. I feel that I've been out there long enough and proven myself enough that the people working at the tournaments should know who I am by now.

We haven't been integrated long enough to erase the institutional notion of white players and black caddies. I don't suppose it will be erased in my lifetime, and I wonder now, when I see so few black players coming up, if it will ever go away. It's a mindset that has been slower to change than the Caucasian clause itself.

It affects other areas of the game. As far as I know, there aren't any black officials on any of the PGA tours: the regular tour, the seniors tour, the Ben Hogan Tour, or the LPGA Tour. To my knowledge Lee Elder is the only black who ever served on a committee of players, and that was for but a brief time.

It annoys the hell out of me that we don't get the same recognition as the white players. Last year Roberto de Vicenzo and I defended our championship for players over 60 at the Legends of Golf. We got on television for the first time all week at the awards ceremony and a slick young white guy stuck a microphone in our face to interview us for ESPN. But instead of talking about our victory and our careers, do you know what he said? Something about how "old Sam Snead is in his seventies and he's still playing and making a great showing out here."

Sure, Sam Snead made a great showing. He and Bob Goalby finished second to us. But they weren't the guys accepting the winners' check, we were. Wasn't there anything he could mention about the way the black man and the Hispanic had played? Somehow we still weren't quite Legend enough to make a story for the reporter. He had to reach right past us to Sam Snead.

I think that because we get so little recognition by the game of golf itself, we're more easily overlooked by all of the things that surround professional golf. The black players are overlooked when it comes time for endorsements and tournament exemptions and special invitations. When that happens, it's not just irritating. That's when it starts to cost us money, and it puts us at a competitive disadvantage with the other pros. And that's what makes me the most angry these days.

For example, there are 35 to 40 of what we call outings held every year. Outings are invitations to play a paid round of golf at a private tournament set up by a business for its clients. To show off and make the day's golf special, the business will hire a bunch of touring professionals to appear at its tournament on Monday and play a round of golf with its clients. For this they pay handsomely—as much as $3,000 to $5,000 for each player for one day's work. The pros will play the round, pose for pictures, have a cocktail, and then head off to play in that week's tournament.

Some players get invited to dozens of outings in a year's time, and they can make over $100,000 a year on outings alone. That's an awfully nice bonus to tour winnings. And how are the players chosen for outings? They're invited by the companies, which ask the PGA for a list of players and make their invitations from the list.

I'm never invited to those things because the word on me is that I'm a troublemaker, although the only place I've ever made trouble is with the PGA when they wouldn't let me play. You can count on both hands the number of outings I've played in the last five years, and half of those are from a military tournament held on a Marine Corps base in Hawaii every year. Guys like Lee Elder and Calvin Peete are seldom invited. Jim Dent may be getting a few invitations lately because he's had a couple of good years, but watch him fall back on the money list and you'll see his name passed over too. White guys who have long since ceased to win any real money on the tour get invited every week. Why can't the black men who are past their prime have the same privileges?

The golf system seems to find new and unusual ways to get at the black players. When Jim Dent won two tournaments in his rookie year on the senior tour, a couple of players circulated a rumor that he wasn't really 50 years old yet and was playing illegally. The rumor got big enough so that a group of players actually got together and wrote away to Augusta, Georgia, Jim's hometown, to get a copy of his birth certificate.